Shakespeare and Conflic

Palgrave Shakespeare Studies

General Editors: Michael Dobson and Dympna Callaghan

Co-founding Editor: Gail Kern Paster

Editorial Advisory Board: Michael Neill, University of Auckland; David Schalkwyk, Folger Shakespeare Library; Lois D. Potter, University of Delaware; Margreta de Grazia, University of Pennsylvania; Peter Holland, University of Notre Dame

Palgrave Shakespeare Studies takes Shakespeare as its focus but strives to understand the significance of his oeuvre in relation to his contemporaries, subsequent writers and historical and political contexts. By extending the scope of Shakespeare and English Renaissance Studies the series will open up the field to examinations of previously neglected aspects or sources in the period's art and thought. Titles in the *Palgrave Shakespeare Studies* series seek to understand anew both where the literary achievements of the English Renaissance came from and where they have brought us.

Titles include:

Pascale Aebischer, Edward J. Esche and Nigel Wheale (*editors*)
REMAKING SHAKESPEARE
Performance across Media, Genres and Cultures

James P. Bednarz
SHAKESPEARE AND THE TRUTH OF LOVE
The Mystery of 'The Phoenix and Turtle'

Mark Thornton Burnett
FILMING SHAKESPEARE IN THE GLOBAL MARKETPLACE

Carla Dente and Sara Soncini (*editors*)
SHAKESPEARE AND CONFLICT
A European Perspective

Lowell Gallagher and Shankar Raman (*editors*)
KNOWING SHAKESPEARE
Senses, Embodiment and Cognition

Stefan Herbrechter and Ivan Callus (*editors*)
POSTHUMANIST SHAKESPEARES

David Hillman
SHAKESPEARE'S ENTRAILS
Belief, Scepticism and the Interior of the Body

Anna Kamaralli
SHAKESPEARE AND THE SHREW
Performing the Defiant Female Voice

Jane Kingsley-Smith
SHAKESPEARE'S DRAMA OF EXILE

Stephen Purcell
POPULAR SHAKESPEARE
Simulation and Subversion on the Modern Stage

Erica Sheen
SHAKESPEARE AND THE INSTITUTION OF THEATRE

Paul Yachnin and Jessica Slights
SHAKESPEARE AND CHARACTER
Theory, History, Performance, and Theatrical Persons

Palgrave Shakespeare Studies
Series Standing Order ISBN 978–1–403–91164–3 (hardback) 978–1–403–91165–0 (paperback)
(*outside North America only*)

You can receive future titles in this series as they are published by placing a standing order. Please contact your bookseller or, in case of difficulty, write to us at the address below with your name and address, the title of the series and the ISBN quoted above.

Customer Services Department, Macmillan Distribution Ltd, Houndmills, Basingstoke, Hampshire RG21 6XS, England

Shakespeare and Conflict

A European Perspective

Edited by

Carla Dente and Sara Soncini

palgrave
macmillan

First published 2013 by
PALGRAVE MACMILLAN

Palgrave Macmillan in the UK is an imprint of Macmillan Publishers Limited, registered in England, company number 785998, of Houndmills, Basingstoke, Hampshire RG21 6XS.

Palgrave Macmillan in the US is a division of St Martin's Press LLC, 175 Fifth Avenue, New York, NY 10010.

Palgrave Macmillan is the global academic imprint of the above companies and has companies and representatives throughout the world.

Palgrave® and Macmillan® are registered trademarks in the United States, the United Kingdom, Europe and other countries.

ISBN 978-1-349-34463-5   ISBN 978-1-137-31134-4 (eBook)
DOI 10.1057/9781137311344

This book is printed on paper suitable for recycling and made from fully managed and sustained forest sources. Logging, pulping and manufacturing processes are expected to conform to the environmental regulations of the country of origin.

A catalogue record for this book is available from the British Library.

A catalog record for this book is available from the Library of Congress.

Transferred to Digital Printing in 2013

Contents

List of Illustrations

Notes on Contributors

Clara Calvo is Professor of English Studies at the University of Murcia (Spain). Her research interests include Shakespeare's afterlives and the role of Shakespeare in a shared European transnational cultural identity. From 1995 to 2005 she was in charge of the stylistics section of *The Year's Work in English Studies*. She is the author of *Power Relations and Fool-Master Discourse in Shakespeare* (1991) and has co-authored, with Jean-Jacques Weber, *The Literature Workbook* (1998). She has edited, with Ton Hoenselaars, a volume on *European Shakespeares* for *The Shakespearean International Yearbook* (2008) and an issue of *Critical Survey* on *Shakespeare and the Cultures of Commemoration* (2011). She is currently engaged in two funded research projects on 'Shakespearean Anniversaries' and 'Shakespeare and the First World War'.

Juan F. Cerdá is Lecturer at the University of Murcia, Spain. He is a member of the research project 'Shakespeare in Spain within the Framework of his European Reception', in which context he has been researching the role of Shakespearean drama in twentieth-century Spanish theatre and film. His latest publications include essays on Shakespeare in García Lorca's early poems (2011), Shakespearean film adaptations at the time of Franco's dictatorship (2011), and newspaper reviews of Shakespearean performances in early twentieth-century Madrid (forthcoming in *Cahiers Élisabéthains*).

Anna Cetera is Associate Professor of English Literature at the University of Warsaw, in Poland. Her publications include two monographs: *Enter Lear. The Translator's Part in Performance* (2008) and *Smak morwy. U źródeł recepcji przekładów Szekspira w Polsce* [*Mulberry Taste: The Beginnings of the Polish Reception of Shakespeare in Translation*] (2009). She has also published in academic journals on Shakespeare and censorship, Shakespeare and war, and drama translation. She is currently editing a new series of Polish translations of Shakespeare (*Richard II*, 2009; *Macbeth*, 2011; *Twelfth Night*, 2012; *The Tempest*, 2012) and a collection of essays entitled *Shakespeare Mania*.

Carla Dente is Professor of English at the University of Pisa, Italy. She has published extensively on theatre studies along the lines of textual analysis and the investigation of specific theatre and cultural phenomena.

She has worked on contemporary, Renaissance and Restoration playwrights. Her essays on Shakespeare include studies on *The Merchant of Venice, The Taming of the Shrew, Hamlet, A Midsummer Night's Dream* and *The Comedy of Errors*. She is the author of *Trittico* and *La recita del diritto* (1995), the editor of *Teatro inglese contemporaneo* (1995) and *Dibattito sul teatro* (2006), and the co-editor of *Hamlet Promptbooks of the Nineteenth Century* (2002; electronic publication), *Conflict Zones: Actions Languages Mediations* (2004), *Proteus: The Languages of Metamorphosis* (2005), *Crossing Time and Space: Shakespeare Translations in Present-day Europe* (2008) and *Translation Practices* (2009). She is currently working on theatre and the law.

Boris Drenkov holds a PhD from the University of Munich with a dissertation on the cult of Elizabeth in sixteenth- and seventeenth-century England. He has taught English literature in Siegen and Munich (Germany) as well as in other parts of Europe and in the United States. He has taken part in numerous conferences on Renaissance literature in Europe and North America and has published articles on the English Renaissance and literary theory in France and Italy.

Małgorzata Grzegorzewska teaches English Literature at the Institute of English Studies, University of Warsaw, Poland. She has published on Renaissance poetry and drama. She is the author of *The Medicine of Cherries. English Renaissance Theories of Poetry* (2003) and three books in Polish, two of which are devoted to Shakespeare's tragedies: *Scena we krwi* [*Stage in Blood*] (2006) and *Kamienny ołtarz* [*The Altar of Stone*] (2007). Her most recent publication, *Trop innego głosu* [*The Voice of the Other*] (2011) discusses the uses of rhetorical prosopopoeia in early modern English poetry.

Ton Hoenselaars is Professor of Early Modern Literature and Culture at Utrecht University, the Netherlands. He is the President of the European Shakespeare Research Association (ESRA). His books include *Shakespeare's History Plays* (2004) and *Shakespeare and the Language of Translation* (2004; revised edition, 2012). Currently, he is one of the editors of the *Cambridge World Shakespeare Encyclopedia*, and is completing a book on Shakespeare at the civilian internment camp of Ruhleben (Berlin) during the First World War.

Alessandra Marino is Research Associate at the Open University (UK) within the project 'Oecumene: Citizenship after Orientalism'. She completed her PhD in Postcolonial and Cultural Studies at the University of Naples, 'L'Orientale'. Her research fields range from postcolonial literature and theory to visual studies and she has published articles on Anita Desai, Nalini Malani, contemporary Indian cinema and video art, and on Shakespearean appropriations in a postcolonial perspective. She is the co-editor, with Lidia Curti, of *Shakespeare in India* (2010).

Alessandra Marzola is Professor of English Literature at the University of Bergamo, Italy. She has published and edited books on Shakespeare; twentieth-century British theatre; the rhetoric of economic discourse in John Maynard Keynes; 'Englishness' in the twentieth century; and literature, war and violence in twentieth-century Britain. Her books on Shakespeare include *L'impossibile puritanesimo di Amleto* (1986), *La parola del Mercante* (1996) and, as editor, *L'altro Shakespeare* (1992) and *The Difference of Shakespeare* (2008). She is also the co-author, with Davide Del Bello, of *Shakespeare and the Power of Difference* (2011).

Monica Matei-Chesnoiu is Associate Professor of English Literature at Ovidius University Constanta, Romania. She is the author of *Shakespeare in the Romanian Cultural Memory*, with an introduction by Arthur F. Kinney (2006), and *Early Modern Drama and the Eastern European Elsewhere: Representations of Liminal Locality in Shakespeare and his Contemporaries* (2009). She is a member of the International Committee of Correspondents for the *World Shakespeare Bibliography*. Her book *Re-imagining Western European Geography in English Renaissance Drama* was published in July 2012 by Palgrave Macmillan.

Georgi Niagolov teaches English Medieval and Renaissance Literature in the Department of British and American Studies at the University of Sofia, in Bulgaria. Recent publications include *The Preposterous Postness of Being* (2011), *An Open Source Hamlet?* (2010), *Cleopatra: Shakespeare's Tragic Woman* (2009), *Plato's Healing Poison, Zeno's Motionless Flight, Shakespeare's Tricky Lies and Schrödinger's Cat's Ghost* (2008) and *Different Ideas about Language* (2008). He is currently experimenting with alternative approaches to teaching Shakespeare.

Manfred Pfister was Professor of English at the Freie Universität Berlin and is a member of the Berlin-Brandenburgische Akademie der Wissenschaften (Germany). He was co-editor of the *Shakespeare Jahrbuch* and *Poetica* and author of *Das Drama. Theorie und Analyse* (Munich, 1982; English edition, 1988). Among his more recent book publications are *Laurence Sterne* (2001), *A History of English Laughter* (2002), *Performing National Identity: Anglo-Italian Transactions* (2008), *William Shakespeare's Sonnets, for the First Time Globally Reprinted. A Quatercentenary Anthology*

(2009) and editions of Bruce Chatwin's *In Patagonia* (2003), Samuel Butler's *Notebooks* (2005) and Shelley's *Zastrozzi* (2009).

Paola Pugliatti was Professor of English Literature at the University of Florence, Italy, and she also taught at the universities of Messina, Bologna and Pisa. Her latest book-length studies on the European Renaissance and on Shakespeare are *Beggary and Theatre in Early Modern England* (2003) and *Shakespeare and the Just War Tradition* (2010). Other fields of interest are the novel and textual genetics, with particular attention to James Joyce's *Ulysses*. She is co-editor, with Donatella Pallotti, of the *Journal of Early Modern Studies*, an open access publication of Firenze University Press.

Miguel Ramalhete Gomes is currently an FCT Fellow engaged in post-doctoral research focusing on the theme of Shakespeare and presentism. He recently finished his PhD dissertation, 'Texts Waiting for History: William Shakespeare Rewritten by Heiner Müller', at Faculdade de Letras da Universidade do Porto (FLUP), in Portugal. He is a researcher at CETAPS (Centre for English, Translation, and Anglo-Portuguese Studies), in the following projects: 'Mapping Dreams: British and North-American Utopianism' and 'Shakespeare and the English Canon: A Research and Translation Project'. His latest project is a translation of *Henry VI, Part 3*.

Francesca Rayner is Assistant Professor at the Universidade do Minho, Portugal, where she teaches Theatre and Performance. Her PhD thesis 'Caught in the Act: The Representation of Sexual Transgression in Three Portuguese Productions of Shakespeare' was published by the university in 2006 and her subsequent research has centred on the cultural politics of Shakespearean performance in Portugal, with a particular interest in questions of gender and sexuality. She has published articles in national and international journals such as the *Luso-Brazilian Review*, *Portuguese Studies* and *The Shakespearean International Yearbook* and is currently working on a book about Shakespearean performance in Portugal in the post-revolutionary period.

Sabine Schülting is Professor of English Literature and Cultural Studies at Freie Universität Berlin, Germany. Her research interests are early modern and nineteenth-century literature and culture, Shakespeare, and Gender Studies. Books include *Wilde Frauen, fremde Welten: Kolonisierungsgeschichten aus Amerika* (1997) and *Geschlechter-Revisionen: Zur Zukunft von Feminismus und Gender Studies in den*

Kultur- und Literaturwissenschaften, co-edited with Sabine L. Müller (2006). She is also the editor of *Shakespeare Jahrbuch*. Her current work is devoted to the cultural reception of Shakespeare's *The Merchant of Venice* in Germany after 1945.

Sara Soncini is Researcher and Lecturer in English Literature at the University of Pisa, Italy. Her research has focused mainly on twentieth- and twenty-first-century British and Irish drama, but she has also written extensively on modern-day appropriations of Shakespeare (translations, adaptations, rewriting). Her book publications include *Playing with(in) the Restoration: Metatheatre as a Strategy of Appropriation in Contemporary Rewritings of Restoration Drama* (1999) and, as co-editor, *Shakespeare Graffiti: Il Cigno di Avon nella cultura di massa* (2002), *Conflict Zones: Actions Languages Mediations* (2004), *Myths of Europe* (2007) and *Crossing Time and Space: Shakespeare Translations in Present-day Europe* (2008). She is currently writing a monograph on the representation of war in contemporary British drama.

Jesús Tronch-Pérez holds a PhD from the University of Valencia, Spain, where he is Senior Lecturer and teaches English Literature and Creative Translation. His main research interests are textual criticism (specifically focusing on Shakespeare and early modern drama) and the presence of Shakespeare in Spain. He has published *A Synoptic 'Hamlet'* (2002), and *Un primer 'Hamlet'* (1994), as well as a number of commissioned essays in book collections and articles in journals such as *Shakespeare Survey*, *TEXT: An Interdisciplinary Annual of Textual Studies* and *SEDERI*. Together with Clara Calvo, he is currently preparing a critical edition of *The Spanish Tragedy* for the Arden Early Modern Drama series. Forthcoming is an online monograph on *Hamlet* in Spain for *Hamlet Works*.

Foreword

Ton Hoenselaars

Europe is a continent whose nation-states are committed to cooperating in a union that recognizes their joint interests in political, economic and cultural terms. Yet, anyone following the current news on Europe's first major euro crisis might be inclined, and rightly so, to think that in times of political or economic emergency, Europe's shared culture is the first victim. Negotiations about the common currency stir up memories of deep political divisions in the past. Familiar national stereotypes – invariably the unpleasant ones – are revived in the media. Views on immigration tend to re-introduce the ancient discussion about the internal borders as well as the frontiers of Fortress Europe as a whole. And as the Continent seeks to restore economic order, the arts are facing severe financial cuts. Museums begin to delve into their own holdings to devise more affordable in-house exhibitions, well-established orchestras are threatened with extinction, and the more experimental the theatre company, the greater its danger of losing government subsidy.

This collection of essays focuses on one of Europe's most influential writers – his lifetime, his work and his afterlives. It demonstrates that conflict and division in Europe are not new, and that, indeed, such conflict and division have been the mainstay of the Continent's distinctly variegated culture. This collection of essays illustrates how, writing his plays and poems, Shakespeare himself negotiated a humanitarian position while, among other things, the religious map of Europe and the world trade map were being effectively redrawn. Moreover, this collection makes the fine point that Shakespeare's stance cannot always be described as passive or pacifist, and that conflict may be read into his language, his action, as well as his silences. These essays recount fascinating tales of the playwright's work as a companion for later rebels with a cultural cause. They tell of the murkier moments in European history, and the astonishing chronicles of those who, even when held captive in times of tyranny and war, kept coming back to Shakespeare to read, to perform, to survive the political conflict as well as their own personal suffering, unbroken, at home or in exile.

What is achieved by this collection of essays – emerging from the 2009 Pisa conference of the European Shakespeare Research Association (ESRA) – is perhaps best described with reference to the American inventor Charlton Joseph Kadio Hinman (1911–77). Hinman's career comes into focus in 1941, when he became the first PhD student of the early modern editor and bibliographer Fredson Bowers at the University of Virginia, and spent his first research fellowship at the Folger Shakespeare Library to collate, by hand, the First Folio text of *Othello*. Following the Japanese attack on Pearl Harbor on 7 December 1941, Hinman had to abandon his Shakespearean research, was trained as a Navy crypt-analyst, and subsequently became an officer in a code-breaking unit in Washington, DC, with none other than Fredson Bowers, his dissertation supervisor, as his commanding officer. As a member of a naval intelligence group that also included other future bibliographers of note, Hinman came to hear about the then current experiments in the field of aerial photography of enemy territory. Aerial photographs would be taken before and after a so-called bombing run. These photographs would then be overlaid on a screen and viewed alternately. As Hinman described it:

> first one picture for a fraction of a second, then the other picture for the same brief period, then the first picture again, and so on. The result was – or at any rate was supposed to be – that wherever there had been no change in the target area since it had first been photographed the screen showed only a single, perfectly motionless picture of that area; but that wherever there had been a change the picture on the screen flickered or wobbled.[1]

Clearly it was only one small step from the basic principles underlying the US experiments with pre- and post-strike aerial photography in wartime to the visionary Hinman Collator, the first experiments with which were conducted at the Folger Shakespeare Library soon after the war, in the summer of 1946. This device enabled a quick and reliable comparison of dozens of seemingly identical pages in Shakespearean Folios and Quartos, so that variant readings could be spotted almost instantly (see Figure).

It would be unsubtle to argue that the machine that revolutionized Shakespeare Studies, and its discipline of Bibliographical Studies in particular, was simply the outcome of aerial reconnaissance practice during the Second World War – of course, the invention represents a synthesis of existing knowledge as well as a range of other developments at the time – but the history of the Hinman Collator does remain the encouraging tale of Shakespeareans engaged in conflict, and an example of

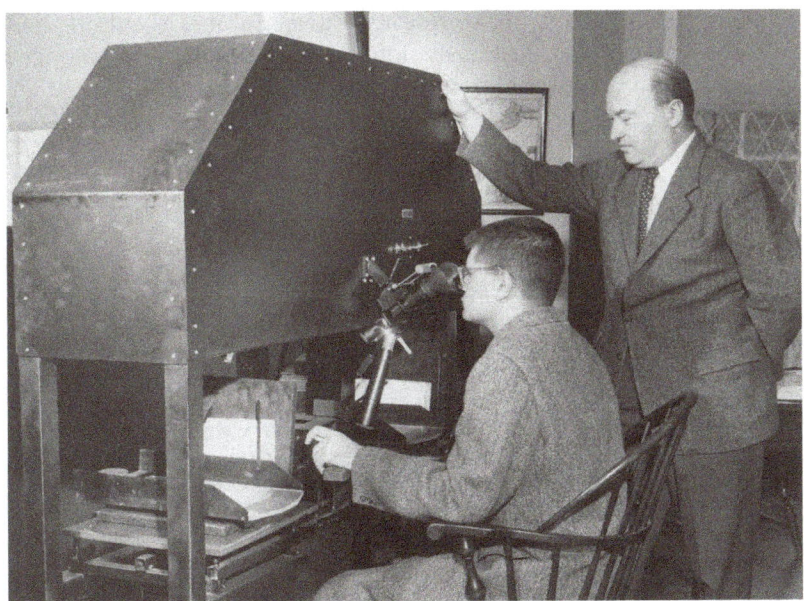

Fredson Bowers and junior researcher, Matthew Bruccoli at the Hinman Collator. Courtesy of Special Collections, University of Virginia

how these Shakespeareans emerged from that same conflict, reaping great rewards. The map of Shakespeare Studies would never look the same after the war.

The essays in this collection devoted to European Shakespeare have much in common with Charlton Hinman's collator project. Both are rooted in the dynamics of *conflict* and both are fascinated with the concomitant notion of *impact*. These projects share a dual focus, a frame of mind, while studying instances of conflict, to look, as Hamlet phrases it, 'before and after'.

Some might unfairly read a certain amount of irony into the relevance of wartime reconnaissance methods in the US Navy in order to appreciate some of the current aims of the European Shakespeare Research Association (ESRA).[2] Over the years, it has been the objective of ESRA to study the contribution of Europe to Shakespeare's conception of the world as well as the formative role of 'Shakespeare' to the development of a European sense of cultural identity. Its complex research mission, however, has never been the privileged property of European scholars. As a research area, European culture and Shakespeare's pivotal place in its long history have always belonged to the world academic community at large. On this rare issue, there should be no conflict.

Notes

1. Charlton Hinman, 'Mechanized Collation: A Preliminary Report', *Papers of the Bibliographical Society of Virginia*, 41 (1947), 99–106 (103). Hinman's description is also quoted in Steven Escar Smith, '"The Eternal Verities Verified": Charlton Hinman and the Roots of Mechanical Collation', *Studies in Bibliography*, 53 (2000), 129–61 (136). Smith notes that there is also another, slightly different, version of events, but both descriptions have the aerial reconnaissance flights as their focus.
2. The European Shakespeare Research Association website at www.um.es/ shakespeare/esra/ describes the aims of the organization and keeps a detailed record of past conferences (since 1990) and their proceedings. Other attractions of the site include its regular updates on current research, news about future conferences, and the possibility to register as a full member, free of charge.

Acknowledgements

This volume stems from the very productive debate among the community of international researchers who convened in Pisa, in November 2009, for the eighth conference of the European Shakespeare Research Association (ESRA). Though this book comprises only a selection of the work presented and discussed on that occasion, we are grateful to all those who took part in the conference for their individual contributions to the stimulating atmosphere which to led to first envisaging this project.

We are also extremely grateful to ESRA for entrusting us with the organization of the conference, and to both ESRA and IASEMS, the Italian Association of Shakespearean and Early Modern Studies, for their joint financial support of the initiative through their offer of bursaries for junior researchers.

The authors who have contributed the chapters and introductory pieces in this volume have been a pleasure to work with: a heartfelt 'thank you' to each one of them for their scholarship, time and dedication.

We also wish to thank Felicity Plester and Benjamin Doyle, our commissioning editors at Palgrave Macmillan, for their support towards the publication of this book, and Michael Dobson and Dympna Callaghan for welcoming it into their Shakespeare Studies series – there is no better venue we could think of. Thanks, too, to Barbara Slater for her invaluable assistance during the production process.

We are extremely thankful to the following institutions and individuals for their help with obtaining the images contained in this volume and securing publication rights: Deej Baker (Digital Services, University of Virginia); the Brotherton Library (Leeds); Waldemar Jerke; Douglas Lanier (University of New Hampshire); Manx National Heritage (Isle of Man); the Polish Center of Mediterranean Archaeology (University of Warsaw); the Romanian Academy Library; João Tuna. We are particularly grateful to Miranda Brigiotti for allowing us to use Ernesto Mussi's painting for the book cover, and to Edizioni ETS in Pisa for providing us with a photograph of the same.

Finally, a very special word of thanks to our friend and colleague Sylvia Greenup, who agreed to revise our script; to her linguistic expertise, professionalism and passionate commitment to the cause, this book owes so much more than a few lines of praise can express.

CARLA DENTE AND SARA SONCINI
PISA, DECEMBER 2012

List of Abbreviations

1H4	*Henry IV Part I*
Ado.	*Much Ado About Nothing*
Cym.	*Cymbeline*
Dream	*A Midsummer Night's Dream*
Ham.	*Hamlet*
JC	*Julius Caesar*
Lr	*The Tragedy of King Lear*
Mac.	*Macbeth*
More	*Sir Thomas More*
Per.	*Pericles*
PhT	'The Phoenix and the Turtle'
R2	*King Richard II*
Rom.	*Romeo and Juliet*
Temp.	*The Tempest*
TN	*Twelfth Night*
TNK	*The Two Noble Kinsmen*
Tro.	*Troilus and Cressida*
Ven.	*Venus and Adonis*
Wiv.	*The Merry Wives of Windsor*

General Introduction

Carla Dente and Sara Soncini

This volume on Shakespeare and conflict originates from the lively – and, as far as we know, perfectly amicable – exchange of ideas among participants in the eighth international conference of ESRA, the European Shakespeare Research Association, which took place in Pisa in 2009. As the local hosts, we felt on that occasion that the time and toil that had gone into organizing the conference had been amply rewarded by the quality of the responses to the proposed topic and by their challenging variety – not to mention the crowning achievement of four sunny days in a row in late November, a matter of no small wonder for those delegates already familiar with the standard Pisan autumn. Through a committed and truly collaborative international network of researchers, the map of Shakespeare's use of the conceptual space of conflict throughout the whole range of his production had been brought into sharper focus. Moreover, in keeping with ESRA's emphasis on approaching Shakespeare as a pan-European (and trans-European) literary and cultural phenomenon, which has historically transcended national boundaries to enjoy a distinctly nomadic afterlife, a fascinatingly complex picture had emerged of the crucial role played by principles, patterns and situations of conflict in the construction, the reproduction and the cross-cultural and cross-historical dissemination of Shakespeare's myth with its attached meanings.

While intended to reflect the broad understanding of the Shakespeare/conflict nexus, which underpinned the conference proceedings and so clearly proved its critical productiveness, the papers selected for publication have since been revised and refocused in order to cohere with the conceptual framework provided by this volume and to allow for a more systematic approach to a field which Paola Pugliatti, in her introduction to Part I, aptly defines as 'a region of infinite opportunities' for the critical reader. The threads of analysis pursued in the individual chapters, while presenting thematic and generic diversity, converge methodologically around three main positions, according to whether the primary emphasis falls on 'Conflict *in* Shakespeare', 'Conflict *through* Shakespeare' or 'Shakespeare in Times of Conflict'. These headings are by no means intended to describe absolute categories drawing fixed, clear-cut lines of delimitation in a taxonomic perspective, but simply serve to provide working hypotheses formulated on an empirical basis; an analytical tool kit that may help to elucidate the nature and the mechanics of the interrelation(s) posited by the conjunction 'and' in the title of this collection. Moreover, the points of intersection between the three areas are clearly as important to the overall perspective of the book as those of divergence; indeed, they are thrown into greater relief by the very fact that they cut across typological divisions. While this accounts for the internal mobility, we felt it was nonetheless important to outline research directions which, in future chartings of the territory, may be further pursued, complemented, reoriented – or even discontinued.

The contributions presented in Part I, devoted to conflict *in* Shakespeare, highlight the variety of conflictive and conflicting dimensions embedded in Shakespeare's texts. The order in which they are arranged mirrors the line of argument of Paola Pugliatti's introductory chapter to this section, which starts with a reflection on the presence of conflict in Shakespeare in its more literal, visible manifestations, as a constant thematic engagement with war and a range of related experiences, and then takes the discussion on to the metaphorical and metacritical plane. The situations and dynamics of conflict explored by the following chapters pursue a similar path in that they move from the negotiations between host and stranger in Shakespeare's dramas of migration and exile (Sabine Schülting), via the performance of duel rituals in the plays and their broader cultural and juridical implications (Pugliatti), on to the investigation of conflicting meanings and uses of silence in *King Lear* (Małgorzata Grzegorzewska), Shakespeare's wordplay as an expression of conceptual opposition and cultural convergence (Georgi Niagolov), and conflict as a stylistic principle informing a poetic text that has in its turn met with an embattled reception (Boris Drenkov on 'The Phoenix and the Turtle').

The second part of the volume ('Conflict *through* Shakespeare') draws a historically and geographically composite picture of the way in which Shakespeare's universe of discourse has been enlisted to dramatize a variety of conflicts of a socio-cultural, political or aesthetic nature (or, more often, a combination of the three). These include the so-called 'language wars' fuelled by situations of diglossia across Europe, and the role or roles played by Shakespeare translations in this context (Jesús Tronch-Pérez); the normative gender boundaries and stale theatrical conventions of 1930s Spain, and García Lorca's attempt to challenge them through his irreverent take on *Romeo and Juliet* (Juan Cerdá); the disruptive effects of *Hamlet* on the discursive texture of Humphrey Jennings's documentary film about the 'People's War', *A Diary for Timothy* (Alessandra Marzola); Heiner Müller's lifelong engagement with Shakespeare as a means of voicing his troubled relationship with the GDR as both a citizen and an intellectual (Miguel Ramalhete Gomes); the re-framing of the economic, sexual and racial conflicts within *The Merchant of Venice* in the light of contemporary debates within the New Europe (Francesca Rayner); and, finally, the cultural tensions surrounding Asian-British identities as expressed through Neil Biswas's recasting of *King Lear* as a TV serial (Alessandra Marino). The progression here develops along two main axes. The first is chronological, and covers a time span from the late nineteenth century (the first instances of Shakespeare translations into minorized languages tracked by Tronch-Pérez) to the present day. The second trajectory traces (inevitably, with some degree of approximation) the departure from the Shakespearean source in terms of the medium of reproduction, moving from textual practices such as interlingual but also intralingual translation (as in the case of Lorca's and Müller's dramaturgical reworkings of canonical texts) to instances of intersemiotic and intermedial transfer: stage productions, a screen adaptation and the engaging case of transmedial hybridization represented by Jennings's film.

Reversing the perspective, the third and final part of the book ('Shakespeare in Times of Conflict') looks at the way Shakespearean meanings have been renegotiated through reception and reproduction in actual historical contexts of strife and/or outright belligerence. While sharing with the previous section a preoccupation with the shaping agency of reconfigurations of Shakespeare in moulding European identities and their attendant mythologies, the emphasis here falls on the ability of conflict situations to unlock new, alternative or dissident meanings in the text, as well as on the negotiations activated by the encounter with Shakespeare in times of social duress and personal struggle. Extreme circumstances, traumatic experiences, tense political or cultural confrontations inevitably entail a changed perception of culture and of its role for individuals and for societies, thereby inviting a far-reaching interrogation of the significance and the potential uses of Shakespeare. This is apparent from the first three chapters in this section with their account of site-specific Shakespeare performances during the First and Second World Wars in various parts of Europe. Whether mounted by British conscientious objectors in Dartmoor prison during the Great War (Clara Calvo), by Second World War German and Austrian internees in British or Allied detention camps (Ton Hoenselaars), or by political prisoners in Fascist-dominated Romania (Monica Matei-Chesnoiu), these apocryphal productions of canonical texts prompt a new perception of the Shakespearean experience whose overall implications for the discipline of Shakespeare Studies are helpfully outlined in Manfred Pfister's introductory chapter. In the final two contributions to this section, the focus shifts towards a more metaphorical conflictive situation, that of the struggle for canonicity and cultural prestige which looms large in the history of Shakespeare translation and retranslation throughout Europe. At the same time, the collective, communal dimension of theatrical production gives way to a more private form of engagement with Shakespeare, as in Anna Cetera's account of Shakespeare translations in Poland and the role played by translators' personal rivalries and professional jealousies in determining aesthetic choices and translation strategies. Manfred Pfister's closing study of the sonnets translated in situations of confinement (such as prisons or detention camps) or displacement (as in the case of exiles), while returning to a model of Shakespeare reception in adversity, similarly emphasizes the psychological, even existential nature of the connection between the individual act of rewriting and the historical situation of conflict.

Conflict/Shakespeare/Europe

To approach Shakespeare through the lens of conflict may appear as an inevitable, one might even say a predictable, choice for a book written at the beginning of the twenty-first century: Shakespeare's experience of a conflict-ridden Europe, reflected in the ubiquitous presence of war in his drama, powerfully resonates with our own awareness, in the era of global terror and 'infinite' war, of the persistence and pervasiveness of violence as a means of addressing social, political, economic and identity conflicts and, more broadly still, as a basic relational modality between individuals as well as groups. The contemporary relevance of conflict as a topic is matched by the growing importance, in the area of Shakespeare Studies, of critical work devoted to war in Shakespeare and/or to wartime Shakespeares, often springing from international research networks,[1] or from nationally-funded research projects involving European partners. Amidst this shared general climate, a focus on conflict seems all the more timely and necessary for a book which openly declares its affiliations with the by now well-established tradition of European Shakespeare research.

As is well known, the political project of a united Europe is historically rooted in the determination, following the bloodshed of two world wars fought mainly on European territory, to prevent future deadly conflicts through joint democratic management within the context of a supranational, independent institution which would be able to transcend competing national interests and transform diversity from a source of contentious divergence into a strength. Equally familiar is the story of the rift between the European ideal of peace-building integration and the reality of division and conflict, but a few of its key moments are probably worth outlining. The foundation stones of today's European Union – the establishment of the ECSC in 1951 and of the EEC in 1957 – were laid in a territory still bearing the scars of the Second World War and freshly bleeding from the wound of the Iron Curtain. When, in February 1992, the by then 12 member states of the EEC signed the Maastricht Treaty in a promisingly Wall-free Europe, civil war was already raging in Croatia, and would spread to Bosnia-Herzegovina within less than two months. That Europe's debut as a political entity on the international scene should be accompanied by the culpable immobilism and ambivalence with which its policymakers addressed the first war fought on European ground since 1945 appeared disconcertingly ironical to Eurosceptics and Europhiles alike, and raised legitimate doubts as to the ability of 'Europe' actually to promote peace, democracy and respect for human rights.

The widespread tendency during the ethnic wars of the 1990s to explain away the violence of aggressive nationalism in terms of atavistic Balkan tribalism and to confine to non-European alterity a bloody war which was raging on the very doorstep of the infant EU is only the largest blot on a generally mediocre record for dealing responsibly and as a united entity with serious political and/or military crises. The pattern at work during NATO's takeover of what should have been Europe's role in Bosnia and Kosovo was repeated after the attacks of 9/11 and George W. Bush's launch of his infinite war on terror. Irritated by French and German reluctance to support American plans for the invasion of Iraq, the then US Secretary of Defense, Donald Rumsfeld, pitted what he disparagingly called 'Old Europe' against a 'New Europe' in which the political centre of gravity would shift to the East with the imminent admission of the new accession states. In Rumsfeld's reformulation, however, European 'newness' no longer referred to the recent conversion of the post-Communist member states-to-be to capitalist democracy, but rather to their governments' willingness to comply with US-dictated foreign policies – a willingness which was by no means confined to Eastern European countries but rather cut across the whole of Europe, since active support for Bush's 'coalition of the willing' also came from the UK, Italy, Spain, Portugal, Denmark and the Netherlands. While Rumsfeld's move is easy to pinpoint as a politically expedient strategy to destabilize, and thereby contain, the potential threat of an emerging and competing superpower on the world scene, Europe's response to an allegedly global conflict was characteristically fractured, both at the interstate level and within those countries where government support of the operations in Iraq met with fierce public dissent. Disproving Francis Fukuyama's authoritative prediction, made less than one year earlier, that 'the West may be cracking'[2] – that a distinctly European aversion to American unilateralism and disregard of international law had turned initial support for the war on terror into an ever-widening political and moral gulf between the two sides of the Atlantic – it was instead Europe that once more showed its cracks, and was left pondering the prospective loss, or at least dilution, of its identity.

As we write these pages, another global crisis is mercilessly exposing the chronic and apparently intractable conflicts in which Europe continues to be enmeshed, and that now more than ever seem to have come dangerously close to breaking point. The so-called Arab Spring of 2011 has once again brought into the open the political fragility of the extended New Europe and its inability to cope humanely and in unity with the problem of refugees and mass migration. Today, with the global financial crisis unresolved and the threat of default looming large, we have reached a point where the existence and the future of Europe as a political entity can no longer be taken for granted. For all the efforts made over the last two decades towards a deeper political, economic and cultural integration, so far it is general disorientation, inveterate myopia and reignited rivalries that have taken the place of the vigorous, unified response and shared vision that are so frequently invoked as the only possible long-term cure for systemic economic crisis. Even for staunch Eurobelievers such as the present writers it has become increasingly difficult, at this particular historical juncture, to dismiss as mere alarmism the spreading fear that following the Arab Spring of 2011, 2012 may go down in history as the year of the European Fall.[3]

Historically, then, the European Union's exposure to conflict situations has thus far worked as a litmus test indicative of its fragile and fractured identity, throwing into ever greater relief the 'symbolic and cultural deficit'[4] at the heart of a construction which has relied too exclusively on the impoverished cement of economic and political-bureaucratic ties, leaving it resting on shaky foundations. It has by now become a widely-shared perception that the future of Europe is to a great extent dependent upon making up this deficit. This was the rationale, for instance, behind the vibrant appeal 'For a Europe Founded on its Culture', issued in July 2004 by the European Writers' Council, in which the governments of the newly-enlarged EU were asked to 'launch an ambitious European project capable of cementing a European cultural identity' as proof of their genuine political commitment.[5]

Boasting both an outstanding historical record for 'cementing' emerging national cultures and an unparalleled cultural mobility, Shakespeare would appear to be a highly eligible candidate to fill the much-needed role of Europe's cultural mediator. He would be able simultaneously to operate as a connective tissue holding together this disjointed, unruly body and to foster an enhanced cosmopolitanism thanks to his unique position in world literature. And yet, there are at least two reasonable objections that can be raised against this candidacy. In the first place, to look at Shakespeare as Europe's champion is an obviously anachronistic gesture. Europe is hardly ever mentioned in the Shakespearean canon, and when it is, the word 'Europe' is used as a simple geographical indication entirely devoid of the kinds of cultural, spiritual or political connotations that were later attached to it.[6] This objection is rather easily overruled by pointing out that Shakespeare's prospective skill as a cultural mediator would lie not so much in some European core essence emanating from his works as in the enhanced intercultural dimension that is embedded both in their composition – Shakespeare as the recycler of countless European sources, myths, genres, cultural practices – and in the history of their diffusion first in Europe and then globally.

However, this unique capability for crossing historical and geographical borders and facilitating intercultural communication may in its turn legitimately raise scepticism as to Shakespeare's suitability for the job. Arguably, that is, the global dimension acquired by Shakespeare may be seen to undermine the very cultural cohesion that he is called upon to provide and promote. What if worldwide dissemination has irremediably watered down Shakespeare's potential to act as a symbolic glue for Europe? And how do we reconcile the phenomenon of a truly borderless Shakespeare with the emphasis on borders that still drives

Europe's attempts at defining and redefining its own identity?[7] What is more, there is surely something incongruous about pressing into the cause of European consciousness-raising a cultural icon that is currently undergoing a full-blown identity crisis. Shakespeare's plural and planetary existence has not merely destabilized previously clear-cut boundaries 'between local and global, original and copy, pure and hybrid, indigenous and foreign, high and low, authentic and inauthentic, hermeneutic and post-hermeneutic',[8] which might help to make sense of his metamorphic afterlife; what has been triggered is an ever-accelerating process of uprooted, deterritorialized reproduction, amounting in some instances to an out-and-out reconfiguration of Shakespeare as a logo or brand name designed for global consumption.[9] The conceptual instability that already inheres in the notion of 'Shakespeare' – a term which can at one and the same time denote 'a particular man, an author, a body of works, a system of cultural institutions and, by extension, a set of attitudes and dispositions',[10] as well as the way they intersect and interconnect – reaches spectacular heights once we turn our gaze towards 'the Shakespearean': that thick mass of references, quotations and hybridizations afloat in contemporary popular culture, which no longer appear traceable to an authorial figure, but strike us rather as an uncontrolled, virus-like proliferation of 'decontextualized, disembodied, unmoored, even hallucinatory references and recreations'.[11] Can one still rely on today's global 'Shakespace'[12] to provide solid enough ground for the cultural and symbolic (re)founding of European identity? Or are we, by investing Shakespeare with this unlikely role, simply holding on to an obsolete myth, and one which smacks dangerously of Eurocentric short-sightedness?

The contributions to this volume are best seen as an attempt to come to grips with these questions. They fully embrace the intercultural slant that has so far driven the ever widening research network promoted today by ESRA and by like-minded initiatives in the past.[13] By focusing on cultural interaction and cultural mobility, they adopt a European perspective that eschews monolithic definitions of both 'Europe' and 'Shakespeare', choosing instead to investigate the fissures and the fault lines that are produced by the encounter of different cultures both in and through Shakespeare. In so doing, they do not claim for Shakespeare the overambitious and ideologically suspect status of a European cultural icon, but rather envisage 'Shakespeare' as an ideal laboratory situation for the study of intercultural dynamics that have both European and global resonance – a 'cultural circuit facilitating motion', to borrow a phrase from Stephen Greenblatt's recent 'Manifesto',[14] which has historically played a prominent role in the cultural construction (and deconstruction) of that fuzzy, elusive concept that we still continue to address as 'Europe'. As the editors of this volume we wholly subscribe to Sonia Massai's call for a provincialization of Europe in the light of the worldwide (re)circulation of Shakespeare;[15] at the same time, however, we believe that the diachronic primacy of Shakespeare's European cosmopolitanism should not be altogether disregarded, as it constitutes one of the root causes of, or at least a crucial enabling factor in, his subsequent planetary spread. Finally, we trust in conflict as a vantage point that, by enhancing contradiction and points of friction, automatically wards off the myth of a transparent, coherent and cohesive 'European Shakespeare' inasmuch as it views this dyad through a prism which maximizes difference and discrepancy both between and within cultures.

The bright side of conflict

The critical fecundity of the conflict-oriented hermeneutics espoused by the contributors to this volume is operative on several levels. As argued above, looking at Shakespeare from the angle of conflict provides a valuable corrective to potentially totalizing approaches to cultural analysis which, in our case, would simply end up replacing the worn-out myth of an English or a national Shakespeare with its more fashionable and 'cutting edge' European or even global version. In this respect, the accent on conflict favours an apprehension of identity formation as a differential and relational process – indeed, a process which is relational in that it *is* differential.[16] Intraculturally, too, the hermeneutic approach adopted in this book commits the researcher to viewing cultural configurations as work in progress, the unstable result of ongoing negotiations that the conflict lens helps to bring into sharper focus: since conflicts involve 'a symbolic encounter that threatens to deeply affect, even to transform, the meanings which make up the fabric of any culture', the conflict zone is one in which, typically, 'the normative mechanisms of a cultural system and the vulnerable, incomplete and provisional character of that normativity' are laid bare.[17]

On a second – and related – level, the productivity of conflict as a critical approach to Shakespeare is testified by the freshness of the scholarly responses it has provoked. Małgorzata Grzegorzewska's thorough and thoughtful analysis of different types of silence in *King Lear*, by shedding light on the variety of meanings produced through their contrapuntal orchestration, aptly reminds us that Shakespeare himself was fully aware of the creative potential of dissonance. In a similar fashion, the other chapters in this book engage with Shakespeare dialectically, and in so doing they often unlock new meanings, point to alternative perspectives, challenge orthodoxies and ultimately broaden the scope of (European) Shakespeare research. The wide-ranging implications for the field of Shakespeare Studies of the critical retrieval of the peripheral, displaced and mostly forgotten Shakespeare performances examined in Part III have already been touched upon above; equally noteworthy, however, are the new cultural connections that were established in these European conflict zones – the unexpected ways in which Shakespeare was made to take on new meaning, and the poignancy acquired by his texts and by the conflicts they dramatize through the encounter with the historical contingencies of war and the dismal reality of pain, loss, trauma and displacement. Similarly, the received image of Shakespeare as a revered, albeit refashioned, model within the modernist movement loses ground before the more multi-dimensional and far less canonical version of bardolatry that emerges from Juan Cerdá's investigation, via García Lorca, of the points of intersection between Shakespeare and the continental avant-gardes. The payoffs of the 'Shakespeare and conflict' methodology may also extend beyond the Shakespearean sphere to acquire general theoretical relevance, as is the case with Anna Cetera's paper on Shakespeare translation in Poland. Her discussion of translation as a battlefield where rival translators fight for primacy, exclusivity and canonicity persuasively exposes the failure of the systemic approach which currently dominates the theory and study of translation to fully account for the shaping agency of personal factors in translators' strategies and, consequently, in the overall dynamics of reception, transmission and canonization that are specific to a given culture.

Last, but by no means least, our narrative of Shakespeare and conflict is also often a narrative of conflict management – of the way conflicts are negotiated thematically, stylistically and structurally inside Shakespeare's works and, in parallel, of the mediating agency which can be or has been assigned to Shakespeare in a number of conflict situations, both actual and metaphorical.

On one level, what emerges from the pages of this book about Shakespeare's record as a mediator in conflict situations is not always a success story. Perhaps ironically, this seems to have been particularly the fate of Shakespeare's third-party interventions in what has historically been the major arena of European cultural interaction, that is to say the field of translation. In the case studies discussed in Jesús Tronch-Pérez's survey of Shakespeare translation in diglossic environments, the expectations raised by Shakespeare's prestige and international standing concerning a possible mediation of the linguistic/political controversies in the Valencian region have ended in disappointment; while in the Polish scenario described in Anna Cetera's chapter, Shakespeare's cultural capital has actually worked to fuel the rivalry among translators and to exacerbate their competing claims to exclusivity and legitimacy. Even her analysis, however, envisages a prospective settlement of these Shakespeare-centred and Shakespeare-propelled controversies by pointing to developments in current editorial practice which might eventually foster a more active mediating role on the part of the editor.

The possibility that the principle of conflict itself might be generative of its own regulation is a powerful theme throughout the collection, starting with Sabine Schülting's opening contribution to the 'Conflict in Shakespeare' section. Her study of Shakespeare's drama of migration and of the different scenarios in which the tensions arising from the insider/outsider dynamics are played out highlights Shakespeare's alertness to the dramatic potential of the negotiation strategies elicited by each different situation but also, most importantly, his awareness of the peculiar suitability of dramatic performance, with its powerful combination of mimesis, embodiedness and role play, as a means of managing or preventing potentially deadly social conflicts – then as today.

The emphasis on patterns or paradigms of conflict – as opposed to simple taxonomic description – which underpins our shared investigation does indeed invite a more general application of the patterns of conflict negotiation which emerge from the particular contexts. One would be tempted, for instance, to connect the conclusions that Georgi Niagolov draws about 'Conflict and convergence in Shakespeare's wordplay' with contemporary debates over European integration and the difficulties involved in the implementation of the 'unity in diversity' model. The way in which, in Sonnet 53 and in *Richard II*, the dichotomy between opposing notions of 'substance' and 'shadow' is simultaneously enforced and transcended reveals the early modern capacity, so magisterially captured by Shakespeare's art, for seeing unity amidst division and discordance, for accepting and embracing contrariety and the potential for dialogue and even harmony that it entails. According to contemporary conflict theory, the pattern at work here would be less one of conflict resolution, with its Hegelian overtones, than the much more radical reconfiguration of positions, relationships and perceptions which is involved in conflict transformation, including its valorization of the relational and cognitive potential of conflict.[18] While no longer recuperable in its historical alterity, the inclusive mode of thinking that regulates Shakespeare's negotiation of rhetorical and conceptual oppositions still has a lesson for the puzzled citizens of Europe as they struggle to come to terms with the apparent paradox at the heart of its identity: it points, perhaps, to an adjustment of the cultural angle from which we view conflict as the precondition for being truly able to envisage, and build, a cosmopolitan culture of difference. We very much hope that this book may prove a small, but helpful, contribution to that process.

Notes

1. See for example the collection edited by Paul Franssen and Ros King, *Shakespeare and War* (Basingstoke: Palgrave Macmillan, 2008), which stemmed from research papers presented and discussed during the Sh:in:E (Shakespeare in Europe) conference on 'Shakespeare and European Politics' that took place in Utrecht in 2003. Simon Barker's *War and Nation in the Theatre of Shakespeare and his Contemporaries* (Edinburgh: Edinburgh University Press, 2007) was also originally presented as a paper on that occasion and later expanded into a full-length study. During the following biennial Sh:in:E conference in Cracow (2005), war-related issues were the focus of many of the papers presented in response to the proposed topic of 'Shakespeare and Memory', among which was an early core of Paola Pugliatti's subsequently developed monograph on *Shakespeare and the Just War Tradition* (Aldershot: Ashgate, 2010). On the other side of the Atlantic, the international conference on 'Wartime Shakespeare in a Global Context / Shakespeare au temps de la guerre' (Ottawa, 2009) inspired the collection edited by Irena R. Makaryk and Marissa McHugh, *Shakespeare and the Second World War: Memory, Culture, Identity* (Toronto: University of Toronto Press, 2012).
2. Francis Fukuyama, 'Europe and America: The West May be Cracking', *New York Times*, 9 August 2002, online at http://www.nytimes.com/2002/08/09/opinion/09iht-edfrancis_ed3_.html?pagewanted=all (accessed 2 October 2012).
3. This possibility was predicted by *Le Monde* editor-in-chief, Erik Izraeliwicz, in a feature which recently appeared on the front page of *Repubblica*, Italy's second-largest circulation daily newspaper: E. Izraeliwicz, 'La nostra scommessa davanti alle tre A', *Repubblica*, 26 January 2012, 1, 13.
4. Luisa Passerini, *Il mito d'Europa: radici antiche per nuovi simboli* (Firenze: Giunti, 2002), 124 (authors' translation). Elsewhere Passerini speaks of Europe's 'missed chances', remarking that 'the idea of Europe has lost, since the Second World War, most of its hopes of regeneration and the aura of utopianism and passion that were still present in the 1930s. By a sort of nemesis, this loss took place at the same time as the actual construction of an institutional European unity began [...] The European construction has been largely an affair of political élites.' See L. Passerini, *Europe in Love, Love in Europe: Imagination and Politics in Britain Between the Wars* (London: Tauris, 1999), 20.
5. Appeal by the Cultural World: 'For a Europe Founded on its Culture' (July 2004), online at http://www.europeanwriters.eu/images/files/1792004211744.pdf (accessed 31 January 2012).

6. Manfred Pfister notes that 'There is a paradox at work here that extends beyond Shakespeare's case: the increased economic, political, cultural and intellectual traffic between the European nations, which was a hallmark of the Renaissance, was not accompanied or underpinned by a programmatic emphasis upon a pointedly "European" cultural identity.' Manfred Pfister, 'Europa/Europe: Myths and Muddles', in *Myths of Europe*, ed. by Richard Littlejohns and Sara Soncini (Amsterdam and New York: Rodopi, 2007), 21–33 (26).

7. The problem of the Continent's territorial configuration was paradoxically revived by the tearing down of the Iron Curtain and the subsequent eastward expansion of the European Union. There is a glaring contradiction between Europe's commitment to act in accordance with its inclusive ethos and the growing anxiety over boundaries expressed by even the most passionate advocates of greater integration.

8. Richard Burt, 'Shakespeare, Glo-cali-zation, Race and the Small Screens of Popular Culture', in *Shakespeare the Movie II*, ed. by Richard Burt and Lynda E. Boose (London and New York: Routledge, 2003), 14–36 (15–16). The quotation also features in Alessandra Marino's chapter in this volume.

9. Among the first pivotal studies tracing this development, see Dennis Kennedy, 'Shakespeare and the Global Spectator', *Shakespeare Jahrbuch*, 131 (1995), 50–64; Barbara Hodgdon, *The Shakespeare Trade: Performances and Appropriations* (Philadelphia: University of Pennsylvania Press, 1998); and Michael D. Bristol, *Big-Time Shakespeare* (London and New York: Routledge, 1996).

10. Bristol, ix. In a later reformulation of the question, Balz Engler wonders whether the term 'Shakespeare' should be referred 'to a person, to a set of printed texts, to a cultural icon, to a theatrical tradition, or to a combination of all of these', concluding that 'it should definitely refer to all of these, and should additionally take into account the way they are related to each other'. See Balz Engler, 'Constructing Shakespeares in Europe', in *Four Hundred Years of Shakespeare in Europe*, ed. by Ton Hoenselaars and A. Luis Pujante (Newark: University of Delaware Press, 2003), 26–39 (27). Drawing on Pierre Bourdieu's notion of the cultural field, Sonia Massai maintains instead that 'Shakespeare can best be understood as the sum of the critical and creative responses elicited by his work'. See Sonia Massai, 'Defining Local Shakespeares', in *World-Wide Shakespeares: Local Appropriations in Film and Performance*, ed. by S. Massai (London: Routledge, 2005), 3–11 (6).

11. Richard Burt, *Unspeakable Shaxxxpeares: Queer Theory and American Kiddie Culture* (New York: St Martin's Press, 1998), xxx.

12. The term 'Shakespace' was coined in 2000 by Donald Hedrick and Brian Reynolds; it contains both the notion of 'Shake space' – of Shakespeare as a territory where different or even opposed forces are played out – and that of 'Shake's pace', that is to say the increasing acceleration produced by the new technologies in the reproduction of the Shakespeare signifier. See 'Shakespeare and Transversal Power', in *Shakespeare Without Class: Misappropriations of Cultural Capital*, ed. by Donald Hedrick and Bryan Reynolds (New York and Basingstoke: Palgrave, 2000), 3–47.

13. Most notably, Balz Engler's initiative at Basel University, the 'Shakespeare in European Culture' or Sh:in:E research project, which was established in 1997. For a historical survey of 'European Shakespeare' as a field of study, the

reader is referred to Ton Hoenselaars and A. Luis Pujante's 'Introduction' to *Four Hundred Years of Shakespeare in Europe*.

14. Stephen Greenblatt et al., *Cultural Mobility: A Manifesto* (Cambridge: Cambridge University Press, 2010), 5.

15. Massai, 10.

16. The notion of conflict as a situation of interaction whereby individual subjects or groups come into contact and become mutually defined and redefined is common to many recent definitions. It can be traced back to the seminal work of German sociologist, Georg Simmel, and forms the backbone of both Erwin Goffman's classic study, *Strategic Interaction* (Philadelphia: University of Pennsylvania Press, 1969) and Jürgen Habermas's theory of communicative action (*Theorie des kommunikativen Handelns* (Frankfurt: Suhrkamp, 1981)). Along similar lines, semiotic theory from Greimas onwards has emphasized the strategic/polemical dimension of social and linguistic interaction and, conversely, semiotically-oriented strategic studies have underscored the interactional/communicative dynamics at work in a conflict situation: for the latter see, for instance, Alain Joxe, 'Stratégie de la dissuasion nucléaire', in *Actes sémiotiques* (Paris: Institut National de la Langue Française, 1983); Lucien Poirier, *Le Chantier stratégique* (Paris: Hachette, 1997); Paolo Fabbri and Federico Montanari, 'Per una semiotica della comunicazione strategica', *E/C, rivista dell'Associazione Italiana di Studi Semiotici On-line* (2004), online at http://www.paolofabbri.it/saggi/comuni cazione.html (accessed 2 October 2012).

17. Cristina Demaria and Colin Wright, 'What is a Post-Conflict Culture?', in *Post-Conflict Cultures: Rituals of Representation*, ed. by C. Demaria and C. Wright (London: Zoilus Press, 2006), 5–12 (6).

18. On the notion of 'conflict transformation' see in particular Hugh Miall, Oliver Ramsbotham and Tom Woodhouse, *Contemporary Conflict Resolution: The Prevention, Management and Transformation of Deadly Conflicts* (Cambridge: Polity Press, 1999); Johan Galtung, 'Introduction: Peace by Peaceful Conflict Transformation – the TRANSCEND Approach', in *Handbook of Peace and Conflict Studies*, ed. by Charles Webel and Johan Galtung (London: Routledge, 2007), 14–32.

Part I
Conflict in Shakespeare

1
Introduction

Paola Pugliatti

Conflict in words

Roget's *Thesaurus* (1987) gives two options for 'conflict': 'contrariety' and 'quarrel'. The first term gives a list of near synonyms which range from words illustrating differences in opinion, such as 'disagreement', and those referring to situations in which some kind of value clash or personal hostility is present, such as 'antagonism' or 'irreconcilability', to those illustrating linguistic, semantic and rhetorical contraposition, such as 'inconsistency', 'antonym' or 'antithesis'. The second term, concentrating more specifically on the semantic field of 'quarrel', obviously includes, alongside other close synonyms, 'war' and 'warfare'.

When applied to the literary experience, therefore, the idea of 'conflict' provides ample ground for discussion, mainly owing to its metaphorical exploitation in different fields over time: to name only a few in the humanities area, linguistics, rhetoric, sociology, anthropology and psychology. As applied to Shakespeare's work, it merely commits the analyst to a point of view, an angle – that of discrepancy and contradiction – from which to observe one of the most unconformable scenarios ever produced in the kind of discourse we call 'literature'. Indeed, it outlines a region of infinite opportunities.

Some of the many possible perspectives that this region offers are pertinently developed in the section that follows. But the basic, etymological meaning of the word 'conflict', which is also prevalent in early modern English, is that which refers to the 'visible bullets' of war. War is ubiquitous in Shakespeare, not only as a staged event but also as the objective correlative of diverse experiences related to warfare, such as attack, defence, siege, opposition, resistance and so on. It is, therefore, an apt cue to start reflecting on conflict *in* Shakespeare.

War versus peace

Onstage as well as off, war was fashionable in the 1590s when Shakespeare started his London career, and theatre audiences enjoyed the loud noise of war which resounds in his early plays. They were excited by the clash of arms and gratified by the revival of untainted national heroes and their unworthy or imperfect rivals. They were thrilled by the turmoil of battle and the dangers of single combat. They shared emotions over the uncertain outcome of sieges, enjoyed stratagems and ambushes, plans to surprise the enemy, conspiracies and truce-breakings and, most of all, they applauded heroism and despised cowardice. In short, they were mesmerized by the magic charm of bloodshed and violence. They appreciated mercy when mercy was required but they were also able to decide when justice should prevail over mercy; and deprecated (as we still do) the 'unjust' aspects of violence: unjustified casualties involving innocent people, dispro-portionate brutality, fratricide, infanticide, rape, unmerciful butchery and unnecessary cruelty – when aptly presented as such – were strongly disapproved of.

Shakespeare gave his audience remarkably contradictory views of war, encompassing both the charm and horror of armed conflict. He staged war both as necessity and as scandal, painted it both as a scourge and a desired condition and even gave voice to an attractive side of cowardice. He penned powerful portraits of military leaders, but also revealed their human weaknesses and their nervous fragility. Some of Shakespeare's common soldiers are conscious of the conflicting issues of responsibility and obedience and capable of challenging them, while others simply see war as an exciting experience. Some are satirically depicted as the prototypes of absurd, ridiculous soldiers or they are criminals who, as was current practice, were recruited in prison; others still are war-manual maniacs; some are worthy of praise and some others deserve utter blame; all of them are indeed 'food for powder'.

The condition of peace is implied in the discourse of war. In Shakespeare's plays peace is seen as a temporary reprieve from the heat of warlike activities, as a preparation for war, as an unattain-able goal and even, in a Machiavellian mood, as a situation in which unforeseeable dangers may loom behind an apparently smooth surface. Indeed, it is even argued that an excess of security may endanger the public weal. That Shakespeare has been described as both a warmonger and as a 'pacifist' ultimately means that his texts enable both these conflicting readings.

Conflict and/or polyphony

Starting from the subject (war) which best shows Shakespeare's tendency to represent conflicting views of reality, we have reached the core of a much-disputed problem in Shakespeare criticism: his perspectivism or, if you like, the many ways in which he staged polyphony.

This is by no means a new issue, but it is probably worth retrieving. It originates in the insightful critical statement by John Keats who, writing about Shakespeare's achievement, but generalizing the idea to achievement in the field of literature, created the famous formula of 'negative capability', defining it as the capacity of 'being in uncertainties, mysteries, doubts, *without any irritable reaching after fact and reason*'.[1] Keats's description of the state of mind of 'being in uncertainties' is one which may be easily found in a dictionary definition of 'conflict', especially when the term is used in either the cognitive or the psychological sphere. What Keats offers the interpretative community, however, is not a negative definition of conflict as carrying the frustration of insolubility, but a positive ability to open up or abandon oneself to a plurality of visions and therefore to a creative and imaginative view of uncertainty.

One of the most interesting twentieth-century developments of Keats's 'negative capability' is Bakhtin's idea of 'polyphony'. In 1929, Bakhtin published the first edition of his book on Dostoevsky. In the same year an article by A.V. Lunacharsky, entitled 'The "Plurality of Voices" in Dostoevsky', appeared. In the largely revised 1963 edition of his book, Bakhtin acknowledges Lunacharsky's contribution to the development of the concept of 'polyphony'. Bakhtin's idea of polyphony also appears in his later 'Discourse in the Novel'. Here, although not mentioning the word 'polyphony', he gives a clear definition of the notion, stating that Dostoevsky's novels constitute 'an arena of neverending struggle with others' words, in all realms of life and creative ideological activity'.[2]

It is interesting to note that Lunacharsky's passages about Shakespeare appear as a development of Keats's idea of 'negative capability'. Shakespeare, Lunacharsky says, is 'an untendentious writer'; he has created 'an incredible variety of personages who are all independent of him' and, he adds, 'one cannot say of Shakespeare that his plays sought to prove a certain thesis, nor that the "voices" introduced into the great polyphony of the Shakespearean dramatic world sacrificed their autonomy for the sake of the dramatic intention or the structure as such'.[3] Surprisingly, Bakhtin and his group were not interested in the study of drama, although drama would seem to be the genre best suited to analysis as 'an arena of never-ending struggles with others' words'. Instead, in his 1963 book, Bakhtin argues against Lunacharsky's idea that Shakespeare's dramatic works constitute an unparalleled example of polyphony, and even affirms that 'the drama is by nature alien to genuine polyphony'.[4]

In a different area, Keats's idea of 'negative capability' has often been evoked in connection with Heidegger's notion of *Gelassenheit*, which has been explained as the 'spirit of *disponibilité* before What-Is which permits us simply to let things be in whatever may be their uncertainty and their mystery'.[5] Heidegger elaborated the idea of *Gelassenheit* in 1959, in a brief text entitled 'Zur Erörterung der Gelassenheit: Aus einem Feldweggespräch über das Denken' (published in English in 1966 as 'Conversation on a Country Path about Thinking').[6] Unsurprisingly, he does not quote Keats as his source but the mystic thought of Meister Eckart.[7] *Gelassenheit* illustrates a speculative attitude which rejects the assurance of technical thinking (what, *mutatis mutandis*, Keats defines as 'the irritable reaching after fact and reason'). In it, Heidegger draws a difference between 'calculative' and 'meditative' thinking. In the 'Memorial Address' which precedes the 'Conversation' in the 1959 German edition, he defines 'meditative thinking' by saying that it 'demands of us not to cling one-sidedly to a single idea, nor to run down a one-track course of ideas'.[8] He suggests an attitude of detachment, releasement and receptivity as the essence of thinking, for 'releasement toward things and openness to the mystery belong together. They grant us the possibility of dwelling in the world in a totally different way.'[9] The textual form in which Heidegger chose to expound the notion of *Gelassenheit* is that of a dialogue between a scientist, a scholar and a teacher. The dialogue form allows, more than any other kind of discourse, illustration of a polyphony of points of view or, as linguists in the Bakhtin circle would say, presentation of words reacting upon others' words. Uncertainties, in a dialogue, take the form of statements that are contrasted by, or even conflict with, other statements, presenting a plurality of voices and viewpoints, thereby allowing doubts to be highlighted instead of being dispersed or resolved.

Keats's 'negative capability' and Bakhtin's 'polyphony', especially as formulated by Heidegger within an inquiry into the nature of thinking, are, I believe, still intriguing and indeed they appear, more or less latently, at the core of much postmodern theoretical and critical elaboration.

A new radicalism?

Appropriationism, the critical approach now largely dominant in Shakespeare Studies, is in part a revision of the New Historicist approach. The critical efforts of New Historicists, it is argued, 'most frequently concentrate on rehistoricising Shakespeare within the political context of the Renaissance', while appropriationism 'delve[s] into the topic of reception'. It examines the many ways in which, through history, the cultural symbol 'Shakespeare' has been used, that is, it suggests 'a view of Shakespeare embedded not only in his own culture but in ours, forcing us to consider both the impact we have on the plays and the impact they have on us'.[10] Appropriation has also been described as *dialogue*, evoking Bakhtin's definition of dialogism as interaction with an alien word.[11] Such an approach is obviously a radical challenge to bardolatry and also tends to deal a serious blow to the idea of authorship, even by enacting gestures of text obliteration. At the same time, however, it strongly confirms the view of an 'adaptable', 'flexible' and 'impressible' Shakespeare, a Shakespeare impregnated with 'negative capability' or with *Gelassenheit*; which, in the final analysis, may appear as a new version of a Shakespeare 'for all times'. Thus, it appears that appropriationism is confined within a paradoxical space, embodying both a historicization and a (new?) form of universalism. Here, it never really succeeds in resolving the conflict between the local and the universal, nor does it provide satisfactory answers to questions such as: what is it that makes the 'adaptability' of Shakespeare's texts? To the question 'why Shakespeare?', Ivo Kamps replies that we do not remove Shakespeare from university curricula because '*Shakespeare serves radical critics just as well as he serves conservative ones.* Shakespeare has accrued so much cultural capital over the years that all sides have equal need of him – professionally, politically and financially.'[12] In other words, Shakespeare's readiness to be appropriated largely depends on the fact that he has been appropriated through time. But where does the adaptability of these texts reside? How is their anachronism manifested? What is that 'something' that makes Shakespeare's plays unendingly updatable? If we do not try to answer these questions, criticism of particular cases of appropriation runs the risk of remaining confined to description. On the other hand, as soon as we try to answer them we inevitably encounter the stubborn ghost of some form of universalism. If we still, using Hawkes's formula, '*mean by* Shakespeare',[13] and mean each time *differently*, then there must be *something* in the texts we attribute to him that has decreed their life beyond their time. Much beyond their time.

Attempts to answer such questions in a non-bardolatric way, that is, by evoking certain modes of thinking which in the Renaissance exploited the paradigm of *contrariety*, were made by a number of texts in the 1970s. Space does not allow me to discuss that critical trend extensively here, therefore I will only quote a passage by Robert Grudin. 'Drama', he says while discussing *contrariety* as a widespread way of thinking in early modern England, 'consistently dwells upon conflict and debate, but few dramatists have tested the potential of contraries as profoundly as Shakespeare, or employed it in such a wide variety of ways.'[14] In an entirely different critical era (the 1990s), T.B. Leinwand formulated a sociological answer to the same set of questions, describing Shakespeare as a cultural and even economic negotiator:

> For every argument enlisting him among the subversives or antiprovidentialists of the period we find an argument for the patriarchal bard or for the keeper of the great chain. Yet it seems clear that he was in many ways an interhierarchical figure: capitalist and artist, bourgeois and artisan, shareholder and actor, urban and provincial. He is perhaps less this or that than a stage for contestation and intermixing.[15]

One feels that the enigma of Shakespeare's uncanny manner of 'dwelling in the world in a totally different way' requires us now to provide new answers, fit for our time.

Notes

1. John Keats, Letter to his brothers, 21 December 1817, in *The Romantics on Shakespeare*, ed. by Jonathan Bate (Harmondsworth: Penguin, 1992), 198; italics mine.
2. Mikhail Bakhtin, 'Discourse in the Novel', in *The Dialogic Imagination*, ed. by Michael Holquist, trans. by Caryl Emerson and Michael Holquist (Austin: University of Texas Press, 1981), 259–422 (349). The Russian edition appeared in 1979.
3. Quoted in Mikhail Bakhtin, *Problems of Dostoevsky's Poetics* (Ann Arbor, Mich.: Hardis, 1973), 27–8. The Russian edition, *Problemy poètiki Dostoevskogo*, appeared in 1963, while Lunacharsky's article ('F.M. Dostoevskii v russkoi kritike') was originally published in *Novi Mir*, 10 (1929). Stefania Pavan has pointed out to me that Lunacharsky's terminology is slightly different from Bakhtin's. Lunacharsky speaks of 'polyphonism' (*polifonizm*) and 'multiplicity of voices' (*mnogogolosnost*).
4. *Problems of Dostoevsky's Poetics*, 28. Bakhtin's idea that Shakespeare and the theatre are not polyphonic is discussed at length in Alessandro Serpieri's essay 'Polifonia shakespeariana' (in *Retorica e immaginario* (Parma: Pratiche, 1986), 109–92).

5. Nathan Scott, *Negative Capability: Studies in the New Literature and the Religious Situation* (New Haven: Yale University Press, 1969), xiii.
6. Martin Heidegger, *Discourse on Thinking* (New York: Harper & Row, 1966). The 1959 German edition appeared in a small volume entitled *Gelassenheit*.
7. Eckart obviously elaborated the notion of *Gelassenheit* in connection with the mystic experience, as the annihilation of one's passions and the complete abandonment to God. Clearly, I am much simplifying Heidegger's idea of *Gelassenheit*, which is a complex and puzzling development in his late thought and one that has been interpreted in various ways. On the one hand, it has appeared as an attempt to overcome his previous ideas on voluntarism and resoluteness which have caused him to be linked with National Socialism. On the other hand, a supposed link with the thought of Eckart and, more generally, with mystic thought has been posited.
8. Heidegger, 53.
9. Heidegger, 55.
10. Jean I. Marsden, 'Introduction', in *The Appropriation of Shakespeare: Post-Renaissance Reconstructions of the Works and the Myth* (New York: St Martin's Press, 1992), 1–10 (5, 8).
11. Christy Desmet, 'Introduction', in *Shakespeare and Appropriation*, ed. by Christy Desmet and Robert Sawyer (London: Routledge, 1999), 1–14 (8).
12. Ivo Kamps, 'Alas, Poor Shakespeare! I Knew Him Well', in *Shakespeare and Appropriation*, 15–32, (20); italics mine. The concept of 'cultural capital' is developed by Pierre Bourdieu in his *La distinction: critique sociale du jugement* (Paris: Minuit, 1979).
13. Terence Hawkes, *Meaning by Shakespeare* (London: Routledge, 1992).
14. Robert Grudin, *Mighty Opposites: Shakespeare and Renaissance Contrariety* (Berkeley and Los Angeles: University of California Press, 1979), 3.
15. Theodore B. Leinwand, 'Negotiation and New Historicism', *PMLA*, 105 (1990), 477–90 (487).

2

'What country, friends, is this?' The Performance of Conflict in Shakespeare's Drama of Migration

Sabine Schülting

'What country, friends, is this?' (*TN*, 1.2.1).[1] Shipwrecked on the coast of Illyria, Viola in *Twelfth Night* is anxious as to how she will be received. Is it hospitality or persecution that is awaiting her? Antonio will later substantiate the fear that the country 'often prove[s] / Rough and unhospitable' to a stranger who is 'unguided and unfriended' (3.3.9–11). Viola's question introduces a recurrent conflict in Shakespearean drama. For Richard Wilson, it 'sets the scene for almost any play by Shakespeare, who repeatedly initiates plots with the mumming gambit of shipwreck, exile, or migration of an alien in an alien land'.[2] The plays explore the precarious situation of the traveller, the migrant or the exile, banished or otherwise separated from family, community or culture: cut loose from structures securing individual identity.

Shakespeare's migrants and exiles have received some scholarly attention in the past, ranging from Jane Kingsley-Smith's discussion of the theatrical aspects of banishment and exile[3] to Richard Wilson's reading of Shakespeare's scenes of exile and migration with, and as anticipations of, Jacques Derrida's concept of unconditional hospitality.[4] In this chapter I seek to reconcile, as it were, these two perspectives. In particular, the chapter highlights the significance of performance for the ethical and political implications of Shakespeare's plays. My main focus is one particular scene of Shakespeare's plot of migration: the moment of arrival, when – like Viola – the migrant anxiously asks what country he or she has come to, and, in turn, the potential host wonders who it is who is coming. It is the precarious instant when the decision between hospitality and inhospitality, but also between the migrant's gratitude and his or her abuse of hospitality, is pending.

Concentrating on *Sir Thomas More*, *The Tempest* and *Pericles*, I aim to show that the plays 'stretch' this moment and open up spaces of potentiality where early modern cultural strategies of coming to terms with the arrival are acted out. Rather than developing a utopian idea of unconditional hospitality, the plays work through the ambiguity resulting from the conflicts between the (early modern) migrant and the community.

Even though the term 'migration' in its modern sense, that is 'the movement of individuals or groups which involves a permanent or semi-permanent change of usual residence',[5] is anachronistic if applied to the early modern age, the phenomenon itself was well known in the sixteenth and seventeenth centuries. Early modern England hosted a considerable number of refugees, vagrants and itinerant workers who had left their homes as a result of colonization, international trade, the Reformation and the Counter-Reformation, as well as in response to the wide-ranging economic changes both within and outside England. However, I will not minutely differentiate between migration, exile and vagrancy here, but rather consider them as comparable phenomena. I will also largely neglect two categories of early modern migrants: first, the so-called 'vagrants' (including strolling actors), whose mobility and social status was drastically curtailed by the vagrancy laws of the sixteenth century; and second, the black population of early modern England, who became the target of anti-migration debates and policies towards the end of Elizabeth's reign. These events were related to, but not congruent with, the cultural controversies with which I am mainly concerned.

Citizens and aliens

The point of departure for my reading of what I call 'the moment of arrival' in Shakespearean drama is *Sir Thomas More*. Shakespeare scholars have traditionally been concerned with the intricate problem of the play's collective authorship. The so-called 'Hand D' passages, now generally believed to have been contributed by Shakespeare,[6] have attracted considerable attention. In fact, it has been argued that the lines of the revised Scene Six 'show Shakespeare playing a significant role in reshaping the overall script'.[7] They are of particular interest to my argument because – as Honigmann and others have suggested – this scene shifts the arguably xenophobic tendency of the first scenes of the play towards a 'most moving plea in defence of foreigners', thus giving ample evidence of 'Shakespeare's generosity of spirit'.[8]

Sir Thomas More is generally related to the anti-alien tensions in the London of the 1590s,[9] very likely the time when the original version of the play was written. The so-called Dutch Church Libel, a 53-line poem in doggerel verse, nailed to the walls of a Dutch churchyard in Broadstreet Ward on 5 May 1593, is frequently viewed as constituting the immediate topical context of the original version of *Sir Thomas More*. The placard threatened strangers living in London with merciless persecution for the hardship they had allegedly brought to the citizens: 'Weele cutte your throtes, in your temples praying / Not paris massacre so much blood did spill.'[10] Xenophobia was widespread among London citizens, and many travellers from abroad explicitly commented on the dislike of foreigners they encountered in the English capital.[11] In 1500, an anonymous Venetian lamented that the English 'have an antipathy to foreigners, and imagine that they never come into their island, but to make themselves masters of it, and to usurp their goods'.[12] Throughout the sixteenth century, anti-alien sentiments regularly flared up, particularly in times of crisis, with peaks in the first two decades of the century, the late 1560s and between the mid-1580s and 1593.[13] By the late sixteenth century the number of 'aliens' in London amounted to about 5000, thus not exceeding 4 to 5 per cent of the urban population,[14] and the majority of these were Dutch and French Protestants whose numbers had risen considerably in the 1560s and 1570s after the intensification of Catholic persecution in the Netherlands and in the aftermath of the massacres of St Bartholomew's night in France. But the Huguenots were not welcomed by everyone. They were prosperous, constituted their own communities, and often settled in the 'liberties' outside the jurisdiction of the city authorities.[15] Migrants (including both foreigners and aliens) living in London did not enjoy 'the freedom', that is, the full political and economic rights of the citizens. Yet English merchants and artisans, who regarded Huguenot economic activities as serious competition to their own businesses, repeatedly complained that strangers and foreigners offended against the restrictions on retail trade and set up workshops.[16] Xenophobic pamphlets as well as physical violence or the threat thereof were complemented 'with lawsuits and parliamentary campaigns to tighten the restrictions on aliens'.[17]

In general, the city authorities successfully managed to suppress anti-alien aggression, so that scenes of *physical* violence were relatively rare. Alien settlement was obviously supported by the upper ranks,[18] and xenophobic resentments were additionally rejected in (Protestant) sermons and homilies, which stressed the Christian obligation to grant hospitality particularly to strangers. '*We must tender hospitality without discretion, lest that the person, who we exclude and shout out of doores, be God himselfe*',[19] writes William Vaughan in *The golden-groue* (1600), a compendium on the moral, political and literary fashions of the time. Identifying the expansion of international trade as the major cause for the lack of hospitality, Vaughan contrasts the economic logic of the time, which construes the needs of the migrant as a financial burden rather than a moral obligation, with a Christian ethics of hospitality and generosity, which has to be granted to everyone. However, Vaughan's ideal of an unqualified hospitality remained a utopian ideal. Encounters with migrants in the early modern age (just as today, one might add) were primarily discussed with regard to the tensions between the migrant (or the group of migrants) and the host community whose norms the migrants allegedly ignored or whose privileges they unabashedly claimed. As David Williams has shown for medieval texts, the figure of the exile stood in opposition to the idea of the community, regarded as 'one without human intercourse', 'an unbinder, undoer, and an uncreator'.[20] Nevertheless early modern Londoners certainly 'experienced conflicting emotions about the strangers who settled in their communities, feeling on the one hand compassion for co-religionists driven from their homeland for refusing to abandon their faith, while at the same time sensing that aliens would compete with them for work and thus threaten their livelihoods'.[21]

The original text of *Sir Thomas More* clearly referred to, or perhaps even sought to capitalize on, the xenophobic tensions of the 1590s, negotiating them in a history play that recorded the events of the so-called Evil May Day of 1517 when anti-alien riots broke out on an unprecedented scale. It was several days before the authorities were able to put an end to the violence. Evil May Day was kept alive in cultural memory, and the Elizabethan authorities feared a repetition of these insurrections through the exacerbation of current anti-alien sentiment.[22] This was certainly one of the main reasons for Master of Revels Edmund Tilney's massive intervention in the manuscript. It was particularly the beginning of the play that caused his objection, succinctly expressed in his oft-quoted command:

> Leave out the insurrection wholly and the cause thereof, and begin with Sir Thomas More at the Mayor's sessions, with a report afterwards of his good service done being Sheriff of London upon a mutiny against the Lombards – only by a short report, and not otherwise, at your own perils.[23]

As Nina Levine has convincingly argued, Tilney's censorship attempted to mitigate the potentially seditious aspects of the play by 'substituting narrative for dramatic form'.[24] Early modern anti-theatrical discourse was driven by a strong concern that spectators might be induced to emulate deviant behaviour they saw performed on stage: 'Stage Plaies [...] move wholy to imitacion & not to the avoyding of those vyces which they represent', as the Lord Mayor complained to the Privy Council on 13 September 1595.[25]

The original text of *Sir Thomas More* closely follows the accounts given in Hall's and Holinshed's chronicles of the events leading to the Evil May Day riots. It adopts not merely the name of the leader of the insurrection, John Lincoln, but also the two incidents on which the complaints of the London citizens against the strangers were based: first, the abduction of a London artisan's wife and plate by the Lombard Fra(u)ncis de Barde, who refused to release her and then boldly demanded that her husband pay for her board; and, second, the theft of two doves which carpenter Willyamson had bought and which were taken from him by a Frenchman, who had Willyamson sent to prison when he complained.[26] In *Sir Thomas More*, these two incidents are conflated, turning Willyamson into the victim of both trickeries. Levine remarks that this would have caused the censor's objection since, in contrast to the narrative told by the chronicles, the actual performance of these abuses on stage would have bridged the historical distance 'with a volatile presentation designed to rile contemporary audiences'. This would have been reinforced by the fact that the play gives a voice to the citizens, thus eliciting sympathy for their protest. Crucially, in the play, the rioters' complaints in Scene One are driven less by xenophobia than by a conflict between citizens and the elite, the former's understandable anger at being exploited by strangers who are not presented 'as refugee artisans but as imperious courtiers gleefully helping themselves to the citizens' property and wives'.[27]

Although the revision of the play does not completely follow the instruction of the censor, who obviously intended to reduce the parts of the rioters even more extensively, the Hand D (that is Shakespeare's) additions have been criticized by recent scholars as 'belittl[ing] the protesters, depriving them of an individuality they possessed earlier in the play and reducing them to the idiotic fear of disease-causing foreign vegetables'.[28] Although Cohen is certainly right in stressing the orthodox justification of the political order at the basis of More's arguments,[29] he somewhat neglects the fact that Shakespeare's additions transform the economic and social strife, the quarrels between citizens and (alien) courtiers into tensions between citizens and migrants, thus shifting the source of the conflict. More describes the impending riots as leading directly to a complete dissolution of social order, a Hobbesian war of all against all, in which 'men, like ravenous fishes / Would feed on one another' (*More*, 6.97–8). However, what eventually convinces the rioters is neither this dystopian vision nor the reference to the divine nature of social order, but rather More's appeal to their empathy with the migrants. He draws a verbal image of the 'wretched strangers' (*More*, 6.85) that is diametrically opposed to their previous appearance on stage and completely shifts their social status. More's strangers are no longer the arrogant cavaliers of Scene One, but poor and homeless migrants, 'Their babies at their backs, with their poor luggage, / Plodding to th' ports and coasts for transportation' (*More*, 6.86–7). Asking his listeners to imagine themselves in the position of the dispossessed, More does not merely confront the citizens with the possible results of their anti-alien insurrection, but also imaginatively redraws the conditions of the first encounter and the power relation between citizens and strangers.

Levine points to the contradiction at the basis of More's speech, which merges 'a subject's obedience with universal brotherhood'.[30] More reminds his audience that they share with the migrants their precarious political position with respect to the authorities, and this is what should prompt them to rethink their behaviour. Having taken part in the insurrection, they might soon share the fate of the migrants, that is banishment:

> [...] whither would you go?
> What country, by the nature of your error,
> Should give you harbour? [...]
> Why, you must needs be strangers. Would you be pleased
> To find a nation of such barbarous temper
> That, breaking out in hideous violence,
> Would not afford you an abode on earth,
> Whet their detested knives against your throats,
> Spurn you like dogs, and like as if that God
> Owed not nor made not you [...]
> What would you think
> To be thus used? This is the strangers' case,
> And this your mountainish inhumanity.
>
> (*More*, 6.141–56)

More's vision places the exiles in a condition reminiscent of Lear's situation on the heath; excluded from all society, reduced to bare existence, and denied not merely the status of citizens but even that of human beings.

Richard Wilson reads this scene as an anticipation of the dream of unconditional hospitality as developed in the late work of Jacques Derrida.[31] However, I would rather agree with Levine that *Sir Thomas More* spells out (not least through the conflicting positions represented by its various authors) the complex tensions between the crown, the citizens of London and the migrants, *without* resolving these conflicts in a conciliatory scenario. Analyses of the scene that proceed on a binary opposition – be it that of xenophobia vs. universal humanism or of conservatism vs. revolt – fail to recognize 'the paradoxical centrality of "the stranger" – not only as a demonized outside of citizen identity, as it is usually understood, but as an unsettling figure for the differences at the heart of civic polity'.[32] In the play, the stranger emerges as a figure that challenges citizenship and the privileges of the citizen while concurrently serving as a foil against which these very concepts are negotiated, affirmed and defended. Whereas the beginning of the play establishes the opposition between the migrant and the community, as well as between citizens and courtiers, More's speech stresses the instability of the first opposition and the unequal distribution of power characterizing the second. More reminds his listeners that the nature of royal authority is unpredictable and can easily redraw the boundary between citizens and exiles.

Significantly, More appeals to the rioters' imagination by invoking a vivid image of 'the wretched strangers [...] / Plodding to th' ports and coasts for transportation' (6.85–7). The moment is not acted out. Instead, it is an effect of rhetoric, of *enargeia*, that is, the power of language to create a vivid (mental) picture of that which is set forth in words. The empathy with the fate of migrants which More demands is dependent on this form of powerful oratory. As a stage manager of sorts, More makes his listeners *see* the strangers, acknowledge their misery, and imagine themselves in their position. In this sense, his language is performative, replacing, as it were, the encounter between citizens and strangers in the first scene of the play with a radically different scenario, whose effect on its audience (on stage) turns out to be even stronger. Performative language thus becomes the means of making the rioters empathize with the emotions experienced by the migrants.

Although a certain degree of anachronism is involved in projecting the relatively recent concept of empathy onto the early modern age,[33] I would nevertheless argue that Shakespearean drama shows an awareness of the processes to which modern philosophy, psychology and cognitive sciences have come to refer as empathy: '"the attempt by one self-aware self to comprehend unjudgmentally the positive and negative experiences of another self", depending on "the use of imaginal and mimetic capacities"'.[34]

David Krasner underscores the capability of theatre to elicit affective reactions in the audience, thus making them imagine the experience of the actor-character '*as potentially actual*' and allowing them '*to transcend the limits of [their] own world*'.³⁵ On the fictional level, More's speech effectively brings about the two stages of empathy Krasner discusses: an 'affective reaction' that leads to cognition.³⁶ To More's question, 'What would you think / To be thus used?', the citizens respond: 'Faith, 'a says true. Let's do as we may be done by' (*More*, 6.157–8). More draws upon the potential of the imagination to bridge the gap between the self and the other, the citizen and the migrant. In this way, the scene shows on stage what Krasner identifies as the power of theatrical performance: that of evoking the audience's empathy with the actions and characters before their eyes.

Performances of the moment of arrival

The fundamental insecurity of arrival so vividly described in More's speech is repeatedly staged in Shakespearean drama: Viola in *Twelfth Night*, Rosalind and Celia in *As You Like It*, the shipwrecked party in *The Tempest*, Egeon in *The Comedy of Errors*, Pericles – all are uncertain as to whether they can hope for hospitality and support in a country where they are strangers. Who is awaiting them? Should they disguise their real identity or even hide themselves? 'What should I do in Illyria?' (*TN*, 1.2.3), asks Viola, and there is no immediate solution to the problem of how the migrant might best be able to cope without any friends or relatives in the foreign land. But the insecurity also affects the host: Leontes in *The Winter's Tale* or Cleon in *Pericles* cannot be sure who is coming. Will the guest bring war or peace? Is he really who he claims to be? How long is he going to stay?

Shakespeare's plays stage this insecurity of the event of arrival as a moment of potentiality both for the migrant and the host community. Although the solution of the conflict is of course to some extent prescribed by the genre and, as a matter of fact, has already been decided upon by the playwright, the performance frequently suspends it. It is acted out by the characters on stage, thereby being postponed for a few lines, a scene or sometimes even the whole play. In *Twelfth Night*, for example, Viola's precarious situation is not immediately resolved, but deferred by the comic scene in Act One, Scene Three. It is only at the beginning of Scene Four that she has become a member of Duke Orsino's household. In *As You Like It*, Rosalind, Celia and Touchstone decide to leave the court 'to liberty, and not to banishment' (1.3.132). It takes some scenes before they reappear on stage (2.4), when they are in the Forest of Arden, weary and exhausted from their journey and unable to walk any further. Another 80 lines later Corin, the old shepherd, offers to share with them the little he possesses (2.4.81–2).

In *The Tempest*, the whole play revolves around the vulnerable situation of the arrivals on Prospero's island and the question of whether any harm will be done to them, whether they will manage to usurp Prospero's power, or whether there will be a final reconciliation. Uprootedness is the universal condition from which every single character suffers in this play, and the island is the stage on which the various relationships between guests and hosts, shipwrecked strangers and native inhabitants are being acted out. From the very beginning of the play, Prospero claims the powerful position of the host who can dictate his laws to his 'guests'. The 'collusion between hospitality [...] and power',[37] stressed by Derrida, could not be more palpable. For a considerable time, hospitality is merely a promise, an effect of Prospero's art of (theatrical) illusion. This becomes most obvious in Act Three, Scene Three, when the exquisite banquet prepared by Prospero's spirits disappears as soon as the group of castaways approaches. But not only is hospitality not granted, its refusal is also *staged*. In *The Tempest*, hospitality is a favour whose potentiality is displayed to the arrivals only to be performatively withdrawn.

In fact, it is the effect of this refusal of hospitality which towards the end of the play evokes Ariel's pity and ultimately makes Prospero change his mind. Ariel has been affected by the scenes of inhospitality he himself has both staged and witnessed:

> Confined together
> In the same fashion as you gave in charge,
> Just as you left them; all prisoners, sir,
> In the lime-grove which weather-fends your cell.
> They cannot budge till your release. The King,
> His brother, and yours, abide all three distracted,
> And the remainder mourning over them,
> Brimful of sorrow and dismay; but chiefly
> Him that you termed, sir, the good old lord Gonzalo:
> His tears run down his beard like winter's drops
> From eaves of reeds. Your charm so strongly works 'em
> That if you now beheld them your affections
> Would become tender.
>
> (*Temp.*, 5.1.7–19)

He adds 'Mine would, sir, were I human' (19). Through Ariel's intervention Prospero eventually realizes what Thomas More also demands of the rioters and what Miranda feels when she observes the shipwreck of Act One: the fact that witnessing the act of migration makes the onlooker sympathize or empathize[38] with the migrant. As in *Sir Thomas More*, in Ariel's speech migration has become a heart-rending visual scenario, a kind of *tableau vivant* which is presented to the sight (or, rather, the imagination) of the listener(s) – both within the play and in the theatre. It is Ariel's invitation to emulate his pity for the strangers that eventually makes Prospero change his mind. On a different level, Ariel's recognition also has implications for a discussion of the affective power of theatre. As Krasner stresses, it is primarily the bodily existence of the actor playing the character that evokes the audience's affective response: 'The actor onstage is not an abstraction but a living organism expressing emotions, actions, gestures, movements, and sounds. [...] I exist in the audience as observer, but I also exist as a body reflecting on the actions and movements of another body.'[39] Ariel's remark that he feels with the castaways despite the lack of any shared bodily experience enhances the effect of his lines on the empathizing (human) listener/spectator.

When Prospero eventually greets his prisoners with 'Welcome my friends all' (5.1.127), it has taken him five acts to come to realize that he and the arrivals on his island share the same fate. This late welcome leads to mutual recognition, forgiveness, the establishment of new communal bonds and the return home – a reconciliation from which Caliban will be forever excluded. In contrast to the early modern alien who may, under certain conditions, demand hospitality, Caliban 'is relegated to an absolute outside, savage, barbaric, precultural, and pre-juridical, outside and prior to the family, the community, the city, the nation, or the State'.[40] In the early modern age, this relation between community and absolute outsider is not regulated by any juridical or moral obligation nor predicated upon emotional ties.

If unconditional hospitality was at best an ideal, both in early modern England and in Shakespeare's plays, the hospitality Pericles enjoys at the court of King Simonides in Persepolis seems to be the only exception to the rule. Having barely survived the shipwreck and having lost every-thing, Pericles, washed ashore, bemoans his fate as 'a prince [bereft] of all his fortunes' (5.49), who does not wish for more than 'death in peace' (51). His identity as Prince of Tyre has become meaningless, so that on encountering the two fishermen, he does not tell them his name, but repeatedly refers to himself as 'a man' (5.95, 108, 112) – thus implicitly asking for their empathy with his situation on the basis of their shared human nature. The fishermen's offer of clothes, food and shelter (5.113–18) establishes a sharp contrast not merely with the welcome Pericles experienced in Antioch, but also with the 'great ones' of Pentapolis of whom the fishermen – somewhat echoing More's picture of 'ravenous fishes' (*More*, 6.97) – complain: 'the great ones eat up the little ones. I can compare our rich misers to nothing so fitly as to a whale: a plays and tumbles, driving the poor fry before him, and at last devours them all at a mouthful' (*Per.*, 5.67–70).

In contrast to *Sir Thomas More*, the conflict between the aristocracy and the common people is here free from any xenophobic undertones. In *Pericles*, aristocratic greed is explicitly contrasted with the poor fishermen's generosity towards the destitute stranger. Moreover, the fishermen's severe social critique is a far cry from the citizens' (and also More's) disobedience to royal authority. Instead, they praise their king as 'good Simonides', claiming that 'he deserves so to be called for his peaceable reign and good government' (*Per.*, 5.137, 139–40). In a way, then, *Pericles* can be read as a revision and rectification of some of the potentially subversive notes of the earlier play which caused the censor's intervention.

When Pericles arrives at court, the lords treat him as a despicable 'stranger' (6.55). They see in him the vagabond or migrant workman who has 'practiced more the whipstock than the lance' (54). But Simonides exhorts them that strangers should not be judged by their outward appearance and princes 'Should live like gods above, who freely give / To everyone that come to honour them' (7.57–8). Despite his obscure identity which he does not disclose to his host, Pericles is granted abundant hospitality at Simonides's court, which goes far beyond the basic needs of a castaway. He participates in the tournament and is welcomed to a courtly banquet where he is offered a place of honour; and he receives valuable presents from the king, who eventually even gives him his daughter in marriage. Simonides's hospitality is excessive and apparently unconditional. It seems to meet the ethical obligation of Derrida's categorical 'yes *to who or what turns up*, before any determination, before any anticipation, before any *identification*'.[41] The questions so crucial in early modern controversies about vagabonds and foreigners – Who is coming? What is his or her background? Does s/he deserve hospitality? How long will s/he be staying? – are not seriously considered by either the fishermen or Simonides. Yet, also in these scenes, hospitality is granted only to strangers who do not question the power of the host. During the banquet, Simonides and Thaisa are captivated by Pericles whose inward virtue, the play seems to suggest, they recognize intuitively – despite his shabby outward appearance.

Whereas Antiochus sees his position endangered by his daughter's suitors, Simonides gives freely to those who have come to honour his sovereignty and, one should add, who 'by nature' deserve it.

In *Pericles*, the moment of arrival and its different possible outcomes are played through Antiochus's perfidy, Cleon's abuse of hospitality, the support granted to Thaisa by Lord Cerimon and to Pericles by the fishermen, Simonides's hospitality, the reduction of hospitality to pandering – these are all variations on the position of the host, whereas the stranger appears as a suitor, a guest relieving the famine of the host, a castaway, a knight in disguise, a slave sold by pirates, and as a customer to a prostitute. Interestingly, the negotiation of the imminent conflict between arrival and host (community) is repeatedly marked by the change from (Gower's) narrative to action. In a recent article on the play, Peter Holland contends that

> Gower is a narrator who, as he identifies, 'stands I'th'gaps' (4.4.8), marking the interstices, those connections which drama does not, sometimes cannot and occasionally refuses to show [...]. In a way that no previous version of this story had had to do, the author or authors of *Pericles* [...] separate narration from action, story-telling from story-showing, turning the narrator into an actor, the author into a performer in 'the text' they have made.[42]

Some of these interstices between narrative and action exactly coincide with what I call the moments of arrival. Gower stops his narrative precisely at the moment of shipwreck – shipwreck of course also being notoriously hard to stage, so there may be a practical element to this – or when the characters arrive in a foreign country. Through the narrator, who draws attention to this moment and the concurrent shift in mode, the crucial relevance of this scene and the necessity to *act out* the situation, to perform it on stage rather than merely narrate it, is stressed. After having left Tarsus, Pericles's fleet is destroyed in a storm and he is shipwrecked on the coast of Pentapolis. Gower comments:

> For now the wind begins to blow;
> Thunder above and deeps below
> Makes such unquiet that the ship
> Should house him safe is wrecked and split,
> And he, good prince, having all lost,
> By waves from coast to coast is tossed,
> All perishen of man, of pelf,

Ne aught escapend but himself,
Till fortune, tired with doing bad,
Threw him ashore to give him glad.
          Enter Pericles wet [and half-naked]
And here he comes. What shall be next
Pardon old Gower; this 'longs the text.

(*Per.*, 5.29–40)

Editor Walter Cohen in the Norton Shakespeare glosses "longs' as follows:
'Continuing would lengthen Gower's speech too much; or, *'longs*:
belongs to'.[43] I would suggest understanding the line as an acknow-
ledgment that 'story-showing' has a greater impact on the audience
than the potentially long-winded, hence wearisome, 'story-telling' of
the scene of arrival. Gower's deixis ('And *here* he comes', emphasis
added) directs the audience's attention to Pericles's visual appearance –
as the pitiable victim of a shipwreck who has lost everything. Theatrical
performance replaces narration – primarily, I would argue, to heighten
the audience's attention towards this particular moment and enhance
its effect. This reading would be corroborated by Act One, Scene Two
of *The Tempest*, where Miranda's reaction to a reverse shift of mode is
shown. Whereas Miranda has been thoroughly affected by the terrible
sight of the shipwreck ('O, I have suffered / With those I saw suffer!'
Temp., 1.2.5–6), she hardly pays attention to Prospero's *narrative*, even
though it is her own life story he tells her. Her emotions during the
storm are not those described by Hans Blumenberg in his *Shipwreck with
Spectator*, namely, an indulging in 'the pleasantness that is said to characterize this sight', not as the 'result of seeing someone else suffer but
of enjoying the safety of one's own standpoint'.[44] Instead, the vivid scenario makes her transcend her own position and 'share [...] a similar [...]
feeling with the object of contemplation'.[45] Returning to the shift of
mode, in *Pericles*, from telling to showing, one may observe that it is
not the opposition between language and acting that is relevant here,
but rather the difference between narrative and (rhetorical or bodily)
performance. It is only the latter that creates powerful images – real
or imaginary – and thus manages to emotionally involve listeners and
spectators, both on stage and in the auditorium.

Conclusion: (stage) managing conflict

Shakespeare's 'drama of migration' not only makes its audience *imagine*
the situation of strangers whose presence provoked severe tensions in

early modern England. The plays performatively enact or play through possible relationships between host community and migrants, self and other, including scenes of hospitality, betrayal or open violence. They evoke and channel affective reactions (ranging from xenophobic hatred to pity and empathy), and – in the case of comedies and romances – eventually reimagine and celebrate the harmony of a restored community. Crucially, the plays stage the hiatus in the moment of arrival when the outcome has not yet been decided upon. Viola's question, 'What country, friends, is this?', captures this precarious moment from the perspective of the migrant, whereas Cleon's enquiry sent to Pericles's fleet represents the same moment from the point of view of the vulnerable community, unsure who comes, 'for what he comes, and whence he comes' (*Per.*, 4.79). The plays 'give time', as it were, to the audience, asking them to rethink the parameters of these encounters by encouraging them to sympathize or empathize with the characters onstage. In this way, Shakespearean drama also reflects on the power of theatre to affectively engage its audience, thereby enabling them imaginatively to cross the gap not merely between fiction and reality, but also between their own and another's experiences. It self-reflexively affirms the crucial social function of theatrical performance for a community's interaction and, in particular, its value as a space for the negotiation of the conflicts arising from migration.

Notes

1. Citations from Shakespeare's plays (except for quotes from *Sir Thomas More*) are all taken from *The Norton Shakespeare*, ed. by Stephen Greenblatt et al. (New York and London: W.W. Norton, 1997).
2. Richard Wilson, *Shakespeare in French Theory: King of Shadows* (London: Routledge, 2007), 254.
3. Jane Kingsley-Smith, *Shakespeare's Drama of Exile* (Basingstoke and New York: Palgrave Macmillan, 2003).
4. Wilson, 242–60.
5. Peter Clark and David Souden, *Migration and Society in Early Modern England* (London: Hutchinson, 1987), 11.
6. See John Jones, *Shakespeare at Work* (Oxford: Clarendon Press, 1995), 7–29.
7. John Jowett, 'Introduction', in Anthony Munday and Henry Chettle, *Sir Thomas More*, ed. by John Jowett, The Arden Shakespeare, Third Series (London: Methuen Drama, 2011), 1–129 (21). All citations from the play follow this edition and will be noted parenthetically in the text.
8. E.A.J. Honigmann, 'Shakespeare, Sir Thomas More and Asylum Seekers', *Shakespeare Survey*, 57 (2004), 226, 235.
9. See for instance Tracey Hill, '"The Cittie is in an uproare": Staging London in *The Booke of Sir Thomas More*', *EMLS*, 11 (2005); Honigmann, 225–6, 233–5; Nina Levine, 'Citizens' Games: Differentiating Collaboration and *Sir Thomas*

More', *Shakespeare Quarterly*, 58 (2007), 31–64; Wilson, 257–8; Jowett, 41–7. William B. Long even suggests that the original play had been commissioned by government officials as an attempt to deal with the anti-alien tensions of the time: see 'The Occasion of *The Book of Sir Thomas More*', in *Shakespeare and 'Sir Thomas More': Essays on the Play and its Shakespearean Interest*, ed. by T.H. Howard-Hill (Cambridge: Cambridge University Press, 1989), 45–56 (49). Jowett questions this 'instrumental view of theatre in relation to those in power', adding that the choice of Thomas More as the protagonist of such a project would not have made much sense (Jowett, 15).

10. *The Dutch Church Libel*, http://www.lesliesilbert.com/churchlibel.html (accessed 27 July 2011).

11. See Ian W. Archer, 'Responses to Alien Immigrants in London, *c*. 1400–1650', in *Le migrazioni in Europa secc. XIII–XVIII: atti della 'venticinquesima settimana di studi'*, ed. by Simonetta Cavaciocchi (Florence: Le Monnier, 1994), 755–74 (755).

12. Quoted in C.W. Chitty, 'Aliens in England in the Sixteenth Century', *Race & Class* 8 (1966), 131.

13. Compare Ian W. Archer, 'Popular Politics in the Sixteenth and Early Seventeenth Centuries', in *Londinopolis: Essays in the Cultural and Social History of Early Modern London*, ed. by Paul Griffiths and Mark S.R. Jenner (Manchester and New York: Manchester University Press, 2000), 26–46 (31).

14. Ian W. Archer, *The Pursuit of Stability: Social Relations in Elizabethan London* (Cambridge: Cambridge University Press, 1991), 132. Early modern terminology differentiated between English-born 'foreigners', who had moved to London but were not citizens, and 'aliens' or 'strangers', who had come from abroad and who were not allowed to set up a workshop or be engaged in retail trade. 'Aliens' could become 'denizens' by royal letters patent, which granted them the right to purchase land. 'Naturalized aliens' held basically the same privileges as Englishmen. See Steve Rappaport, *Worlds Within Worlds: Structures of Life in Sixteenth-Century London* (Cambridge: Cambridge University Press, 1989), 42; Chitty, 132. In the following, I will use the terms in their early modern sense.

15. Jowett, 42.

16. Rappaport, 42–60; Archer, *The Pursuit of Stability*, 131–40.

17. Archer, 'Popular Politics', 30–1.

18. See Archer, 'Responses to Alien Immigrants', 755 *passim*, 766.

19. William Vaughan, *The golden-groue moralized in three bookes: a worke very necessary for all such, as would know how to gouerne themselues, their houses, or their countrey. Made by W. Vaughan, Master of Artes, and student in the ciuill law* (London: Simon Stafford, 1600), sig. P6^r. Italics in original.

20. David Williams, 'The Exile as Uncreator', *Mosaic*, 8 (1975), 1–14 (8–9).

21. Rappaport, 57.

22. See Lloyd Edward Kermode, *Aliens and Englishness in Elizabethan Drama* (Cambridge: Cambridge University Press, 2009), 77.

23. Quoted in Anthony Munday and Henry Chettle, *Sir Thomas More*, ed. by John Jowett (London: Methuen Drama, 2011), p. 139. This instruction was added by Tilney in the margin to the play's opening lines.

24. Levine, 42.

25. 'Complaint from the Lord Mayor and Aldermen to the Privy Council', 13 September 1595, repr. in E.K. Chambers, *The Elizabethan Stage*, 4 vols (Oxford: Clarendon Press, 1923), IV, 317–18 (318).

26. Edward Hall, *The Vnion of the Two Noble and Illustre Famelies of Lancastre [and] Yorke* (London, 1550), sig. 49ᵛ.

27. Levine, 48.

28. Walter Cohen, '*Sir Thomas More*: Passages Attributed to Shakespeare', in *The Norton Shakespeare*, 2011–14 (2013). For similar arguments see also Hill and Kathleen McLuskie, *Dekker and Heywood: Professional Dramatists* (Basingstoke: St Martin's Press, 1984), 30–1.

29. Cohen, 2013.

30. Levine, 59.

31. Wilson, 257–8.

32. Levine, 61. Levine suggests parallels between More's demand for a collaboration between citizens and strangers and the collaborative nature of the play text.

33. The term only entered the English language in the early twentieth century, as a translation of the German *Einfühlung*. See: 'empathy', *Oxford English Dictionary*, 2nd edn (1989), online version, http://www.oed.com/view/Entry/61284 (accessed 2 August 2011).

34. David Krasner, 'Empathy and Theater', in *Staging Philosophy: Intersections of Theater, Performance, and Philosophy*, ed. by David Krasner (Ann Arbor, Mich.: University of Michigan Press, 2006), 265. Krasner quotes from an article by Lauren Wispé on the distinction between sympathy and empathy.

35. Krasner, 264, 256. Italics in original.

36. Krasner, 257.

37. Jacques Derrida, *Of Hospitality. Anne Dufourmantielle Invites Jacques Derrida to Respond*, trans. by Rachel Bowlby (Stanford: Stanford University Press, 2000), 55.

38. *The Tempest* is probably less concerned with empathy than with sympathy, the latter term being defined by Krasner as 'the heightened awareness of the suffering of another person as something to be alleviated' (Krasner, 264). Sympathy evoked by Ariel (and earlier on by Miranda) establishes an ethical position from which the effects of Prospero's power are criticized. However, I do not differentiate sharply between empathy and sympathy since I am primarily interested in the ways in which the plays affectively involve the spectators both onstage and in the audience, and this applies to both empathy and sympathy.

39. Krasner, 270–1.

40. Derrida, 73.

41. Derrida, 77.

42. Peter Holland, 'Coasting in the Mediterranean: The Journeyings of Pericles', *Angles on the English-Speaking World*, 5 (2005), 11–29 (26–7).

43. *The Norton Shakespeare*, p. 2731.

44. Hans Blumenberg, *Shipwreck with Spectator: Paradigm of a Metaphor for Existence*, trans. by Steven Rendall (Cambridge, Mass.: MIT Press, 1997), 26.

45. Krasner, 257.

3

Killing by the Book: Scenes from the Duel Ritual

Paola Pugliatti

Continuity/discontinuity of models

The debate about the persistence of chivalric values in the European Renaissance has produced contrasting theories. Generally speaking, the alternatives underlying all constructions are whether the traces which the romantic medieval world bequeathed to the more realistic Renaissance culture are to be considered as signs of continuity and permanence or of discontinuity and complete change.

Classical interpretations of this issue (such as those of Huizinga and Hauser) describe, respectively, the *waning* of the Middle Ages and the *second defeat* of chivalry; it therefore seems that both authors argue for a reading of the transition as a radical change. However, on nearly every page in which they deal with this issue we find examples of the persistence of significant traces of earlier practices, ideas and representations. For instance, after arguing that in an age of realism 'as a military principle chivalry was no longer sufficient', Huizinga says that chivalric ideas, 'in so far as they formed a system of rules of *honour* and precepts of *virtue* [...] exercised a certain influence on the evolution of the laws of war'.[1] Hauser, in turn, describes a transition rather than a break, significant changes rather than the appearance of entirely new discourses; a sort of *conversion* which allowed the chivalric spirit to survive. He also suggests that in order to survive it must incorporate the unequivocal marks of its defeat, and that irony is one of the conditions of such a survival. Shakespeare and Cervantes, he argues, 'merely proclaim what is everywhere apparent, that chivalry has outlived its day and that its creative force has become a fiction'. Indeed, 'the agreement between them is nowhere so significant as in reference to chivalry, which they both consider out of date and decadent'.[2] In other words, the chivalric ideals and their ethical force can be resumed only in representations which contain the marks of their defeat.

The idea of a 'discontinuous continuity' also informs a more recent study by Mario Domenichelli, who argues for the 'obstinate persistence' of the chivalric model and examines its extraordinary capacity for adaptation to the changing times through different forms which, by adding or subtracting certain marks, by constructing high-mimetic celebrations or low-mimetic degradations, gradually build up different versions of that model.[3]

Being one of chivalry's leftovers, the micro-issue of the duel falls inevitably within this pattern of discussion. Sydney Anglo argues that 'the [Renaissance] duelling craze was chivalric honour gone rotten'[4] and characterizes the early modern duel as prescribed by fencing manuals as 'balletic homicide', 'mathematical dance' and 'terpsichorean combat';[5] a kind of practice, he says, which had 'nothing to do with loyalty, service or battle'[6] or with the military character of the traditional knightly skills.

Discontinuity is also privileged by Markku Peltonen, who argues that the Renaissance revival of duelling was exclusively connected with the diffusion of Italian courtesy books such as Castiglione's *Il cortegiano* and Guazzo's *La civil conversazione* with their debate on courtesy, civility and politeness which considered honour and reputation as necessary attributes of the perfect courtier.[7]

Mervyn James establishes a relationship between the endemic violence of the Tudor world and 'the mentality defined by the concept of honour'. 'Honour', James explains, 'could both legitimize and provide moral reinforcement for a politics of violence'. James develops this idea while, at the same time, describing a process which he defines as 'the moralization of politics' under the Tudors; that is, 'a process whereby a system of social controls and moral sanctions was effectively internalized'. The duel, he argues, was one of the most characteristic expressions of 'honour violence' and also one of the most longeval, for 'the belief persisted that every gentleman had the right to defend his honour by the sword, which alone could define disputes in which it was brought into question'.[8]

Part of this system of social control concerns the regularization of the duel ritual. As Lawrence Stone remarked, 'a powerful cause of the decline of casual and unregulated violence [...] was the development in the minds of the landed classes of a new ethical code – the code of the duel'.[9] In other words the duel, once it was controlled by rules which assured its fair performance, established a new moral code which substituted the medieval right to violence of the upper classes and was, therefore, instrumental in limiting private turbulence. Indeed, the attitude of the authorities was often ambiguous: in spite of the many proclamations and verbal and written condemnations, even during the reign of James I single combat was tolerated because it solved, in a neat and sparing way, disputes that might otherwise have involved whole families with their groups of quarrelsome supporters, to the detriment of social security and public order. Thus, while formally rules and prescriptions were imposed in order to limit the arbitrariness of unregulated conflict, in reality these same rules ended up legitimizing a bloody institution, which thus became a form of authorized violence.

These readings, although producing different evaluations, all outline a *chevalerie-gentillesse* model and life ideal which proved extraordinarily persistent both because it was based on an enduring class ideology, and because its forms were mutable and adaptable; clearly, the duel ritual was one of the most emblematic ingredients of that model. Indeed, as Robert Baldick remarks, the ritual persisted in spite of the formal condemnations pronounced by kings, popes, jurists, divines, civic authorities, moral pamphleteers and even public opinion; in spite of the intense debate over its moral and legal aspects, of the biblical injunction 'Thou shalt not kill', of the prohibition decreed by canon law, and in spite of the ironic treatment it received in the pages of novels and on the stage.[10]

Whether it was a practice influenced by courtesy books, a lifestyle conducted under the banner of 'honour', a pathetic residue of the dying chivalric spirit, an attempt to reaffirm the privileged status of a caste which was undergoing an epochal crisis, a new Italianate courtly spectacle, or even a way to repress private violence, the fact remains that the ritual persisted in spite of all opposition.

Chivalric generosity

Palamon and Arcite are two perfect knights. Hegel does not mention them in the chapter of his *Ästhetik* devoted to chivalry, but he would have acknowledged that they embody to perfection the ideals of honour, love and loyalty which he discusses as constitutive of knightly culture. They are imbued with high chivalric values: the bond between them is strong, their valour absolute, their youth untainted; they show extreme courage in war but are ready to lament the 'Scars and bare weeds / The gain o' the martialist' (*TNK*, 1.2.15–16)[11] which war has left on Thebes. Love for the same woman will unbalance their reciprocal loyalties, but in the end those loyalties are reaffirmed. When Palamon, newly escaped from prison, offers to fight his cousin for his disloyal conquest of Emilia, he recalls Arcite's chivalric endowments ('you were called / A good knight and a bold', 3.1.65–6) and only asks to be fed and armed: 'give me a sword, / Though it be rusty, and the charity / Of one meal lend me' (73–5). But Arcite will do much more than what is asked of him; he will bring 'wholesome viands' (85) and he promises: 'You shall have garments and / Perfumes to kill the smell o'the prison' (86–7). Most importantly, 'there shall be at your choice / Both sword and armour' (89–90).

When they are armed, it appears clearly that they mean the duel as a judicial combat which will establish 'to whom the birthright of this beauty / Truly pertains' (3.6.31–2). But the duel is interrupted by the arrival of Theseus, Hippolyta, Emilia and others. Later on, Palamon and Arcite are allowed to fight in strict accordance with the rites and ceremonies of the judicial duel; but the fact that Arcite is victorious does not pronounce the final verdict. In the end, Emilia will be Palamon's, thanks to Arcite's supreme act of loyalty (fortunately for her, she likes both of them!) If we agree with Palamon, who thinks that Arcite has treacherously plotted against him, then we must conclude that the judicial duel has assigned the victory to the less deserving, but in the end poetic justice is done: Arcite, trampled by his own horse, is dying and, through an extreme act of chivalric generosity, he bequeaths Emilia to his friend. The moral of the story is that when the gods prove to be incompetent, chivalric ideals are still able to redress their mistakes.

God's judgement

The judicial duel, or trial by battle, derives from the Germanic 'trial by ordeal', which substituted for a court's examination and verdict a hard trial, indeed an ordeal, which the persons under indictment had to overcome in order to clear themselves. Similarly, in the judicial duel, right and wrong were in reality attributed on the basis of the skill and luck of the two contenders, but, as in the trial by ordeal, the outcome was indisputable because it was considered God's verdict.

However, the judicial duel soon started to be condemned. In a book written about 1410, Christine de Pisan questions her mentor, Honoré Bouvet, author of *L'arbre des batailles*, about whether the judicial duel is 'just and permitted by law'. In Christine's account, Bouvet answers that 'giving a wager for such an encounter or accepting it' is condemned under all forms of law for, 'as judicial combat seeks to discover if God will help the right cause, so it is like tempting God's will'. The victorious party wins 'by chance and not because they have any right to it'. Indeed, 'it has often been seen, that the one who was right has lost'.[12]

The only proper Shakespearean trial by combat whose outcome establishes on which side God and truth militate is in *Henry VI Part II*. Ironically, however, the duel is not performed by two noblemen but by two plebeians. Peter, the armourer's servant, is challenged by his master Horner, whom he has accused 'for saying that the Duke of York was rightful heir to the crown' (1.3.28–9). Against all expectations, Peter mortally wounds his master who, before dying, reveals the truth of Peter's assertion: 'Hold, Peter, hold! I confess, I confess treason!' (98). The combat, in this case, reveals its nature as ordeal for, although both socially and physically the stronger, Horner is morally the weaker and he is also a presumptuous liar: he boasts of an easy victory, but is easily overcome by his servant, whose hand is directed not by a superior fencing skill, but by God's sense of justice.[13]

The duel to which Edmund is challenged by Edgar in *King Lear* is readable as a judicial combat. We know on whose side right is and we therefore expect the text to allow Edgar to purge all offences. The anomalous element, however, is that Edmund does not know who the challenger is: 'Know, my name is lost', Edgar says (*Lr*, 5.3.112). Edmund knows well what the rules of chivalry are, but he accepts the challenge. Edgar's warlike and noble aspect does not admit a refusal:

> In wisdom I should ask thy name,
> But since thy outside looks so fair and warlike,
> And that thy tongue some say of breeding breathes,
> What safe and nicely I might well demand
> By rule of knighthood I disdain and spurn.

> (*Lr*, 5.3.132–6)

When Edmund falls, Goneril reminds him that the duel has not been performed regularly: 'By th' law of arms thou wast not bound to answer / An unknown opposite. Thou art not vanquished, / But cozened and beguiled' (144–6).

A number of other challenges, also bearing similarity to the medieval judicial combat, are to be found, especially in the history plays. King Richard (*R2*, 1.3.119–43), offending both contenders, stops the judicial duel between Bolingbroke and Mowbray. Act Four of *Richard II* opens with another such challenge (4.1.19 *ff.*): Bagot, Fitzwater and Percy accuse Aumerle of complicity in Gloucester's murder, while Surrey stands up for him. Aumerle throws his gage at Bagot, but Bolingbroke forbids Bagot to take it; then, as often happens whenever hot-blooded noblemen are present, Percy and another Lord, too, throw their gages at Aumerle, at which Surrey, incensed, throws his pawn at Fitzwater, but Bolingbroke succeeds in calming the gang warfare. In *Henry VI Part I* (4.1.78 *ff.*) Vernon and Bassett, a Yorkist and a Lancastrian, ask Henry to grant them a duel because each accuses the other of slandering their masters (York and Somerset). Henry refuses; then York and Somerset, who are present, suggest solving the contention themselves and challenge one another; upon this, Henry pronounces a forceful speech about the evils of internal dissension which temporarily soothes the contention, and no duel actually takes place.

A rough count reveals that out of the twelve judicial combats that we find in Shakespeare's plays none is performed 'by the book'. The first one in *The Two Noble Kinsmen* is interrupted; the second gives the victory to the less deserving contestant and, in the end, poetic justice must be summoned to obtain a fair verdict; the trial between Peter and Horner in *Henry VI Part II* is anomalous because fought by two plebeians; the judicial combat between Edgar and Edmund should not have taken place at all. Goneril is right: the righteous Edgar has played foul. The challenge launched by Bolingbroke to Mowbray, at first granted and then denied, not only stops God's pronouncement of his verdict, but becomes a tragic gesture, opening the path to Richard's deposition. None of the challenges launched in Act Four of *Richard II* is permitted by Bolingbroke; and the same happens with those in *Henry VI Part I*. It is indeed possible to say that stopping these combats is the only authoritative act performed successfully by the pious Henry.

There are more 'public' duels, such as those meant for the common good in which two outstanding figures belonging to adverse parties in a war heroically pose as champions of the two armies, risking their own lives in order to save the lives of their people. These duels, too, carry traces of the judicial combat, for they imply some sense of fatality. Although he says 'I may speak it to my shame, / I have a truant been to chivalry' (*IH4*, 5.1.93–4), Hal challenges Hotspur before the battle of Shrewsbury, but the suggested combat, which is Shakespeare's invention, does not take place. Acts Four and Five of *Troilus and Cressida* are crammed with ineffectual duels: Hector launches a challenge without naming his adversary, thus creating great confusion in the Greek camp. Then, when Ajax is chosen to meet the Trojan champion, Hector refuses to fight because Ajax is his cousin; Troilus, who has witnessed Cressida's unfaithfulness, challenges Diomede, but their duel, too, is not brought to a conclusion. Finally, Hector meets Achilles but, after exchanging a few blows, Achilles retires to prepare the most unchivalrous act imaginable. In Act One, Scene Nine of *Coriolanus*, Martius and Aufidius engage in single combat; but they do so out of inveterate hatred rather than to put an end to the war between Rome and Corioles. In the end, however, neither is hatred satisfied nor excellence shown on the side of either party because the Volsces arrive to rescue Aufidius and take him away.

Private disputes and the duel of honour

Giovanni da Legnano, a fourteenth-century professor of law in the Bologna Studium, devotes the last part of his *De bello* to single combats and provides one of the most perspicuous definitions of the duel:

> a duel is a corporeal fight between two persons, deliberate on both sides, designed for compurgation, glory, or exaggeration of hatred. I said 'a fight'. This is the genus to which it belongs. I said 'deliberate on both sides'. This distinguishes it from a fight in necessary self-defence. [...] For in a fight of that kind there is ordinarily no deliberation on the part of the attacked, but only on the part of the attacker [...]. But in a duel there is deliberation on both sides. [...] And I said 'corporeal' to distinguish it from a judicial fight, which also takes place between two persons, as plaintiff and defendant.[14]

Other types of combat, we may agree with Legnano, are not duels fought 'by the book'. As Robert Baldick says, 'it is important to make a distinction between the hot-blooded combat, fought on the spur of the moment, and the duel proper, which is fought in cold blood, before witnesses, with a certain ceremony and in accordance with a strict code of law and honour'.[15]

Hot-blooded combats are what we see in the opening scene of *Romeo and Juliet*, where supporters of the two enemy households engage in a violent fray in which, as the Chorus says, 'civil blood makes civil hands unclean' (Prologue, 4). The quarrel is picked by servants of the Capulet house who are skilled in provocation, but those of the Montague house are more than willing to respond to any instigation which may come from their rivals. When Benvolio and Tybalt turn up they, too, start fighting, as do a few citizens who join in for no other reason than the sheer pleasure of the rumble, until the heads of the two houses reach them and they, too, offer to fight. The Prince intervenes and stops the fray, calling both factions 'Rebellious subjects' and 'enemies to peace'

(1.1.79). But, as we know, the private war continues. Mercutio describes Tybalt as a 'duellist' and mocks his fencing skills: he is 'the very butcher of a silk button' (2.4.24); then, in technical terms taken from Vincenzo Saviolo's treatise,[16] he makes fun of Tybalt's 'immortal passado, the punto reverso, the hay!' (25–6). Benvolio accuses Mercutio of fostering the same attitude:

> Thou – why, thou wilt quarrel with a man that hath a hair more or a hair less in his beard than thou hast. Thou wilt quarrel with a man for cracking nuts, having no other reason but because thou hast hazel eyes. [...] Thou hast quarrelled with a man for coughing in the street, because he hath wakened thy dog that has lain asleep in the sun.
>
> (*Rom.*, 3.1.16–26)

A few minutes later, Tybalt provokes Romeo calling him 'villain'; Romeo ignores Tybalt's provocation but, after a while, he unsheathes his sword and kills him to avenge Mercutio's death; none of these combats is – either ideally or formally – a proper duel.

There are, however, in Shakespeare duels that come closer to the Renaissance 'duel of honour', that form of combat meant to cancel an offence to one's reputation (Legnano's 'compurgation' – in canon law, the action of clearing a person of a charge). In these cases, although God is not a party in the quarrel, the mystical conviction that the victory of the injured party and his adversary's death will wash clean the offence is absolute. The perfect challenge for 'compurgation' is Benedick's to Claudio in *Much Ado About Nothing*. Claudio has slandered Hero thus causing her (simulated) death. What moves Benedick to challenge his friend is not only the desire to avenge Hero but also the service due to Beatrice. She has stirred his sense of honour by hinting at the decay of the chivalric spirit and at his tendency towards effeminacy: 'manhood is melted into courtesies, valour into compliment, and men are only turned into tongue, and trim ones, too' (*Ado*, 4.1.319–21). Benedick immediately agrees to challenge Claudio: 'By this hand, Claudio shall render me a dear account' (332–3). The challenge will be launched but the duel will never take place.

In *Cymbeline* Iachimo, vanquished and disarmed by Posthumus, seems to attribute his discomfiture to the disloyal trick he has played on Imogen. Part of his reason for complaining is that he has been not only disarmed, but doubly dishonoured because Posthumous, who has beaten him, is disguised as a peasant: 'The heaviness and guilt within my bosom / Takes off my manhood' (5.2.1–2); otherwise, he says, how could 'this carl, / A very drudge of nature's, have subdued me / In my profession? Knighthood and honours borne / As I wear mine are titles but of scorn' (4–7). Strictly speaking, however, 'knighthood and honour' should have prevented him from coming to arms with an inferior in the first place.

There are several other cases in which duels are planned but never performed. In *Twelfth Night*, the duel between Viola-Cesario and Sir Andrew cannot take place – the unspoken reason being her womanhood, the ostensible one his/her abhorrence of violence: 'I am no fighter', she says; and 'I am one that had rather go with Sir Priest than with Sir Knight' (*TN*, 3.4.236, 263–4). In *The Merry Wives of Windsor* the issue of the duel to avenge a personal offence is pervasive but, again, no duel is ever performed. Shallow, 'who writes himself "Armigero" in any bill' (*Wiv.*, 1.1.8–9), complains that age does not permit him to challenge Sir John Falstaff: 'Ha! O' my life, if I were young again, the sword should end it' (1.1.36–7). Later, the idea of a duel between Sir Hugh and Caius to avenge a personal offence is introduced. Again, the duel will never take place, but is constantly awaited and constantly averted or postponed; in one of these moments, when Sir Hugh is expected to engage in the proposed duel with Caius, the Host gives evidence of technical expertise in the art of fencing. To Caius, who asks 'Vat be all you, one, two, three, four, come for?', he replies: 'To see thee fight, to see thee foin, to see thee traverse, to see thee here, to see thee there; to see thee pass thy punto, thy stock, thy reverse, thy distance, thy montant' (2.3.222–5; we may recall that Beatrice mockingly calls Benedick 'Signior Mountanto').

Hamlet and Laertes, we are told, are good fencers and Hamlet has been 'in continual practice' since Laertes went to France (*Ham.*, 5.2.157). We also know that Laertes's weapons are 'rapier and dagger' (110). The contenders do everything according to the rules: there has been a formal challenge (falsely, a friendly challenge); and when the two young men are face to face they choose foils, comparing their length and weight; the duel has judges who act as seconds and 'bear a wary eye' (226). Hits are duly marked and loyally acknowledged and, before treachery is revealed, we are actually shown a realistic, rule-abiding duel as nowhere else in Shakespeare. What we see are two noble youths, well trained in the art of fencing, who engage in a combat that, supposedly, is not meant to be mortal but only to show the contenders' skills in realistic technical terms: indeed, by the book. From a social point of view, their duel is the most acceptable of armed encounters, for it provides entertainment and a good performance. Were it not that there is *venenum in cauda* or, rather, on the tip, the exchange of rapiers, too, would show us a possible, and probably frequent, turn in a single combat. But at the end we know that honour, the law of arms, the chivalric ideal and the rites of knighthood have all been tragically betrayed.

What shall we do, then, with this impressive catalogue of failures? Let us broaden the field a little and see if similar ruffles disturb the surface of the concept which is at the basis of the whole construction: the concept of honour.

Honour and cowardice

'I love / The name of honour more than I fear death', Brutus tells Cassius (*JC*, 1.2.90–1). The declaration harmonizes with what we know of Roman honour as part of manly behaviour. Brutus, however, is drawing a distinction: 'death' is, for him, a fact; it is *simply* death, a concept whose meaning all mortals are more or less able to grasp. 'Honour', instead, is 'a name' ('I love *the name* of honour'); 'name', here, means 'reputation', something that is acquired by doing noble deeds but may be lost by a single disreputable act. As Hegel says, 'The measure of honour [...] does not depend on what the man actually is but on what this idea of himself is', that is, on what one is in other people's representation. This, in the end, means that 'Honour is only a show [*Schein*]'.[17] Although it is blasphemous to liken Brutus to Falstaff, for whom, too, honour is 'a word' (*1H4*, 5.1.134), and perhaps even more blasphemous to associate both to Hegel's thought, it is clear that what is being recalled in all these cases is the frailty, transience and fugacity of honour.

We may be surprised when we hear 'brave' Macbeth, in the final stage of his desperate resistance, utter the lines: 'Why should I play the Roman fool, and die / On mine own sword?' (*Mac.*, 5.10.1–2). Does he, although besieged, still believe that he may overcome his enemies? Perhaps he does; but more relevant than his contingent position is the fact that he is questioning an age-old model of military honour and would prefer to save his life if it is in danger of being taken. The text, in other words, suggests that there can be a different reading of the proverbial Roman resolution, one that risks disrupting a whole cultural construction of what has been presented for centuries as a supreme value: a reading that views the resolution to die in order to preserve one's honour as foolishness, even perhaps as a form of cowardice.

Troilus is defined as 'the prince of chivalry' (*Tro.*, 1.2.225–6) but his sense of honour is far from unshakable. In Act Two, Scene Two Hector and his brothers argue about the honour that can derive from the present war. Hector and Troilus hold different opinions: Troilus argues that the quarrel 'hath our several honours all engaged' (2.2.122–3); Hector, on the contrary, says that "'tis a cause that hath no mean dependence / Upon our joint and several dignities' (191–2). In his monologue in Act One, Scene Two, however, Troilus had expressed an altogether different view, calling fools those who had engaged in the war and therefore feeling that his 'honour' was abased by the futility of the cause: 'Fools on both sides, Helen must needs be fair / When with your blood you daily paint her thus. / I cannot fight upon this argument. / It is too starved a subject for my sword' (1.1.90–3). Here, in other words, he seems to share the opinion of Thersites, who says that as regards that war 'All the argument is a whore and a cuckold' (2.3.71).

The play in which honour and cowardice are most efficaciously presented as problematic and unstable categories is *Henry IV Part I*. We know from the first scene that Hotspur is a most valiant warrior. Not unlike Macbeth, he has quenched a rebellion and Henry praises his valour, expressing his envy of Northumberland for having such a son, 'A son who is the theme of honour's tongue, / Amongst a grove the very straightest plant' (1.1.80–1). But Hotspur's valour will soon be made fun of. It is Hal who dramatizes Hotspur's warlike disposition in comedic terms and in plain prose:

> I am not yet of Percy's mind, the Hotspur of the north, he that kills me some six or seven dozen of Scots at a breakfast, washes his hands, and says to his wife, 'Fie upon this quiet life, I want work'. 'O my sweet Harry', says she, 'how many hast thou killed today?' 'Give my roan horse a drench', says he, and answers, 'Some fourteen', an hour after; 'a trifle, a trifle'.
>
> (*1H4*, 2.5.102–9)

But it is Falstaff who most seriously questions the idea of honour. Falstaff, undoubtedly, is a coward; this definition certainly applies to his behaviour. However, there is a huge difference between the moments in which Falstaff provokes laughter by *performing* acts of cowardice and those in which we find the fat knight *reflecting on* the idea of honour. In such moments, Falstaff presents a sensible and even attractive side of cowardice. His famous monologue on honour (*1H4*, 5.1.127–40) sounds less like the expression of cowardice than a serious meditation on the frailty of fame and its uselessness once one is in the grave. Honour is 'a word' (134), 'Honour is a mere scutcheon' (140). Falstaff is going to feign death in order to avoid being slain and he is also

trying to catch some spark of fame (and honour) when he brags that
he has killed Hotspur. But these facts belong to his comedic *staging of*
cowardice; his *reflections on* the issue, instead, are not far from those of
warlike Macbeth on the foolishness and emptiness of the 'heroic' suicide advertised by Roman war culture. We may go back to Hegel who,
more than two hundred years later, would teach his students that the
man of honour 'fabricates capricious aims for himself, presents himself
in a certain [assumed] character, and therefore binds himself in his own
eyes and those of others to something which has neither obligatoriness
nor necessity in itself'. Thus, 'it becomes a point of honour to uphold
the character he has assumed'. Honour therefore remains linked to contingency and arbitrariness and it 'may also become something entirely
formal and without worth'.[18]

Belarius, in *Cymbeline*, seems to share these ideas about the incon-
sistent, illusory and arbitrary character of honour, especially when
obtained through taking up arms. Though he is a minor character in the
play, the text does not allow us to question his honesty:

> [...] the toil o'th' war,
> A pain that only seems to seek out danger
> I'th' name of fame and honour, which dies i'th' search
> And hath as oft a sland'rous epitaph
> As record of fair act.
>
> (*Cym.*, 3.3.49–53)

Masculinity

I am aware that such a collection of 'sland'rous epitaphs' about honour
and of failures to perform its most characteristic ritual – the duel –
as those I have mustered up from Shakespeare's plays may appear a
guileful argument for there are, obviously, innumerable statements to
the contrary both in Shakespeare's plays and in the literature of the time
which show conformity to the old chivalric ideals. After all, at a time
in which the rites of chivalry were disintegrating, their deconstruction
only shows conformity to a widespread way of thinking; and, when we
read the scholarly comments about the demise of chivalry, we are led
to conclude that it was simply too late in European culture to celebrate
those rites without resorting, as Hauser suggests, to irony or to outright
negation. After all, Ariosto, Pulci, Boiardo and others had attempted the
same kind of deconstruction before the appearance of Shakespeare; and
Shakespeare's contemporary, Cervantes, was doing the same in the most

radical form ever imagined. But did their irony really pronounce a final defeat of the chivalric spirit? The argument, it seems, cannot be sealed by such a soothing and sensible conclusion. There is indeed another ingredient which contributed significantly to the persistence of certain forms of organized violence and which, although it cannot be discussed at length here, deserves at least to be mentioned.

'Warlike aristocracies', Huizinga suggests, 'need an ideal form of manly perfection'.[19] Indeed, an important component of the chivalric spirit was a certain idea of masculinity, an idea that was surfacing in a conscious way only by the end of the sixteenth century and which was seen as a vital cultural trait of both class and gender. In a book entitled *The Image of Man*, George L. Mosse places the birth of the modern and late modern idea of masculinity between the second half of the eighteenth century and the beginning of the nineteenth; however, although the idea was 'systematized, formed into stereotype, only at the start of the modern age', its 'building blocks', Mosse says, already existed. Mosse considers the birth of this stereotype as a fundamental element in the construction of nationality and nationalism; he draws a careful distinction between the early modern and the modern version of the idea and says that the old conceptions of masculinity 'were, to a large extent, based upon a warrior caste', although 'the refinement and ritual of court society had tempered such an image of masculinity long before the end of the eighteenth century'.[20] He acknowledges, however, that the old warrior-courtier ideal type made a significant contribution to the formulation of the modern stereotype, a bourgeois version in which the body became an essential component of the ideal type of man. Speaking more specifically of the duel, Mosse argues that it remains a significant practice in the aristocratic conception of masculine honour, a conception that was going to last, and that contributed significantly to the construction of the modern ideal type of man, which was seasoned with fundamental moral and physical characteristics.[21]

Jennifer Low, in turn, argues that the duel represents a crucial element in the very acquisition of rank and masculinity: 'the practice was so central to the notion of the courtier that its meaning helped to define the aristocracy of the period as a whole. The construct of the duel enabled male aristocrats and members of the gentry to figure themselves in ways consistent with both the old military ideal and that of the courtier.'[22]

Indeed, the duel ritual and the concept of honour outlived the death of chivalry, and the fact that they were vital components of an idea of masculinity which was then dawning in its modern version contributed to their permanence throughout modified cultural and social contexts.

We know that even in England trial by combat and the right to appeal to the judgement of God remained in force until the first decades of the nineteenth century. The last time it was invoked was in 1817; on that occasion, the court granted this form of judgement stating that 'The general law of the land is in favour of the wager of battle, and it is our duty to pronounce the law as it is, not as we may wish it to be.'[23] The appellant won the combat and was thereby acquitted of murder. It was only on 22 March 1819 that the English Parliament abolished the right to prove one's truth and innocence by performing an act of violence and to be absolved of a crime by appealing to the judgement of God.

Notes

1. Johann Huizinga, *The Waning of the Middle Ages* (Harmondsworth: Penguin, 2001), 99–100.
2. Arnold Hauser, *The Social History of Art*, 2 vols (London: Routledge and Kegan Paul, 1951), I, 397, 401.
3. Mario Domenichelli, *Cavaliere e gentiluomo* (Roma: Bulzoni, 2002), 36, 51–2.
4. Sidney Anglo, 'Introduction', in *Chivalry in the Renaissance*, ed. by Sydney Anglo (Woodbridge: Boydell Press, 1990), xi–xvi (xiii).
5. Sydney Anglo, 'How to Kill a Man at your Ease: Fencing Books and Duelling Ethic', in *Chivalry in the Renaissance*, 1–12 (2, 7).
6. Anglo, 'Introduction', xiii.
7. Markku Peltonen, *The Duel in Early Modern England* (Cambridge: Cambridge University Press, 1986). *The Courtyer*, Thomas Hoby's first English version of *Il cortegiano*, was published in 1561; George Pettie's *The ciuile conuersation*, his translation from the French of the first three books of Guazzo's text, appeared in 1581, and was followed five years later by the fourth and final book translated by Bartholomew Young (who worked directly from the Italian original).
8. Mervyn James, *Society, Politics and Culture in Early Modern England* (Cambridge: Cambridge University Press, 1986), 308, 309, 322.
9. Lawrence Stone, *The Crisis of Aristocracy, 1558–1641* (Oxford: Clarendon Press, 1965), 243.
10. Robert Baldick, *The Duel* (New York: Barnes and Noble, 1965).
11. All Shakespeare quotations are from William Shakespeare, *The Complete Works*, ed. by Stanley Wells and Gary Taylor (Oxford: Clarendon Press, 1990).
12. Christine de Pisan, *The Book of Deeds of Arms and of Chivalry*, trans. by Sumner Willard (University Park: Pennsylvania University Press, 1999), 197, 198.
13. The legal aspects of the trial by battle in Shakespeare are discussed by George W. Keeton who, in *Shakespeare's Legal and Political Background* (London: Pitman, 1967), examines this episode (214–16). On single combat in Shakespeare, see Theodor Meron, *Bloody Constraint: War and Chivalry in Shakespeare* (Oxford: Oxford University Press, 1998), 86–93; on the rites of chivalry, see James T. Johnson, *Just War Tradition and the Restraint of War: A Moral and Historical Inquiry* (Princeton: Princeton University Press, 1981),

131–50. J.R. Hale argues that the duel as ritualized form of violence implied that 'there was an ideal, a really true law that existed for the man who saw himself as exceptional [...] that would permit him to give rein to his aggressiveness but at the same time protect him from its full consequences by a ritualization of the preliminaries to and the actual forms of combat'. See 'Sixteenth-Century Explanations of War and Violence', in John R. Hale, *Renaissance War Studies* (London: Humbledon Press, 1983), 335–58 (344).

14. Joannes de Legnano, *Tractatus de bello, de represaliis et de duello*, trans. by James L. Brierly (Oxford: Oxford University Press, 1917), 331–2.

15. Baldick, 22.

16. Vincentio Saviolo, *Vincentio Saviolo his Practice* (London, 1595).

17. G.W.F. Hegel, *Esthetics*, trans. by T.M. Knox, 2 vols (Oxford: Clarendon Press, 1975), I, 558.

18. Hegel, I, 559.

19. Huizinga, 75.

20. George L. Mosse, *The Image of Man: The Creation of Modern Masculinity* (New York and Oxford: Oxford University Press, 1966), 5.

21. Mosse, 17–23 *et passim*.

22. Jennifer Low, *Manhood and the Duel: Masculinity in Early Modern Drama and Culture* (Basingstoke: Palgrave Macmillan, 2003), 9.

23. Baldick, 19–20.

4

The War of 'Nothings' in *The Tragedy of King Lear*

Małgorzata Grzegorzewska

Silence in word and deed

The Polish language contains a number of words that disclose the secret nuances of silence and are untranslatable into non-Slavonic languages, English included. When we want to describe objective reality in which no sound is heard we use the noun *cisza*; whereas when we refer to the voluntary act of declining to speak or remaining silent as a consequence of not knowing what to say, we have a different verb to describe this non-action (*milczeć*) and a noun related to this verb (*milczenie*). The silence that may surround us (*cisza*) is then different from the silence between two people who are not speaking (*milczenie*). The former can have a specific resonance ('the sound of silence' can be translated as *brzmienie ciszy*), the latter is always embarrassingly voiceless, mute, dead (in Polish we also say *głuche milczenie* which literally translates as 'deaf silence'). Moreover, we can express the subtle difference between complete silence and the strategies which permit something to be passed over in the utterance (*przemilczeć*) or suddenly to break it (*zamilknąć*).

Whichever of these meanings is taken into consideration, we immediately discover the fact that silence (in all its guises) is among the most creative and, at the same time, the most unpredictable of theatrical signifiers; one of the most persuasive *logoi* uttered on stage. Its success, however, cannot be taken for granted. Dramatic conflicts are expressed and resolved through dialogues that are rarely limited to an innocent exchange of ideas. Most often, onstage discourses become the site of struggle between opposing characters or ideas. Yet this focus on the spoken word should not diminish our sensitivity to the operations of another powerful weapon that may be used in those dramatic encounters, namely, intentional silence. Intentional silence can either be inscribed in the rhetorical texture of the play (in the form of those cunning figures of speech which stealthily take advantage of the listener's curiosity and make the most of the unsaid), or employed by the actor as a means of articulating the character's emotions or state of mind: surprise or delight, shy meekness or stubborn defiance, joy or sorrow. Furthermore, the actor's 'speechlessness' or moments of stage calm may either foreground or downplay the importance of the rhetorical means designed by the playwright. In any case, however, the effectiveness of silence largely depends on rhetorical allusion, on the actor's gesture, or on other articulate signs that allow us to overcome its innate vagueness and endow it with some conventional, recognizable meaning. Bare silence, like naked truth and simple-hearted affection, does not lend itself to theatrical games. When it *signifies* nothing, it cannot *do* anything. Perhaps, however, it can disclose something other than itself.

It is a critical commonplace that silence plays different roles in a performance text and in a written text:

> The key differences [...] between reading from the page and reading from the stage include the visualization of character, space and situations; the possibility of keeping more strands of the multiple narrative in view. There is, however, another crucial difference: in a theatrical production the silence of characters can be as significant as their speech.[1]

Moreover, within a theatrical production there are different kinds of silence: Jerzy Limon argues, for instance, that 'we should distinguish between silence as an acoustic reality on the stage, and fictional silence as the acoustic reality within the created realm'.[2] It is a distinction worth keeping in mind, as it will later be of use in interpreting the situations in which a character addresses the audience in an aside, breaking the silence that is an 'acoustic reality on the stage', that is to say in the theatre, while remaining unheard within 'the created realm', the world of the play. First, however, I will argue that Shakespeare makes silence resonate powerfully in the very text of his plays, that is 'on the page', before its manifold nature, ranging from treacherous to magnanimous, is fully exposed in theatre auditoriums. This is best evidenced in *The Tragedy of King Lear*, a play which carefully explores the potential of sophisticated rhetorical silence while at the same time exposing the sterility and inherent vulnerability of plain silence, which in fact signifies far more than speech ever can.

'Rhetorical' vs. 'bare' silence

When the king encourages his daughters to win his favour by flattering him, both Goneril and Regan claim that words cannot express, and still less 'contain', their love. Their protestations prove, however, to be careful rhetorical constructs which disclose the material impact of well-chosen words. Goneril, Lear's 'eldest born' daughter, speaks first, and declares:

> Sir, I do love you more than word can wield the matter,
> Dearer than eyesight, space and liberty,
> Beyond what can be valued, rich or rare,
> No less than life, with grace, health, beauty, honour.
> As much as child e'er loved, or father found,
> A love that makes breath poor and speech unable,
> Beyond all manner of so much I love you.

$$(Lr., 1.1.61)^3$$

Her distrust of language appears insincere, as she manages to respond in a way that points to the infinite abundance, rather than scarcity, of *all* the possibilities enclosed in the commonplace and facile declaration of love: sincerity and deceit, earnestness and hypocrisy, naturalness and artificiality, restlessness and calm, excitement and boredom, anticipation and love weariness. So, although she states that brevity can be more eloquent than the most elaborate oration, because affections elude the finitude of spoken words, she cannot refrain from speaking. And though the qualification 'dearer than eyesight' seems to render well the measure of true love, especially in the context of the subplot in which we see a father blinded by an ungrateful son, the expression *'no less* than life' surely precludes something that, as we shall see, true love demands, that is the giving up even of one's life for the sake of the beloved.

Ernest A. Horsman explains in his annotated edition of Shakespeare's great tragedy that the enigmatic expression 'all manner of so much' which is the gist of Goneril's speech includes 'all kinds of answer to the question "how much"'.[4] A rhetorician would conclude from this that Goneril employs the figure of preterition. This is closely related to aposiopesis, which denotes an interruption (as in music, where it can express the moment of parting or death), and through eloquent use of silence intensifies what is passed over: what remains is nevertheless proffered without words. If somebody breaks off mid-sentence evoking the impression that s/he is so overwhelmed by emotions that s/he cannot speak, then we are dealing with rhetorical aposiopesis or *reticentia*, reticence.[5] Silvia Montiglio argues, for instance, that aposiopesis always results in 'a silent suspension that leaves the sentence unfinished'.[6] Preterition, on the other hand, consists in an announcement of silence that draws our attention to the abundance of possibilities that hamper the fluency of expression. For instance, the sentence 'Truly I am at a loss where I should begin' suggests that the speaker is faced with too great a choice to be able to decide on one word, one expression or one sentence.[7]

Goneril relies precisely on the latter strategy, and Lear's munificent reward for her answer shows that the king is pleased with such an expression of filial love. Goneril's use of rhetoric is highly appreciated and generously remunerated. A great part of the kingdom, which Lear metaphorically holds in his hands in the form of a map, passes into the possession of his eldest daughter, who has just proved her aptness as a successor to the throne through her publicly-deployed skills as an able orator and rhetorician. The figure of overabundant silence materializes in the form of a copious gift. Plenitude breeds plenitude, and the map is the 'ocular proof', to borrow a phrase from *Othello*, of this fecund and continual succession:

> Of *all these bounds, even from this line to this,*
> With shadowy forest and with champaigns *riched,*
> With *plenteous* rivers and *wide-skirted* meads,
> We make thee lady. To thine and Albany's issues
> Be this perpetual.

> (*Lr.*, 1.1.63–6; italics mine)

Lear's second daughter, his 'dear Regan', uses a slightly different means to win her father's favour, but in fact she only multiplies Goneril's cornucopian audacity. She claims her sister has already named her own 'deed of love' (as indeed Goneril's answer includes all possibilities), 'only she comes too short' (1.1.71–2). Regan adds infinity to infinity, implying that her love both exceeds and equals that of Goneril.

The third contestant, however, refuses to comply with the rules established by her father and her sisters, dangerously failing to acknowledge the political implications of her refusal. Lear's exchange with Cordelia suddenly breaks the abundant flow of empty signifiers. Worse still, Lear's beloved daughter refuses to adorn her silence with any expedient attire.

Not only does she challenge her sisters (whose rhetoric she considers but 'glib and oily art', 1.1.226) and her father (whom she wants to strip of illusions), but she ventures to dispose of the very process of signification itself. This premeditated, self-imposed voicelessness is the main reason for her defeat, but the point she intends to make demands such sacrifice:

> LEAR: [...] what can you say to draw
> A third more opulent than your sisters? Speak.
> CORDELIA: Nothing, my lord.
> LEAR: Nothing?
> CORDELIA: Nothing.

> (*Lr.*, 1.1.85–9)

The issue at stake is not only, as some critics would have it, the contrast between Cordelia's honest plainness and her sister's ornate, but deceitful rhetoric. It is rather the contrast between the opulence and poverty of different kinds of silence; or, as we could also say, different means of expressing silence. It may seem that Cordelia's message does not differ from Goneril's pronouncement: 'love makes breath poor and speech unable'. Yet what Goneril utters only in words, Cordelia fulfils in reality. She proves that self-sufficient 'breath', which signifies both 'speech' and 'life', can indeed be placed under threat by unselfish love which renders words poor, ineffectual and inadequate. Moreover, love destabilizes the rudimentary environment of an egoistic individual: 'space and liberty'; seen in the light of post-Heideggerian philosophical discourse (an angle that will be further developed in the following paragraphs), unselfish love assails the very site of *Dasein*.[8]

While Goneril and Regan use rhetorical silence for active self-promotion, Cordelia accepts the possibility of self-annihilation. Not only is her retirement into bare silence utterly sterile (if we measure its efficiency by the standards imposed on us by the mercantile minded, self-seeking Lear), but it leads directly from the death of language to the death of the character. Speechlessness, exile and death are then the necessary consequences of Cordelia's decision which can be neither encompassed by reason nor articulated in any language.

The stunning effect of the quoted dialogue is further intensified by the triple repetition of the unacceptably blank 'nothing', which reverberates like an ominous echo in an empty room. Encouraged to follow in the footsteps of her sisters, Cordelia chooses to lay bare a deficiency, rather than yield to an abundance of words. It is as if she realized that the *every*thing contained in her sisters' declarations cannot suffice for the articulation of true love as demanded by her father; in order to express love truly she needs more than words can say, *more* than everything. So the message that Cordelia fails to convey, at least at this stage, is that the love which stands for absolute dissipation and excess must surfeit the confident completeness of the world and language. Struck mute by true affection, Lear's loving and beloved daughter cannot win any favour.

Surely, silence could easily serve a skilful flatterer, as Thomas More recorded in his *Dialogue of Comfort Against Tribulations*, written in 1535, when he described a sly parish priest who, despite his want of fluency in Latin and lack of eloquence, managed to praise a vainglorious prelate better than the most accomplished orators. The priest's recipe for success proved much simpler than anyone might have expected and consisted in a plain but comprehensible histrionic gesture. On the professional stage where actors 'honestly employ their crafts and the understanding of the medium to the best of their capabilities to describe characters',[9] this amateur performance might win small approval, but 'at the table of the great'[10] it paved the way for success. We may deem the priest a sham actor, since he was pretending to be (acting *as if*) rather than honestly performing (acting *out*) an admiring person, but he certainly was an accomplished flatterer:

> For when he saw that he could find no words of praise that would surpass all that had been spoken before already, the wily fox would speak never a word. But as one who were ravished heavenward with the wonder of the wisdom and eloquence that my lord's grace had uttered in that oration, he set up a long sigh with an 'Oh!' from the bottom of his breast, and held up both his hands, and lifted up his head, and cast up his eyes into the welkin, and wept.[11]

The studied silence of the priest was thus carefully clothed in body language which in real life helped this cunning sycophant convey the meaning of his praise-above-words.

Cordelia's candid and 'naked' silence, on the other hand, becomes susceptible to misunderstanding in the true-to-life world brought on stage by the playwright and the director of the performance. Her guileless, bare 'nothing' also stands in sharp contrast with Goneril's and Regan's eloquent use of rhetorical silence. No wonder then that Lear finds her silence disturbingly hollow and hopelessly unproductive: 'How, nothing will come of nothing. Speak again' (1.1.90). Given a second chance, she therefore measures her own expression by the limits of convention:

> Unhappy that I am, I cannot heave
> My heart into my mouth. I love your majesty
> According to my bond, no more nor less.

(Lr., 1.1.91–3)

Forced to express herself in words which Lear would have liked to be translatable into material reality, Cordelia can speak only of legal contracts. Her tongue is thus literally tied ('bound') by her social role, which she audaciously pronounces 'according to her bond'; and her silence is set within meticulously defined limits ('no more nor less') which contrast with the boundless, that is to say bountiful and therefore overflowing silences which opened up in Regan's and Goneril's proclamations of love.

This is, however, only one aspect of Cordelia's silence, which complies with her public self and which she decides to bring into the open. It is preceded by two carefully designed asides in which she provides a slightly different explanation of her behaviour. The first of them, articulated in the form of question and answer, refers precisely to the very same incommensurability of the interpersonal and the private, of (public) words and (subjective) affections which her sisters weave into rhetorical figurations of silence: 'What shall Cordelia speak? Love, and *be* silent' (1.1.62). There is a lesson to learn from this difference between the soundless (in the double sense of infinite and inaudible) silence in rhetoric, which in effect turns out but an empty word, and the sudden break in stage speech, which has the impact of a real deed. This double sense of Cordelia's behaviour is confirmed by her second aside which is a perfect example of resolute self-portrayal: 'Then poor Cordelia / And yet not so, since I am sure my love's / More ponderous than my tongue' (1.1.76–8). The Arden Shakespeare tells us that 'ponderous' should be understood in this context as 'weighty' and 'substantial', thus foregrounding the material effect of silence in stage performance.[12] It is nevertheless equally important to recall other meanings of this adjective, strictly connected with the art of rhetoric, for 'ponderous' denotes also 'wordy' and 'loquacious' expression, the very opposite of reticence. Thus, Cordelia confirms indeed (or rather in *deed*) what her sisters have just said about silence.

And yet, her statements stand apart (quite literally *askew* or *aside*) from Goneril's and Regan's rhetorical tricks. The very nature of theatrical aside is brought here into the foreground. As Jerzy Limon has argued, 'the essential meanings in theatre are created through the juxtaposition between at least two models of perceiving reality (that of the figures and of the audience)'. In the aside, 'an actor is factually saying something but is not heard, although, considering the proxemic distance, he or she should be heard by other figures, just as the utterance is heard by the spectators'. Since such a situation violates 'the laws of the acoustics and becomes a common stage marker of the way we are supposed to perceive a given scene in accordance with the convention introduced', the critic calls this kind of silence 'conventional', as opposed to the 'dialogical silence', which 'results from a conscious [...] decision of a figure not to say something'.[13] In other words, the aside takes place in the 'fifth dimension' of the stage, where one character's speech or whisper is audible to the audience, but at the same time does not get through the soundproof barrier which for the time of this utterance separates the persona from the imaginary world of the play, as if placing him or her in another space and time, simultaneously present but not overlapping with the fictional world of the characters.

It is as if Cordelia 'steps out of the play' in order not only to articulate her doubts, but also to break the illusion of the play. The query 'What shall Cordelia speak?' sounds like a question posed by the actress who wants to find some justification for the behaviour of the character whom she enacts.[14] Thus, although Cordelia remains physically present on stage, and we hear her thoughts vocalized, to other characters she remains a silent enigma. And of course even we, who can hear her speak, do not know whether 'vocalization', that is making her inner-most secrets audible, amounts to self-revelation, rendering those secrets understandable for herself and others. In short, theatrical aside exposes the (soundless) depths of the character's reticence, rather than opening up the channel of communication. Within the reality of the stage it remains an invisible (inaudible) gesture without any chance of becoming the common experience shared by all the characters.

Indeed, Cordelia never gives away her thoughts or feelings precisely because they cannot be expressed. Instead of trying to disambiguate her silence by giving preference either to her public refusal to speak or to her private pronouncements; to her public straightforward audacity or to her helplessness ('What shall Cordelia speak?'), we can profit greatly from comparing Shakespeare's play with some crucial ideas which pervade the tradition of apophatic theology, from Pseudo-Dionysius's early medieval mystical treatises to the contemporary post-phenomenological thought of Jean-Luc Marion. As both Wittgenstein and Heidegger agreed, when something eludes words, it should not be talked about (*darüber muss man schweigen*),[15] but their apparent consensus is challenged by Marion, who in his seminal project of post-Heideggerian and post-Derridean apophatic theology highlights different meanings of silence. The issue at stake, then, is not to reach the point, as Wittgenstein and Heidegger did, where one reasonably gives up talking about the inexpressible (God, for instance), but rather to distinguish between the silences 'of contempt and joy, of pain and pleasure, of consent and of solitude' (although in Cordelia's case we should rather speak of the silent paradox of love and dissent). 'The greatest difficulty', observes Marion, 'doubtless consists in deciding what the silence says: contempt, renunciation, the avowal of impotence, the highest honor rendered, the only one neither unworthy nor "dangerous"'.[16] This line of argument leads to a conclusion which sets the tone of my analysis:

> The silence concerning silence [...] conceals from us that, finally, nothing demands more of interpretation than the nothingness of speech. To have done with silence, keeping silence does not suffice. *Silence, because it does not explain itself, exposes itself to an infinite equivocation of meaning.*[17]

In other words, when talking about silence we must abandon the safe concept of places or spots of indeterminacy, for silence, like love, releases indeterminacy from these imagined spatial constraints operating within human language; it therefore inundates our very existence with deathlike shadowiness. It conveys infinite vagueness; in the world held in check by a system of cartographic coordinates (represented by the map which Lear brings on stage) it is a voiceless call coming from an unmapped, unknown wilderness. To quote Marion once again: 'Death, pre-eminently, imposes silence; the emptiness of infinite spaces opposes its suffocating vacuity, like an eternal silence; aphasia, desertlike, grows with its silence.'[18]

Marion's argument thus prepares us for a better understanding of Cordelia's subtle triangulation of unselfish love, unconditional silence, and the ineffable, lavish nonbeing. 'For that which crosses Being', claims the philosopher, 'eventually has the name *agapē*. *Agapē* surpasses all knowledge, with a hyperbole that defines it and, indissolubly, prohibits access to it.'[19] Hence the insurmountable difference between love and the world:

> Love strikes the world with vanity in all indifference to its virtues – it is an extrinsic vanity; in the same way, it touches certain beings

with a grace just as extrinsic, according to which it associates with its incommensurable action the most trivial of beings: the cobblestone that one passes, a child's sleigh, an invented proper name, the being matters little, provided that it stem from a love to which, in any case, it will remain foreign. [...] The difference [foreignness] does not at all pass between beings and nonbeings, or even between those who indeed wish to join the polarization of love, and the others; it passes between love itself and the world – being – by itself.[20]

I would like to argue that it is precisely this difference that Shakespeare illustrates in the first act of *King Lear*. Goneril and Regan turn out the winners of the game because they play safe when they define the indefinite, while Cordelia risks all and loses all. It happens so, because instead of resorting to the prolific figures of preterition or aposiopesis, which after all are *figures of speech*, she gives in to apophasis, which is the only real name for speechlessness; not just the mere insufficiency of words, but the ultimate and irrevocable nonexistence of speech. While Goneril and Reagan seize the opportunity to speak about the feeling that exceeds the limits of a single utterance, Cordelia surrenders to the negativity of love which she equates with the ineffable Absolute of the theologians. Only her love equals this mighty Nothing which, paradoxically, appears an insignificant no-thing in 'the world by itself'.

Staging the nothingness of silence

But this is not all that Shakespeare tells us about the conflicting meanings of silence in *The Tragedy of King Lear*. Cordelia's answer is echoed by the words uttered by the wicked, 'base-born' Edmund:

> GLOUCESTER: Edmund, how now, what news?
> EDMUND (*Pockets the letter*): So please your lordship, *none*.
> GLOUCESTER: Why so earnestly seek you to put up that letter?
> EDMUND: I know *no* news, my lord.
> GLOUCESTER: What paper were you reading?
> EDMUND: *Nothing*, my Lord.
> GLOUCESTER: No? What needed then that terrible dispatch of it into your pocket? *The quality of nothing hath not such need to hide itself.*
>
> (*Lr.*, 1.2.26–35; italics mine)

Here Shakespeare achieves something virtually impossible; he not only dramatizes silence, but renders it visible by devising dramatic action which illustrates the moment of deliberate concealment. This gesture stimulates Gloucester's curiosity and then raises his suspicions. 'No news' read from a letter which Edmund hides in haste thus becomes a perfect instance of silence aligned with stealth and dangerous scheming. Moreover, it contradicts the economy of Lear's judgement ('nothing will come of nothing'), as we remember from Edmund's soliloquy that he hopes to win much by staging his spectacle ('Legitimate Edward, I must have your land', 1.2.16), and we also know that this well-staged 'nothing' will yield the desired fruit, exactly that which Cordelia has just lost through her reticence.

This is connected with another inverted parallel employed by Shakespeare in this scene. Like Cordelia before him, Edmund also speaks about love in his soliloquy: 'Our father's love is to the bastard Edmund / As to the legitimate' (1.2.17–18). He does not, however, sound his own feelings, but instead weighs the affection of his father, and, of course, he thinks it not only a perfectly reckonable, but even a quantifiable reality which can be exchanged for other profits. This attitude stands in sharp contrast with the apophatic concept of love that informs Cordelia's behaviour in Act One. Her 'nothing' entails an absolute resignation to negativity which makes her 'poor, and yet not so' for she alone truly realizes her love to be 'more ponderous than [her] tongue'. But even Cordelia realizes that her silence demands explanation, and this is why her refusal to speak is carefully foretold in a series of asides. It is only through this specific device that she may provide her explanation in the form of (silent) utterances that no other character will hear, but which will be perfectly audible to the audience. Whether speaking 'to herself' (which in the real world would be considered a mark of unreason) or reasonably addressing us, she can thus speak about silence without betraying it, that is without curbing its vagueness with the help of cleverly designed rhetorical figures. Apart from saying 'nothing', she may indeed refrain from saying anything, after her sisters have elaborated on the ineffability of love in their eloquent speeches, and she has exposed the inherent duplicity of rhetoric in the aside, directed outside the world presented on stage. Her aside thus provides us with the 'information that is necessary to increase our awareness and understanding of the fictional world'.[21] In this particular case, Shakespeare uses his in-depth knowledge of the theatre to perform the impossible, that is to show love *extrinsic* to the world. In order to express the ineffable, he allows Cordelia a peculiar insight into the vanity of her father's desire and her sister's efforts, as well as the grace which 'surpasses all knowledge' and therefore can be accessed only in the 'fifth dimension' by those who watch the stage world from the outside, that is from the perspective of the auditorium.

The *Tragedy of King Lear* thus serves to show the complementary and quarrelsome claims of silence as inscribed in the text and rehearsed on the stage. Clearly, the decision to juxtapose the rhetorical devices employed by Goneril and Regan with Cordelia's apophatic love foregrounds the efficacy of the measures they deploy, but at the same time it also lends depth to Cordelia's silence. Their references to silence remain fully incorporated into the system of communication; her silence breaks away from reason and language. Yet another important contrast surfaces between Edmund's and Cordelia's 'nothings'. Prefaced by a soliloquy and an aside, respectively, both Edmund's and Cordelia's 'nothings' mean to us something different from what they denote for the characters who hear them within the fictional world presented on stage, like Lear or Gloucester. Whereas Edmund proves that he can influence 'the quality of nothing', and reminds us that silence can be used as a theatrical signifier, Cordelia surrenders herself to emptiness, which swallows her entirely. Edmund's denial is a form of deliberate silencing, employed to suggest foul play and cause harm; Cordelia's refutation, on the other hand, allows her to keep silence about the ineffable, and thus belongs to the *via negativa*. Lear's beloved and betrayed daughter shows us that in drama and theology alike, bare silence admits no final pronouncements, no definitive closures, no univocal meaning. So, before we ask ourselves once again what we can make of Cordelia's audacious and loving 'nothing', we should come to terms with the fact that whenever it is uttered on the theatre stage, this single word taken from the page of Shakespeare's play will *always* be a source of turmoil and puzzlement.

Notes

1. Brian Woolland, 'The Gift of Silence', in *Ben Jonson and Theatre: Performance, Practice and Theory*, ed. by Richard A. Cave, Elizabeth Schafer and Brian Woolland (London and New York: Routledge, 1999), 125–42 (126).
2. Jerzy Limon, 'The Fifth Wall: Words of Silence in Shakespeare's Soliloquies and Asides', *Shakespeare Jahrbuch*, 144 (2008), 47–65 (48).
3. All quotations are taken from William Shakespeare, *King Lear*, ed. by R.A. Foakes, The Arden Shakespeare, Third Series (Walton-on-Thames: Nelson, 1977).
4. *The Tragedy of King Lear*, ed. by Ernest A. Horsman (Indianapolis and New York: Bobbs-Merrill, 1973), quoted in the Arden Shakespeare edition, 162.
5. Heinrich Lausberg, *Handbook of Literary Rhetoric: A Foundation for Literary Study*, trans. by Matthew T. Bliss, Annemiek Jansen and David E. Orton (Leiden: Brill, 1998), 396.

6. Silvia Montiglio, *Silence in the Land of Logos* (Princeton: Princeton University Press, 2000), 133.

7. Montiglio, 137.

8. This assumption derives directly from Emmanuel Levinas's response to the existentialist philosophy of Martin Heidegger. According to Levinas, every ethical relation stems from the fear of occupying somebody else's 'place under the sun'. Thus, if I agree that the *Da* of my *Dasein* occupies the space that belongs to another human being, every instance of selfless love must then entail a necessary sacrifice on the part of *Dasein*. See Merold Westphal, *Levinas and Kierkegaard in Dialogue* (Bloomington and Indianapolis: Indiana University Press, 2008), 16.

9. Eli Rozik, *Generating Theatre Meaning* (Brighton and Portland: Sussex Academic Press, 2008), 87.

10. I am referring here to the title of a chapter devoted to More, 'At the Table of the Great: More's Self-Fashioning and Self-Cancellation', in Stephen Greenblatt, *Renaissance Self-Fashioning from More to Shakespeare* (Chicago and London: Chicago University Press, 1984), 11–73 (11).

11. Thomas More, *A Dialogue of Comfort against Tribulation*, ed. by Louis L. Martz and Frank Manley (New Haven: Yale University Press, 1976), 213.

12. *King Lear*, The Arden Shakespeare, 163.

13. Limon, 'Fifth Wall', 53.

14. The observation that 'the ontology of whoever utters an aside is different from the figure hitherto enacted by the actor' plays a crucial role in Jerzy Limon's distinction between the aside and the soliloquy: see *The Chemistry of the Theatre: Performativity of Time* (Basingstoke and New York: Palgrave Macmillan, 2010), 171. It is also vital for my argument that Cordelia's 'nothing' transcends the deixis of her world; for, if we follow Limon's line of argument, and agree that in the aside which foreshadows her rebuttal Cordelia is indeed aware of the presence of the audience, then the aside proves a particularly fitting device to imply the possibility of some extrinsic knowledge on Cordelia's part, which allows her to point *outside* the text of the play and *beyond* the fictional reality created on the stage.

15. Ludwig Wittgenstein, *Tractatus logico-philosophicus*, trans. by D.F. Pears and B.F. McGuinness (London: Routledge and Kegan Paul, 1961); Martin Heidegger, *Identity and Difference*, trans. by Joan Stambaugh (New York: Harper & Row, 1969). Both references are quoted in Jean-Luc Marion, *God without Being: Hors-Texte*, trans. by Thomas A. Carlson (Chicago and London: University of Chicago Press,1991), 234–6.

16. Marion, 54.

17. Marion, 54; italics mine.

18. Marion, 54.

19. Marion, 108.

20. Marion, 137–8.

21. Limon, *Chemistry*, 168.

5

Conflict and Convergence in Shakespeare's Wordplay

Georgi Niagolov

An extended understanding of wordplay

'Wordplay' is typically used as a portmanteau term for a whole arsenal of stylistic devices which, although their formal properties may vary slightly, usually operate according to a common technical principle: a polysemous feature of linguistic structure, which may be a single word or a larger syntactic scheme, combines two or more apparently unrelated meanings usually with a short-lived humorous effect.[1] Whereas many of Shakespeare's puns undeniably fall under such a definition, some seem to go beyond its bounds. First, Shakespeare's wordplay is not always funny – often puns appear in tragic contexts and do not have a cheering effect on the spectator/reader. Second, Shakespeare's wordplay is not always local – sometimes an important word recurs in a work and its multiple meanings communicate with each other over larger stretches of text, even occasionally exceeding the boundaries of a single text to reverberate across the corpus. Third, the alternative senses activated by Shakespeare's puns are not always isolated from their textual environment – very often they interact meaningfully with other stylistic devices and patterns such as metaphors, dramatic irony, imagery, plot and character development.

These observations call for an extended understanding of Shakespeare's wordplay that can account for two more complex cognitive phenomena. On the one hand, in cases where alternative senses of polysemous words and ambiguous phrases consistently cohere with each other and also entangle other features of their textual environment in their coherences, they establish alternative, often conflicting, contexts, that is to say alternative versions of the message/story, and thus hold the potential of changing the spectator/reader's overall interpretation of the work. On the other hand, the simultaneous existence of multiple, typically incompatible versions of the same message/story, along with the spontaneous hesitation on the part of the spectator/reader as to which way to take, may result in cognitive traffic between such possibilities and the convergence of logically heterogeneous concepts into multifarious mental constructs.

The aim of this chapter is to approach Shakespeare's more complex use of wordplay through the early modern dichotomy of 'substance' and 'shadows' – an idea that was evidently popular with Shakespeare since even a conservative count yields at least 20 intriguing uses of the dual concept in his poetic and dramatic works.[2] The main argument is that a closer examination of this philosophical notion can throw some new light on early modern conceptualization of poetic polysemy. My specific focus is the use of the dichotomy of 'substance' and 'shadows' in two works, Sonnet 53 and *Richard II*, in both of which it is involved in the complex play of language, but at the same time projects into a metapoetic and metadramatic space to comment pithily on the resultant high-dimensional effects.

Conflicting shadows

> What is your *substance*, whereof are you made,
> That millions of strange *shadows* on you tend?
> Since every one, hath every one, one shade,
> And you but one, can every *shadow* lend:
> Describe Adonis and the counterfeit,
> Is poorly imitated after you,
> On Helen's cheek all art of beauty set,
> And you in Grecian tires are painted new:
> Speak of the spring, and foison of the year,
> The one doth *shadow* of your beauty show,
> The other as your bounty doth appear,
> And you in every blessed shape we know.
> In all external grace you have some part,
> But you like none, none you for constant heart.[3]

The carefully-wrought central conceit of Shakespeare's Sonnet 53 is evidently spun around the distinction between 'substance' and 'shadows', which here operates on two discernible levels: on the one hand, it underpins the larger philosophical framework of the poem and, on the other, it engages in the sonnet's wordplay, producing multiple puns and expanding the possibilities for interpretation.

The philosophical distinction between 'substance' and 'shadows' must have reached Shakespeare and his contemporaries as a blend of related ideas. The earliest traces of the theoretical notion of a constant essence moving through fleeting shapes goes back to Heraclitus, Parmenides and Pythagoras and it was through Ovid's illustrious narrativization of the latter's doctrine of reincarnation, in his *Metamorphoses*, that it was disseminated widely throughout the early modern world. Plato's theory of forms (or ideas), which was rediscovered and reconsidered along with his other works during the Renaissance, abstracts an a-spatial and atemporal reality of absolute being, conceivable only through the intellect, from an illusionary and essentially mimetic material and temporal reality perceived by the senses. In *The Republic* Plato uses for the latter the image of 'shadows': 'For they are mere shadows and pictures of the true, and are colored by contrast, which exaggerates both light and shade.'[4] Finally, Aristotle's theory of substances, which was taught all the way through the medieval period and which still held its place in the curriculum in Shakespeare's time, views 'substances' as imperceptible, yet intelligible, universal and complete epistemological concepts, as opposed to the perceptible, particular, and inherently incomplete manifestations of such substances in the material world, that is their 'accidents'. This theory provides the groundwork for many early modern textbooks on logic and rhetoric such as Thomas Wilson's *The Rule of Reason* (1551), where one reads: 'No substaunce can be seen with our yies, but onelie the outewarde Accidentes, whereby we iudge and knowe, euerie seuerall creature.'[5]

Hence, at first glance, Sonnet 53 seems to be a straightforward compliment to the addressee's true 'substance' of absolute *kalokaghathia*. This 'substance' can merely be hinted at through a multiplicity of describable 'shadows': Adonis, Helen, the spring, the autumn. Each of these 'shadows', however, reflects only a fraction of the complete perfection of the ultimate 'substance', and all of them are therefore arranged in antitheses – the most beautiful man and the most beautiful woman in classical mythology, the fresh and youthful birth of the year and the rich and mellow prelude to its expiration – so that their scope can be expanded as much as possible. Nevertheless, at the end of the poem it becomes clear that no matter how hard the poet tries to convey the addressee's perfection by describing his outward gloss, he can only prove that it is impossible in this way to do justice to the ultimate perfection concealed in the addressee's constant heart.

However, the search for a deeper hidden meaning and the intuitive mistrust of face values, activated by the philosophical significance of 'substance' and 'shadows', draw the reader's attention to the entanglement of the concept in question with the wordplay of the sonnet. 'Substance' (1) establishes the idea of 'essential nature' only through the antagonistic notion of 'the material of which a body is formed', evoked by the clause 'whereof are you made'. It also resonates with 'tend' (attend), 'lend', and 'bounty' projecting its meaning of 'wealth, estate'. 'Strange' (2) suggests both 'not pertaining to you' and 'fantastical, outlandish'. The ambiguous context constructed by the first two lines of the poem extracts from the first mention of 'shadows' (2) its full array of meanings: (a) 'images cast by bodies intercepting the light'; (b) 'reflected images'; (c) 'unreal images, delusive appearances, imitations, counterfeits'; (d) 'portraits, counterfeits'; (e) 'supernatural spirits, phantoms'; (f) 'theatrical players, actors'; and (g) 'servants, followers'. This multiplicity of meaning unlocks the polysemous nature of nearly all words henceforth and provides a wide range of possibilities for 'shade' (3), 'shadow' (4, 10), and 'shape' (12). Lines 3 and 4 allow for various interpretations: (a) every person has just one shade / shadow / appearance / reflection / ghost / servant / follower, while you can lend one of your lot to each one of your servants / followers, but also imitations / reflections; (b) every complete person has one shade / shadow, while you, though being complete, can cast all your shadows / appearances / reflections away; and (c) although each creature has only one form / appearance / reflection, you may appear in the likeness of and thus share the existence of each creature, and so on. The image of Adonis (5), apparently employed to convey the idea of perfect male beauty (as in *Ven.*, 2.8–10: 'The field's chief flower, sweet above compare, / Stain to all nymphs, more lovely than a man, / More white and red than doves or roses are'), because of its multifacetedness elicits a sense of distance and coldness ('lifeless picture, cold and senseless stone, / Well-painted idol, image dun and dead, / Statue contenting but the eye alone'; *Ven.*, 2.211–13). Similarly, the image of Helen (7), employed to convey the idea of perfect female beauty, cannot escape the blot of her betrayal and the woe she brought to Trojans and Greeks alike ('Helen must needs be fair, / When with your blood you daily paint her thus'; *Tro.*, 1.1.91–2). 'Counterfeit' (5), apparently used in the sense of 'verbal picture, image', and reinforced by 'poorly imitated' (6), retains its inherent notions of 'pretence, deceit and disguise', and from there assumes another possible sense of 'impersonation of a theatrical character'. The 'art of beauty' (7) that is to be set on Helen's cheek points to the art of make-up and artificial beauty presented in Ovid's *Medicamina faciei femineae*,[6] as does 'painted' (8). 'Tires' (8) are basically clothes but also 'disguises, theatrical costumes'. 'Show' (10) and 'appear' (11), besides their obvious senses of 'display' and 'represent', also convey the histri-onic ideas of 'act, perform' and 'impersonate'. 'Part' (13) contains the meaning of 'dramatic role' and influences retrospectively the semantic aura of 'shape', in the previous line, bringing to the front its early modern sense of 'part, character impersonated; the make up and cos-tume suited to a particular part'[7] – see for instance Samuel Pepys' *Diary*, 7 January 1661: 'Kinaston the boy; had the good turn to appear in three shapes: first, as a poor woman in ordinary clothes, to please Morose; then in fine clothes, as a gallant, and in them was clearly the prettiest woman in the whole house, and lastly, as a man; and then likewise did appear the handsomest man in the house.'[8] The linguistic ambiguity of Sonnet 53 casts a final shadow on 'like' (14), which is intuitively construed as a preposition sustaining the comparison between 'you' and 'none', but may also be interpreted as a verb.[9] This possibility could give the last line an entirely different reading: 'you like no one and no one likes you for your constant heart', implying that it is the 'external grace' from line 13 that everyone likes 'you' for.

A retrospective reconsideration of the poem from this semantically unfolded perspective discovers two important things. On the one hand, the reader becomes aware of the ease with which each conceit yields to complete reversal: 'In all external grace you have some part' does not mean only 'you partake of all outward perfection', but could also mean 'you are trying to act out, to resemble, each external grace'. 'And you in every blessed shape we know' does not mean only 'we recognize your perfection in each divine form', but also 'we have often seen how, actor-like, you impersonate every beautiful personage'. Spring and autumn as well as Helen and Adonis in the poem are just artificial images, shadows, of the things they represent. This is clearly marked by 'speak' (9), 'painted' (8), 'set' (7), 'imitate' (6), and 'describe' (5). Therefore, in Platonic terms they may be seen as 'shadows of shadows', an interpre-tation that throws a different light on 'shadow' (4): 'And you but one, can every shadow lend' suggesting that 'for all your seeming beauty and grace, you are nothing but an artificial pretender, whose true substance is governed by fluctuation, change, and falseness'. On the other hand, when confronted with such a mishmash of possibilities, the reader instinctively tries to organize them into logically coherent schemata or scenarios. For example, the sequence of alternative meanings pointing at the theatre is remarkably consistent. It starts with shadow's possible meaning of 'actor, player' (2) and continues with the possible inter-pretations of 'describe' and 'counterfeit' (5), 'imitated' (6), the image of making up and dressing up (7, 8), once again 'shadow' (10) and 'show' (10), 'appear' (11), 'shape' (12), and 'part' (13). This results in a possible schema that portrays the addressee of the sonnet as a versatile Elizabethan actor who, just like Edward Kynaston, could play various parts ranging from that of the most beautiful man to that of the most beautiful woman.

The combination of these two effects of wordplay projects an alternative overall interpretation of the sonnet – in which the sonnet inquires into the addressee's nature, by which he can actor-like assume the shape of every external beauty, to discover, rather bitterly, at the end that the utmost substance of the addressee is the fickle stuff of change itself – that runs counter to the primary, more intuitive interpretation: the sonnet inquires into the essence of the addressee's perfect beauty by comparing the latter's outward gloss to conventional blazons only to confirm the opinion that they are merely dross, incomplete reflections of the ultimate Platonic form of perfection rooted in the addressee's constant heart. To us, as to most representatives of our rational age, these two interpretations obviously appear as conflicting. In the worldviews that we use in order to make sense of our everyday, someone's heart is either constant or inconstant, someone is either honest or pretending, either in love or not. Moreover, we are driven by a strong desire to know which one of these possibilities is realized, so each time we try to make sense of an inherently ambivalent work, like Sonnet 53, our understanding collapses into one of many conflicting states. Arguably, this was not entirely the case with readers in the early modern period. As the above analysis of the notions of 'substance' and 'shadows' shows, their conceptualization may have been less restrained by outward form than ours is today, and they may have been more inclined to look for a deeper reality beyond the obvious, for a mystical complexity beyond oppositions, for a unifying absolute.

Converging substance

So far, the discussion of the wordplay in Sonnet 53 shows how alternative meanings of words may cohere with each other, as well as with other tropes and imagery, to produce parallel schemata and scenarios that resemble 'shadows', linked together by possibility in order to reveal a more complex 'substance'. This section focuses on another intriguing use of the dual concept in *Richard II*, through which the complex notion of 'grief' is problematized. The latter seems important even on quantitative grounds – the word itself, its derivatives and its closest synonyms are repeated more than 80 times in the text of the play. Even if the spectator/reader has failed to notice the emphasis on the grief of the Duchess of Gloucester (Act One, Scene Two), Mowbray (Act One, Scene Three), Bolingbroke (Act One, Scene Three), Gaunt (Act One, Scene Three and Act Two, Scene One), and York (Act Two, Scene One), or in any way link them together, the exchange between the Queen and Bushy (Act Two, Scene Two) draws serious attention to the concept and suggests a connection between these and later uses of the word 'grief' in the play:

> QUEEN: [...] I know no cause
> Why I should welcome such a guest as grief,
> Save bidding farewell to so sweet a guest
> As my sweet Richard. Yet again methinks
> Some unborn sorrow, ripe in fortune's womb,
> Is coming towards me, and my inward soul
> With nothing trembles. At some thing it grieves
> More than with parting from my lord the King.
> BUSHY: Each *substance* of a grief hath twenty *shadows*,
> Which shows like grief itself, but is not so;
> For Sorrow's eye, glazed with blinding tears,
> Divides one thing entire to many objects,
> Like perspectives which, rightly gaz'd upon,
> Show nothing but confusion; ey'd awry,
> Distinguish form. So your sweet Majesty,
> Looking awry upon your lord's departure,
> Find shapes of grief more than himself to wail;
> Which, look'd on as it is, is nought but *shadows*
> Of what it is not. Then, thrice-gracious Queen,
> More than your lord's departure weep not. More is not seen;
> Or if it be, 'tis with false Sorrow's eye,
> Which for things true weeps things imaginary.
>
>   (*R2*, 2.2.6–27; italics mine)

Before this scene we learn that, after seizing the property of the dead Gaunt to finance a war in Ireland, Richard is sailing off with his newly-raised army, while at the same time Bolingbroke, furnished with a French army and the support of an ever-increasing number of English lords, is about to touch the northern shores of England to reclaim the title and estate of Lancaster. Neither the Queen nor Bushy know the news yet, so the Queen's intuitive grief seems to be a classic example of dramatic irony, which foreshadows events that at this stage are merely brewing.

Bushy, on the other hand, is apparently trying to allay her fears. Very much in the fashion of a sophisticated Elizabethan courtier, he wields his rhetorical skill employing complex imagery with the intention both to delight and persuade. What he seems to say is that what looks like a real reason for grief is not necessarily one because grieved minds tend to exaggerate and find coherence in meaningless happenstance. A closer look at Bushy's speech, however, discovers a twist of ambiguity in the language he uses, which attributes a different meaning to his words and from there to the whole situation.

Bushy opens his speech with the image of 'substance' and 'shadows', apparently ascribing to the shadows of grief responsibility for the Queen's discomfort, and stating that they are not true substances, that is not genuine reasons for sorrow. He develops this thought in the following image of the Queen's vision distorted by tears and dividing an entire thing into many objects, thus exaggerating the causes of pain (16–17). In line 18, however, Bushy uses the image of 'perspectives', which points towards two possible meanings. The first one – that of a glass cut to produce the optical illusion of multiple reflections of the thing observed through it – coheres with the preceding image of Sorrow's eyes, glazed with tears that act as such perspectives (16, 17); while the second meaning – a particular type of painting or drawing that, when looked at directly, appears as a disfigured mass of incomprehensible shapes but, when viewed from an angle ('awry'), shows a clear form[10] – is consistent with the notion expressed immediately after: 'which, rightly gazed upon, / Show nothing but confusion; eyed awry, / Distinguish form' (18–20). Even though the transition from one image to the other within this single word is motivated by a certain similarity – both types of perspectives seem to present a distorted vision of what they are showing – the second image develops the idea by offering a possibility for grasping the true shape beyond such apparent confusion, namely, eyeing confusion awry. Bushy seizes this idea and relates it back to the Queen's grief: 'So your sweet Majesty, / Looking awry upon your lord's departure, / Find shapes of grief more than himself to wail; / Which, look'd on as it is, is nought but shadows / Of what it is not' (20–4). The effect of the juxtaposition of these lines with the latter image of perspectives presents a logical paradox: while, in the case of the picture, an uninformed observation would merely result in pointless bafflement at meaningless shapes, but an informed viewing from a particular angle would give access to the true encrypted image, in the case of the Queen's distress, it is her 'looking awry' upon the departure of the King that results in multiple unreal 'shapes of grief', and it is her refusal to look at the situation directly that leads her to the shadows of what, according to Bushy, 'it is not'.

The reversal in valorization of these two types of viewing the perspectives creates a meaningful tension within the structure of Bushy's speech and calls into question the validity of its straightforward interpretation. Thus biased, we find that his decorative rhetoric readily yields to deconstruction: Bushy's insistence on 'naught', 'not', 'not', 'not' (23–5) is undermined by his eventual surrendering to the possibility 'or if it be' (26), which seems to lead to a straightforward thought ("'tis with false Sorrow's eye'), but is dissolved into the ambiguous syntax of line 27 ('Which for things true weeps things imaginary'). This can be interpreted as either: (a) deceiving Sorrow's eye, which erroneously bewails imaginary causes, seeing them as true; or (b), in relation to lines 16–17, Sorrow's eye, which is glazed with tears and therefore prone to dividing one entire thing into many objects, laments the imaginable reflections of a true cause. The latter interpretation points to the early modern idea of *divisio*, or amplification, to explain which John Hoskins's *Directions for Speech and Style* (1599) quotes Francis Bacon: 'A way to amplify anything is to break it and make an anatomy of it into several parts, and to examine it according to several circumstances.'[11] As we can see from Bacon's words, the notion in question is twofold: on the one hand, it is a rhetorical device that can be used for intensification and exaggeration, but on the other, it functions as an epistemological approach that offers better insight into the nature of things. This possibility, in turn, promptly increases the complexity of the seemingly unproblematic use of 'substance' and 'shadows' in lines 14–15, and expands its significance to the dimensions of the cognitive concept discussed in the first part of the chapter. Thus, 'Each substance of a grief hath twenty shadows, / Which shows like grief itself, but is not so' acquires another possible interpretation: the 'substance' of grief is a complex abstract phenomenon – what we can see, touch, feel are grief's 'shadows'. We are used to taking these shadows for grief itself, but they are just fractions of what grief really is; yet the 'shadows' of grief are interrelated and form part of a wider, and more complete, perception of grief's 'substance'.

What makes this observation even more important in the context of the play is the realization that the whole plot revolves around the notion of grief: first it is the grief of the Duchess of Gloucester, then Mowbray's grief, then Bolingbroke's, then Gaunt's, then York's, then the Queen's. If examined closely, all these representations of grief follow the same pattern – two incompatible versions of the world are projected by means of wordplay and set against each other. Inevitably, it is revealed that the character responsible for each individual predicament is Richard himself. So, the complexity of the situation becomes even greater when his own grief is brought into the equation, especially since his grief is not an ordinary one – it is a giant's grief, which consumes the grief of the other characters in the play and, somewhat surprisingly, is transformed into the moving humanity of a genuine Shakespearean villain.

A closer consideration of the conceptual dichotomy between 'substance' and 'shadows' therefore suggests that, unlike us today, Shakespeare and his contemporaries may have possessed a mode of thinking which, unrestrained by the desire for rationality and non-contradiction, would be flexible enough to move easily beyond 'shadows' and stretch out into cognitive space in search for a transcendental 'substance'. Moreover, the dichotomy seems to provide an abstract structural model of what actually happens in the spectator/ reader's mind when confronted with conflicting possibilities for interpretation such as those activated by Shakespeare's wordplay. Finally, it shows how poetic ambiguity locks meaning in perpetually wavering cruces, suggesting that this, and not the still, one-sided, momentary appearances of people and things we are so accustomed to, might be the true nature of what actually surrounds us.

Notes

1. Paul Simpson, *Stylistics: A Resource Book for Students* (London: Routledge, 2004), 45.
2. The idea in question was evidently commonplace in Shakespeare's time as many of his contemporaries, such as John Lyly, Robert Greene, Thomas Nashe, Thomas Lodge, George Peele, Edmund Spenser and Philip Sidney, used the distinction between 'substance' and 'shadow' to express a wide range of opinions and feelings. This only increases the notion's cultural significance and justifies a deeper analysis of the conceptual framework that underlies it.
3. All Shakespeare quotations are from *The Riverside Shakespeare*, ed. by Gwynne Blakemore Evans (Boston: Houghton Mifflin Harcourt, 1997); italics mine.
4. Plato, *The Republic*, in *The Dialogues of Plato in Five Volumes*, trans. by Benjamin Jowett (Oxford: Oxford University Press, 1892), II, 303–416 (369). Plato's theory of forms can also be found in *Phaedo*.
5. Thomas Wilson, *The Rule of Reason, conteinynge the Arte of Logique set forth in Englishe* (London: John Kingston, 1563), 10.
6. Later translated as 'The Art of Beauty', and possibly known under this title in Shakespeare's time. See Stuart Gillespie and Robert Cummings, 'A Bibliography of Ovidian Translations and Imitations in English', *Translation and Literature*, 13 (2004), 207–18.
7. See: 'shape, *n.*', *Oxford English Dictionary*, 2nd edn (1989).

8. Samuel Pepys, *The Diary of Samuel Pepys*, ed. by Robert Latham, William Matthews and William A. Armstrong (Berkeley: University of California Press, 2000), 7.

9. Such an interpretation is made possible by the fact that what may be the third person singular form of the verb 'like', that is 'likes', is elided from the second part of the chiasmus: 'none you'.

10. This duplicity of the image of 'perspectives' has been recognized by critics: see the introduction to the Arden Shakespeare edition of *King Richard II*, ed. by Charles R. Forker (London: Thomson Learning, 2005), 55–90.

11. John Hoskins, *Directions for Speech and Style*, ed. by Hoyt H. Hudson (Princeton: Princeton University Press, 1935), 76.

6
Stage and Conflict in 'The Phoenix and the Turtle'

Boris Drenkov

Regardless of the fact that generally 'The Phoenix and the Turtle' is not among the most popular works by Shakespeare, critical views of the poem have always expressed polar positions. In this chapter I would like to explore various dimensions of conflict that characterize both the textuality of the work and its reception among scholars of different periods and academic backgrounds. It is my assertion that the poem has not only provoked disagreement among critical readers who have approached this fragmented and challenging text, but also that Shakespeare's text itself stages a conflict discernible on several levels. It does this, first of all, by distancing itself from – and thereby creating tension with – certain readerly expectations originating from the immediate textual context in which it first appeared: Robert Chester's anthology *Loves Martyr* (1601). At the same time, Shakespeare's contribution to this large-scale literary project by a rather unknown poet can be viewed as a site of internal conflict, that of the lyrical speaker with the empty reality which results from the death of the departed ideal, and the loss of inspiration and value. The present study is developed, therefore, in two parts. Whereas the first concentrates on the opposing opinions the enigmatic text has generated in critical appraisals, the second part exposes the performance of internal conflict and the tragedy of the lyrical speaker in the poetic text itself.

Centuries of misconception

It is undisputed that the poem by Shakespeare appended to *Loves Martyr* is one of the most controversial of his works. What is more important is that the views expressed by critics throughout the history of its existence have never reached a consensus on its artistic value. While Colin Burrow and Wolfgang Weiss consider it as one of Shakespeare's most important works,[1] other academics regard the poem as a mistake, if not indeed a failure – too enigmatic, too incomprehensible to be of any poetic importance. Hazelton Spencer, among those who uphold this view, maintains that 'Shakespeare's contribution is a poor thing, but no doubt his own.'[2] For Hardin Craig, 'It is a puzzling poem which may have some hidden topical significance. As it stands, it adds little to Shakespeare's fame';[3] finally, according to Frayne Williams, 'the poem is so obscure thematically that it has won few admirers'.[4] To this basic dispute over the text's intrinsic quality can be added the debates surrounding its authorship, which, while remaining a secondary concern of the principal scholarly contributions, continue to have their followers and remain a site for academic conflict. Richard Grant White, for example, points out that

> There is no other external evidence that these verses are Shakespeare's than their appearance with his signature in a collection of poems published in London while he was living there in the height of his reputation. The style, however, is at least a happy imitation, especially in the bold and original use of epithet.[5]

However, even in those critical appraisals that are positively inclined towards 'The Phoenix and the Turtle', the keywords that are used to describe the poem remain 'mystery', 'enigma', 'insoluble puzzle' – an inescapable fact that naturally affects its public appreciation.[6]

Nevertheless, the difficulties in evaluating the poem derive from centuries of obscured contextual connections, and the problems that scholars experience on encountering the verses originate in a complex web of reasons. One of the most significant causes of confusion is the common practice of presenting 'The Phoenix and the Turtle' as a freestanding text although the poem is far too short to develop persuasive images. The elegy is meant as a part of the larger-scale text by Chester and it is only in that context that it emerges as a meaningful entity.

The publication as an individual work of 'Let the bird of loudest lay', which I shall henceforth refer to by its opening line, can be dated as early as 1640, when John Benson published a collection of Shakespeare's poetic works, in which the short poem found a place. It appeared there, however, without a title, and even more importantly, without any reference to the source from which it was taken. In 1710 the poem was included in a new edition of Shakespeare's verses, edited by Gildon, again without a reference to Chester's poem. But matters became increasingly muddled in 1780, when, for some unknown reason, Edmund Malone placed 'Let the bird of loudest lay' as the twentieth poem of *The Passionate Pilgrim*. This was felt to be a logical editorial solution and was therefore repeated in several editions of Shakespeare's lyrics in the eighteenth and nineteenth centuries, with the poem bearing the title proposed by Malone – 'The Phoenix and the Turtle'. The first signs of a changing awareness occurred in the very short note on the poem written by Halliwell in 1865. Even nowadays, scholars rarely tend to give a more detailed account of the different contexts in which the poem appeared. One of the most striking proofs that this disregard in fact obscures a proper reading of the poem is the continuing popularity of the false title under which the stanzas have gained popularity. 'The Phoenix and the Turtle' is by no means the correct heading, as the poem does not deal with these characters: these birds are only referred to in Shakespeare's verses in that they are buried. The title therefore leads the reader in a false direction and creates false expectations that remain unfulfilled at the close of the poem, as the celebrated birds are mentioned only twice. The publication tradition and the disrupted links with the original source of the text then logically hamper the perception of the poem.

A further reason for the controversial public reception of the work lies in the traditional interpretation established by numerous important Shakespearean scholars. The allegorical approach has been markedly favoured from its very first modern publication up to the present. Heinrich Straumann distinguishes three different trends in the various approaches to the poem, which themselves present conflicting sites and ambivalent interpretations that draw the public's attention in contrasting directions:

> First there are those who are above all interested in what they consider to be the personal allegory of the poem. [...] The second group of interpreters try to approach the poem by putting it in the context of the traditions and conventions of that genre (elegy – B. D.). [...] Finally there is a third group of critics whom for lack of a better term, we may refer to as idealists. The idealists stress the intellectual and thematic aspect of the poem, i.e. for them the theme of the poem is the miracle of fulfilled love [...][7]

Of these three groups, however, even 50 years or so after Straumann's publication, the strongest remains the first. The names put forward for the allegorical characters of Chester's poem were usually first developed as hypotheses for Shakespeare's text, and were then conveniently accommodated to the rest of *Loves Martyr*. The century-long exegetical history has produced a long list of names, starting with the earliest hypothesis formulated by Grosart – the first modern editor of Chester's anthology – who associated the allegorical images with Queen Elizabeth and the Earl of Essex.

The suggestion that the same real figures should stand behind both Shakespeare's and Chester's allegories, however, seldom worked, and logically enough, one of the poets was to blame – either Shakespeare for not knowing *Loves Martyr* or Chester for not being as skilled a creator of allegories. Nevertheless, it can be concluded that both Shakespeare's and Chester's texts are destined to remain a perpetual source of conflicting interpretation for readers of the Bard's poetry.

Rioting contexts

The contentious nature of 'Let the bird of loudest lay', as anticipated above, is discernible on several levels. One of these is its position in Chester's large-scale literary project. That Shakespeare intended to create a poem which should be remembered for its mysterious and impenetrable influence is obvious not only from the content itself, but from the friction with the context in which it first appeared – *Loves Martyr*. One of the reasons for the impenetrability of the text is that it does not fulfil certain expectations (and this is without considering the above-mentioned additional difficulties arising from the misleading publication tradition) which the reader places on the text even before s/he begins reading. Of course, an important part of these expectations is connected to *Loves Martyr*.

Unfortunately, within the framework of a single chapter it is impossible sufficiently to develop a reading of such a challenging text as Robert Chester's anthology. For this reason I will simply assume that this work is devoted to Elizabeth I. *Loves Martyr* seems to be an example of that representational typology which depicts the last Tudor monarch as a sacred icon. Chester's poem, clearly a work of praise, participates in this tradition, which had been inaugurated decades earlier with Elizabeth's accession, and culminates in Chester's project where the monarch is represented as a divinity in the vision of the immortal phoenix that will reign eternally over England. Although this interpretation of the main textual corpus should logically apply to Shakespeare's poem as well, once we read the text this potential expectation collapses. At first glance, 'Let the bird of loudest lay' offers anything but the enthusiastic praise so vividly present in Chester's text.

In the context of the proposed reading of Chester's poem, Shakespeare's contribution draws even more contrastive attention to itself, primarily because the Bard had otherwise remained mysteriously silent on the death of the queen under whose reign he was born and had prospered as a writer, and additionally, because it interestingly illuminates some new aspects of the vaguely explored relations between the greatest dramatist and the 'Holy Virgin' of early modern England. The structure of the anthology reserved for Shakespeare, as the most popular of the featured poets, the most prominent place. He is the Bard who opens the cycle of appended works. In this way, Chester's text ends with the death of the birds, but a resurrection is never depicted, mainly because Shakespeare must have been considered the most worthy of the living generation to perform this act. Even Ignoto, the anonymous writer whose poem stands between Chester's text and the collection of additional poems, expects the Bard to praise the resurrection of the phoenix. Ignoto's poem ends with a prolific description of the burning, so that the tense expectation of the resurrection reaches its peak:

> Suppose here burnes this wonder of a breath,
> In righteous flames, and holy-heated fires:
> [...] The flame that eates her, feedes the others life:
> Her rare-dead ashes, fill a rare-live urne:
> One Phoenix borne, another Phoenix burne.[8]

The allusions to Elizabeth I are numerous here: the vision of the pelican, who feeds her children with her own flesh, is one of the favourite allegorical descriptions of the queen.[9] The last phrase of the quotation hints at one of the main doctrines of monarchy: the accession of the heir to the throne and the royal institution that never loses substance. In this connection, the logical continuance of the cycle would be the celebration of the restoration – the Phoenix, who rises from the ashes in all her glory and royal grace. But we see something else, something totally unexpected: a grief, a denunciation of the mission with which the poet is burdened, a most painful apprehension of reality, a funeral elegy, a prayer for a burial ritual. Shakespeare's poem thus inevitably attracts even more attention to itself, but it also becomes one of the main focuses of the cycle on account of its extraordinary density and complexity.

Rejecting poetry

The unrealized anticipations of the reader are not exhausted in the issue of subject matter. Such a prominent writer as Shakespeare would surely have been expected to contribute to the cycle with a poem which would, with its elaborate forms and ornaments, prove a lasting example of his mastery; the benchmark by which all the other texts in the collection would be measured. Yet, even at first reading one cannot help but notice the (at best) extravagant poetic style of the verses: it is a poem of dissolute, at times dull, language choice. In this respect, the work openly opposes Renaissance conventions of stylistic register. In fact, the text is a formal rejection of the popularly celebrated characteristics of poetry. 'Rejection' is not too strong a term here, as the text, with its fragmented imagery and complicated symbolism, addresses its allusions not to the audience but inwardly, to itself. Furthermore, it does not attempt to create any aesthetic appeal for the language in the form of rhetorical devices or tropes. It is this shift in the lyrical voice that hampers the reading of the poem.

As Puttenham puts it, the task of poetry is above all to 'delight and allure as well the mynde as the eare of the hearers with a certaine noueltie and strange maner of conueyance'.[10] Puttenham also postulates that the ornament is an integral part of the poetic language where 'this ornament we speake of is giuen to it by figures and figuratiue speaches, which be the flowers as it were and coulours that a Poet setteth vpon his language by arte'.[11] Of this brightness of ornamentation there is no trace in the poem – and this characteristic of the text isolates it from the mainstream courtly poems of the period centring on the figure of the queen.[12] These lines suggest instead a poet who confines the verse within a harsher, less decorative mould.[13]

The problem posed, however, is not merely that of the absence of ornamental conventions; but also of the fragmented, knotted structure and expression which makes the experience of reading an adventurous endeavour. For all its brevity the poem boasts a very complicated structure. Formally, the text can be divided into four separate parts: the first one ends with 'Here the anthem doth commence [...]', the second with 'Either was the others mine [...]', the third begins with 'Propertie was thus appalled [...]', and the fourth is also graphically marked by the beginning of the *Threnos*. Each of these subsections has its own topic, culmination and characters. In the first, the lyrical voice constructs a funeral ritual, in which the mourners are indicated as birds. In the second, a revelation of a miracle takes place, and the main characters – apart from the Phoenix and the Turtle – become abstract notions such as Number or Division. In the third section, the lyrical voice turns to the witnesses of the ritual, and Propertie is appalled, Reason is confounded. The intricacy continues in the last part of the main text, where the chromatic notions celebrated as animate objects prevail as characters, and the narrative perspective is conveyed by a character who is no longer the voice to which the reader had become accustomed, but a new voice, that of Reason. This textual complexity does nothing to help the reader understand the poem; it does not clarify through the writer's logic the core of meaning around which the text is centred. On the contrary, it distances the readers from the meaning, thereby creating a tension between the lyrical text and its recipient. It is an anti-structure: the many parts within the relatively short poem make the subtexts open and close over and over again, creating a sense of stage effects, of various scenes continuously beginning and ending. It is precisely this poetical structure which conveys the blurred voice one hears in the poem and makes the reception of the work so much more challenging.

In the construction of the poem there is an obvious gradation, though not a positive one, which might help us to consolidate the dissolving structures and meaning. There is a gradual dissipation of the concreteness, of the tangible images created by the text. The clearest part is the first one, mainly because of the reference to common birds which poses no difficulty in comprehension and works easily upon the reader's imagination. Yet, even the beginning of the poem introduces indefinite allusions at the same time as it assigns dramatic roles: 'Let the bird of loudest lay, / On the sole Arabian tree, / Herauld sad and trumpet be' (1–3) does not specify a particular bird, and this has caused a series of problems in the scholarly perception of the poem.[14] The second part begins in a promising way, as we are brought to the plot of Chester's poem ('Phoenix and the Turtle fled', 23), but this is only a momentary feeling. The poet's voice leads the reader in unpredictable directions: abstract notions, tautologies and repetitions fill the lines. The vagueness progresses in the following part where we have abstract notions, Propertie and Reason, as characters participating in the action. The persistence of the abstract nouns continues – 'Saw Division grow together' (42), 'Love hath Reason, Reason none' (47) – and culminates in the final part, *Threnos*, in which the style is that of a dramatic epilogue – 'Beautie, Truth and Raritie, / Grace in all simplicitie' (53–4); 'It was married Chastitie' (61); 'Truth and Beautie buried be' (64) – where the birds are formally buried in the impenetrable meaning. The purposeful obscurity becomes obvious from the structure of the poem: the text does not yield up its sense at a first reading, inviting us instead to rethink the performance and dramatically reconstruct the images in our mind if we are to grasp, eventually, the poem's overall meaning.

Problematic beauty

Shakespeare's rejection of textual logic is paralleled by an equally resolute rejection of poetic logic. A characteristic feature of the verses is their lack of any ornamental or decorative tropes. There are no true epithets to dim the robust expression and few adjectives. The latter are predominantly dramatic intensifiers of the strained emotional situation staged by the narrator's voice, and are used exclusively in the first part of the poem: 'herauld sad' (3), 'foule precurrer' (6), 'fevers end' (7). The only adjective that has some visual semantic value, which might give more clarity to the imagery apparatus, is 'white' in 'Let the Priest in Surples white' (13). Yet, the visual connotation here is undermined by the reference to the priest's 'surples' in a funeral procession, a fact that again undeniably insists on emotional conceptualization. The absence of visual specification, the compression of the emotional colour scheme through the adjectives demonstrates that it is not a poem of images that we are dealing with, but one of rising tensions, culminating emotions.

The first part of the poem, as we have seen, appoints certain birds as participants in a funeral ritual, and it is the very act of designation that is symptomatic of the way tropes are employed within the poem. Although these first stanzas have been interpreted as allegories,[15] to my understanding they are exactly the opposite – it is the deconstruction of the trope that we experience here:

> Let the Priest in Surples white,
> That defunctive Musicke can,
> Be the death-divining Swan,
> Lest the Requiem lack his right.

> (*PhT*, 13–16)

The author leads us into the creative process of staging the dramatic event in order to help the reader experience something as a symbol, to make it perform as a symbol in a literary discourse. The birds do not inhabit the text as signs to be decoded. There is an unambiguous insistence that they should not be read as signs at all – there is no deviation from the language norms or the semantic values, there is not even an integration of the symbol in the structure of the text, which is a necessary feature for the construction of an allegory.[16] What we find here is merely a speech act appointing some birds to perform as heralds in a ritual, or simply in the consciousness of the narrator's voice, a fact which disentangles the mysterious appeal of the trope. The allegory is therefore not fully executed, it does not exist as an element of style in the text. This obviously demonstrates the poet's denial, his lack of intention or will to achieve a lyrical tone.

The triumph of the non-poetical can be found on every level of the poem. The rhythmical pattern, for example, does not emphasize meaning in any special way, nor does it sustain any musical effect which might support the poetic imagery. The rhythmical pattern established in the first line is followed rigorously with only very few exceptions until the end. The four-stressed trochees create the feeling of a tired, monotonous line, especially after the first two parts, when the ear has become completely accustomed to the pattern. This rhythmical ennui does not correspond to the idiosyncratic thoughts expressed in the text, and this further obscures the perception of the narrative voice.

A very interesting aspect for the interpretation of 'Let the bird of loudest lay' is undoubtedly its setting and characters. As we have seen, in the first part a funeral ritual is being depicted, and certain birds are assigned the positions of mourners. But although these birds are respected typographically, thanks to the capitalization, as readers we never actually see them fulfil their parts in the ritual. Nor, as they have 'fled' (23), are the Phoenix and the Turtle directly represented as characters. It is only Propertie and Reason that really participate in the events to which the narrator refers. The former serves as an intensifier of the dramatic situation after the revelation of the miracle; the latter is a true character in that it takes over the function of the lyrical voice in the last part of the work – a choice of vital importance for the understanding of the text. Both Propertie and Reason can be understood as aspects of the human mind, or of the human being in general. We might say that they are actually different realizations of one and the same self.

So far we have not, however, discussed the most important character in the poem – the narrative voice – that is the true determiner/director of the action, the constructor of the text. As it happens, this is the character about whom the reader knows most. The lyrical voice experiences an extreme internal conflict caused by the reality in which he must now exist and which is conveyed by the text. As if to show us or to make us experience the pain suffered at the thought of the departed birds, Shakespeare leads us through the emotional chaos of his lyrical voice, a breakdown that is reflected on every level of the text.

The very opening hints at catastrophe. The emphasis is on imperatives and superlatives; the prescribed emotion for the bird that is to announce the death of the Phoenix and the Turtle expresses the tension of the narrator's emotional state to an extreme. Hardly any time is given to the readers to accommodate that picture in their mind before they are presented with another bird – this time a 'foule' (6) one. We are thus introduced to a dramatic conflict, but this conflict between reality and self is not performed, it takes place only in the imagination of the narrator. The unchaste birds do not seem to make any attempt to disrupt the funeral procession, yet the lyrical voice continues to insist: 'From this Session interdict / Every foule of tyrant wing, / Save the Eagle feathered King' (9–11). The complicated syntax of this stanza does not clarify whether the Eagle belongs to the evil or the chaste group and as it turns out, this does not matter: the voice quickly appoints another participant, another character in the funeral cast, another location, without stating any reason. In the second part, the mood of the voice changes dramatically – the uncontrolled viewpoint and syntax shift to a triumphant, somewhat declaratory tone, as demonstrated by the short, simple and clear sentences (20–2). But this sense of relief in the introductory part of the second subdivision is quickly abandoned and the movement of the lyrical voice takes yet another dramatic direction.

The announcement of the miracle, which will distress so many of the witnesses in the procession, makes absolutely no sense. In three stanzas the narrator constructs semantic obscurity on an unbelievable scale of linguistic inconsistency and emotional turmoil: 'Two distincts, Division none / Number there in love was slaine' (27–8); 'Hearts remote, yet not asunder, / Distance and no space was seene' (29–30); 'Single Natures double name' (39). The hectic paradoxical repetitions are supported by the sense of a dialogue with an implicit participant, addressed through the repetition of 'so' ('So they loved as love in twaine', 25; 'So between them love did shine', 33). This feeling of a staged dialogue corresponds to the bewilderment of the reader confronted by the obscure lines: the logic seems to follow some mysterious dramatic path. The frenetic pitch in the description of the miracle creates no clarity, but rather more confusion as the thoughts expressed by the voice are obviously contradictory: 'Two distincts, Division none' (27), 'Single Natures double name' (39). The various attempts made to decode the philosophic sense of these rambling thoughts have proved unfruitful. They even represent, as already ascertained by Furnivall,[17] a disordered mosaic of intertextual references – those listed and discussed in Wilson Knight's authoritative account include Plato, Aristophanes, Socrates, Virgil, Dante, Michelangelo, the Bible,[18] to which Eriksen and Marrapodi also convincingly add Giordano Bruno.[19] That these lines should be perceived as a performative chaos intended to demonstrate the psychic disturbance of the narrator's voice is clearly within the author's intention.

In the third part this tendency reaches its peak. The self is split, and we experience the rupture of the lyrical character in several ways: Propertie is appalled, Reason is confounded. The abstract nouns referring to parts of the human mind eventually convey the suggestion that the conflict being staged occurs within the consciousness of the narrating person. One aspect of this consciousness (the self) accepts and announces the miracle, the other rejects it and withdraws from the narrative – the death of the birds is an unbelievable, unimaginable finale. The tension in the situation in which the lyrical voice finds itself is released in the final section of the poem, where one of the shards of its fragmented personification takes the stage to sing the final lamentation for the Phoenix and the Turtle, assuming the role of a tragic chorus.

It is the last part, the *Threnos*, that constitutes the announcement of a miracle, but this wonder turns out to be one of the most painful revelations in the Shakespearean corpus, lamenting as it does the collapse of the creative individual under the overwhelming evidence of the reality in which he is forced to exist – a reality without poetry, beauty and truth (53–9). With the wondrous bird everything real and beautiful has died and what remains are the ruins of a true world, a lie, an ugly deception:

> Truth may seeme, but cannot be,
> Beautie bragge, but tis not she,
> Truth and Beautie buried be.
>
> (*PhT*, 62–4)

It is not until these lines that we experience the narrator-Reason as a demiurge. Here the imperative acquires a real power: the virtues must remain buried; as there is nothing substantial enough to resurrect them, any return to the ideals would be useless. Shakespeare has ingeniously found a way to praise the Phoenix and the Turtle by showing that for his poetic persona existence without them is beyond belief. To him, death appears as salvation from the loss of authenticity. In an unanticipated, unique manner, Shakespeare's poem thus fulfils the original expectations related to Chester's poem. The text is the ultimate form of praise for the creative existence made possible in Elizabethan England.

The narrator's voice is the element in the poem through which the text should be approached. The internal conflict, the total breakdown which results from the realization that the birds of impossible chastity are dead is the main idea the poet implies throughout his text, the dramatized insanity of the self-conscious narrative voice, its textual realization: from the rash, abrupt changes of viewpoints to the discrepancy between the rhythmical pattern and the semantic content of the lines, from the increasingly blurred images to the mixture of concrete and abstract characters. The poem comes across as the ultimate performative rejection of the poetic mood: beauty is removed from every word and every level of the structure. Through its poignant staging of the conflict within the lyrical voice, 'Let the bird of loudest lay' strikes us as one of the most demanding and valuable texts of the English Renaissance – a powerful counterpoint to the mainstream works associated with the epoch.

Notes

1. See William Shakespeare, *The Complete Sonnets and Poems*, ed. by Colin Burrow (New York: Oxford University Press, 2002); William Shakespeare, *Sonette / Epen und die kleineren Dichtungen*, ed. by Wolfgang Weiss (Darmstadt: Wissenschaftliche Buchgesellschaft, 1968), 460–5 (461).
2. Hazelton Spencer, *The Art and Life of William Shakespeare* (New York: Harcourt, Brace, 1940), 55.
3. Hardin Craig, *An Interpretation of Shakespeare* (New York: Citadel Press, 1949), 106–7.
4. Frayne Williams, *Mr. Shakespeare of the Globe* (New York: Dutton, 1941), 181.
5. Richard G. White, *Memoirs of the Life of W. Shakespeare, with an Essay toward the Expression of his Genius, and an Account of the Rise of the English Drama* (Boston: Cambridge, 1865), 260.
6. Brian Green starts his essay with the words: 'The poem is quite an astonishing one, a perplexing love-elegy, traditional and yet obscure.' See Brian Green, '"Single Nature's Double Name": An Exegesis of "The Phoenix and the Turtle"', in *Generous Lovers: English Essays in Memory of Edward Davis*, ed. by Brian Green (Cape Town: Oxford University Press, 1980), 44–54 (44).
7. Heinrich Straumann, '"The Phoenix and the Turtle" in its Dramatic Context', *English Studies, Netherlands*, 58 (1977), 494–500 (494–6).
8. Robert Chester, *Robert Chester's 'Loves martyr, or, Rosalins complaint' (1601): With Its Supplement, 'Diverse poeticall essaies' on the Turtle and Phoenix by Shakspere, Ben Jonson, George Chapman, John Marston*, ed. by Alexander B. Grosart (London: Trübner for the New Shakespeare Society, 1878), 181. All subsequent quotations are taken from this edition and will be noted parenthetically in the text through line number(s).
9. See, for example Louis A. Montrose, *The Subject of Elizabeth: Authority, Gender, and Representation* (Chicago, Ill. and London: University of Chicago Press, 2006), 53.
10. George Puttenham, *The Arte of English Poesie* (Menston: Scolar Press, 1968), 114.
11. Puttenham, 115.
12. Ina Schabert observes that in the 1590s, when worries concerning the queen's succession grew stronger, the regime commissioned the composition

of literary works and the execution of portraits that depicted the monarch as everlasting and never-changing. These artifacts took advantage of a myriad of mythological characters such as, for instance, Astraea. See Ina Schabert, *Englische Literaturgeschichte: eine neue Darstellung aus der Sicht der Geschlechterforschung* (Stuttgart: Kröner, 1997), 109.

13. Matchett notes that there are three words in the poem which, according to the New English Dictionary, not only are used by Shakespeare for the first time, but uniquely in the English language. These words are: 'precurrer', 'defunctive', and 'distinct' (as a noun). See William H. Matchett, *The Phoenix and the Turtle: Shakespeare's Poem and Chester's Loues Martyr* (The Hague: Mouton & Co, 1965), 35. From a semantic point of view this renders the language tense, considering the shortness of the text, and thereby provokes the reader to decode the innovative vocabulary within the verses.

14. See, for example, Burrow, 37; Matchett, 37; Peter Dronke, 'The Phoenix and the Turtle', *Orbis Literarum*, 22 (1968), 199–220 (208). Shahani identifies the bird with the nightingale which, to me personally, makes the least sense. See Ranjee Shahani, 'The Phoenix and the Turtle', *Notes and Queries*, 191 (1946), 99–101, 120–3 (101).

15. For example in Shahani,101, and A. Alvarez, 'The Phoenix and the Turtle', in *Interpretations*, ed. by John E. Wain (London: Routledge and Kegan Paul, 1955), 4–5.

16. The deviation of meaning is one of the core definitions of tropes. As for the allegory Quintilian says: 'A trope is an expression transferred from its natural and principal signification to another, for the sake of embellishing speech'; quoted in *Metaphor, Allegory, and the Classical Tradition*, ed. by G.R. Boys-Stones (Oxford: Oxford University Press, 2003), 1.

17. In Frederick James Furnivall, 'On Chester's "Love's Martyr": Essex is not the Turtle-Dove of Shakespeare's "Phoenix and Turtle"', *New Shakespeare Society's Transactions*, 1 (1879), 451–5 (451).

18. See George Wilson Knight, *The Mutual Flame: On Shakespeare's Sonnets and 'The Phoenix and the Turtle'* (London: Methuen & Co, 1955), 191–224. The word that Knight uses is not disorder but 'obscurities' (194) in the meanings created by the Shakespeare text (in this he is followed by Matchett, 128). These additionally hamper the sense through 'a series of paralyzing posers' (Knight, 168). Again according to Knight, 'Let the bird of loudest lay' is a part of the stream of '*coterie poetry*' (188, italics in the original), which is described as poems on a homosexual theme, or as Knight expresses it, works of men with 'the higher, or bisexual, integration' (179).

19. Both Eriksen and Marrapodi discover unquestionable similarities in the ideas of the Shakespearean poem and Giordano Bruno's *Degli eroici furori*. The theory is also supported by the fact that Bruno was burnt at the stake in 1600, which is very close to the date of publication of *Loves Martyr*. See Roy T. Eriksen, '"Un certo amoroso martire": Shakespeare's "The Phoenix and the Turtle" and Giordano Bruno's *De gli eroici furori*', *Spenser Studies*, 2 (1981), 193–215; and Michele Marrapodi, 'Simbolo, archetipo e mito in "The Phoenix and the Turtle"', *Nuovi Annali della Facoltà di Magistero dell'Università di Messina*, 1 (1983), 337–58.

Part II
Conflict through Shakespeare

7
Introduction

Carla Dente

Shakespeare 'in motion'

In today's age of global cultural mobility, marked by widespread hybridization and an incessant flux of ideas, knowledge, goods and finances, 'Shakespeare' provides a truly paradigmatic case of a matrix that has operated across different historical and national contexts as a crucial factor shaping people's ways of experiencing, conceptualizing and (re-)imagining reality. This pliancy has resulted moreover in the rise of transcultural critical, theatrical or editorial practices that have further enhanced Shakespeare's versatility, the readiness of his works to give voice to an exceptionally broad range of historical and cultural issues that are alien to the context in which they were originally produced. As brilliantly remarked by Terence Hawkes in the early 1990s, we keep 'meaning by Shakespeare'.[1] Hawkes's observation rested on the assumption that there is no intrinsic meaning to a text, but rather a certain range of meanings, that signification is a process which is essentially based on the agency of readers/critics whose interpretative skills are moulded by the culture and the historical context in which they operate, and whose meaning-making process invests all the texts belonging to each specific literary system.

The critic's position is similar to that of the author who writes a new text based on his/her own specific reading of a previous text. In the case of Shakespeare's work, this propensity towards giving new shape and new meanings to an existing literary corpus has notably manifested itself with a greater degree of freedom when acts of rereading and revision have taken place outside Britain and hence at one remove from his source culture. As a transcultural myth in perpetual motion, 'Shakespeare' suggests metaphorically a comparison with the non-linear reading practice fostered by hypertexts, and the cultural capital which it embodies has likewise both invited and enabled non-linear readings of entire cross-sections in the history of culture and of ideas, resulting at one and the same time in a 'better understanding' and a 'potential misreading'.[2] It is thanks to reading practices of this kind that a whole set of assumptions regarding the completeness and compactness of the text, but also its ethnic and cultural stability, have been dismantled.

The critics read Shakespeare

To quote Hawkes again, 'like it or not, all we can ever do is use Shakespeare as a powerful element in specific ideological strategies'.[3] The versatility of the Shakespearean corpus has fuelled a proliferation of critical perspectives and educational projects that can only partially be comprised within the field of so-called 'Shakespeare criticism'. These mechanics of mobility are in some ways similar to the ones at work in postcolonial contexts, where a moment of tension and conflict – responding polemically to the reality of dispossession and ideologically-biased representations of native culture – is sometimes followed by an attempt to renegotiate Shakespeare as a source of authority and authoritativeness within a new national compact. Postcolonial studies have indeed had the merit of illuminating a process which, albeit in less conspicuous ways, is also detectable in the history of continental Europe itself: a process whereby acts of appropriation have been carried out under the thrust of a complex tangle of social, cultural and political factors which have given rise to different combinations across changing historical frameworks. Shakespeare's work is therefore turned into a convenient resource available to the critic for expressing his/her ideas about texts, themes and values, but also a resource available to successive writers for generating novel meanings from established narratives.

This complex and multifarious production drawing on 'Shakespeare' affords the opportunity to both ponder and test the possibility of extending its methods to research in the humanities, with possible repercussions on teaching; it also provides fertile ground for an investigation, today, of the issue of authorship as a transition from the spoken to the written word, of that of collaborative authorship (in the Renaissance period as well as later), and of the mechanics of textual construction. Shakespeare is also a reliable asset to be drawn upon in case of 'need', when internal or external tensions threaten to crush individual or group identities, testifying to a state of conflict. And this is exactly the process which triggers, time and again, the transition from Shakespeare to 'Shakespeare'.

The use of conflict in critical practice

While the last thirty years have seen a major expansion in the reading of Shakespeare's work side by side with conflict-dominated themes, scholarly approaches whereby Shakespeare's texts are investigated through the lens of conflict – in its thematic, linguistic and ideological declensions – have long figured in the history of criticism.

Starting with Aristotle, conflict has been identified as the structuring principle of drama, not only because of the essentially dialectical and oppositional model underpinning its most obvious linguistic manifestation, that is to say the dialogic form, but also because conflict, as a critical standpoint, has been able to generate thematic categories and ideological orthodoxies that can be applied to the Shakespearean text. Usually, the starting point is a survey of the quantity, quality and function of recurrent argumentative figures across the macrotext. These can take the shape of binary oppositions, contraries, antitheses, paradoxes, or dissociative phenomena which are embedded in the verbal texture of individual texts and are therefore taken as reflections of the presence of conflict on the thematic level.

The historical persistence of this attitude may be verified even from a sketchy mapping of the most representative critical works in this area. Theodore Spencer's *Shakespeare and the Nature of Man*, published in 1943 as the Second World War was raging, significantly detected the overarching presence, in the Shakespearean canon, of a distinctive trait of the early modern episteme, that is to say the notion of the dissociation of sensibility.[4] A couple of decades later, the same approach informed Bodwell Smith's *Dualities in Shakespeare* (1966), and Rosalie L. Coolie's *Paradoxia Epidemica* (1966). Hard on their heels, Norman Rabkin's *Shakespeare and the Common Understanding* (1967) similarly interpreted the frequency of oppositional binarism in Shakespeare's work as a symptom of the ambivalence of their author's perception, or even of the multivalent nature of reality itself.[5]

The impression one derives from this close sequence of like-minded studies is that of an overall approach which, while attempting to locate the texts within their actual context of production, offers up an interpretation that reflects the critical, and more broadly cultural, climate at the middle of the twentieth century rather than a Renaissance mode of thinking. It is a critical attitude that points to the need for ideological repositioning and reappropriation after the devastating effects of the war on a whole episteme. While showing greater awareness of the risk of making Shakespeare too much our contemporary, Robert Grudin, in *Mighty Opposites: Shakespeare and Renaissance Contrariety* (1979), gathers examples of representations of reality that are shaped by the inter-action of conflicting forces, according to documented philosophical influences that can be traced back to Montaigne and Bruno, but also to post-Kantian idealism, a current clearly nearer to the critic's own culture.[6] Philosophy also plays a major role in Jennifer Bates's much more recent *Hegel and Shakespeare on Moral Imagination* (2010), a study which looks at Shakespeare through the categories developed by the German thinker, placing particular emphasis on his ethical view of aesthetics (drama as a form of Absolute spirit and hence the highest form of art) because of its capacity to attain a dialectical synthesis that can account for human experience.[7]

Following the thread of conflict, one can identify a second group of critical works, characterized by interpretations which single out con-trasting elements and illustrate their specific dynamics on the textual or the scenic level: as a significant example one could mention the opposition between the young and the old in *King Lear* or *Romeo and Juliet*, or the inner dialectic of Macbeth, a character whose representa-tion alternates between the two extreme polarities of brave warrior and power-thirsty criminal.[8]

Conflict through Shakespeare

Two main attitudes can be traced in this respect: on the one hand, the text is used to invite audiences to discover parallels between actual situations of conflict belonging to their own historical reality and the models presented by Shakespeare, while on the other, the 'tendentious' rewriting of a text points to a problem of which the actual historical receivers are not yet aware, and which is brought into sharper focus through the allusion to Shakespeare.

Critical readings which testify to the use of Shakespeare in times of war fall under the first type of attitude. Much has been written and said about E.M.W. Tillyard's *The Elizabethan World Picture* (1945) and about the way it gives voice to the author's passionate yearning for the resto-ration of some kind of order and harmony into the grating dissonance of the Second World War. This attempt at pacification, as is well known, was predicated on the critic's monolithic view of the cultural paradigm of canonical literature, a view that was equally distant from the multifarious reality of the Renaissance and from the actual historical context in which his study was composed.

An important chapter in the history of the use of Shakespeare in times of war is the one written by a number of mainstream film productions, of which Laurence Olivier's *Henry V* (1944) still remains the most prominent instance. A distinguished precedent for Olivier's use of Shakespeare to boost the nation's morale through a unified and unifying vision of England at war may be found in *This Sceptred Isle: Shakespeare's Message for England at War*, a pamphlet published by G. Wilson Knight shortly after the outbreak of hostilities. The text of the lecture from which the booklet originated reconstructs the historical context alluded to in *Richard II*, stressing the pivotal importance of the defeat of the Spanish Armada in the formation of the concept of England as a nation. Shakespeare's words contain a promise of better times to come, and it is to these words that the English people are invited by the critic to turn, to heed their passionate call for the preservation of national unity. Wilson Knight's argument hinges upon the famed, vibrant speech Gaunt delivers on the point of death, which, he believes, offers a definition of 'What England is', 'How England should act', 'What England must oppose' and 'What England stands for'. Knight's commentary explicitly bridges the distance between Shakespeare's times and the present: 'How poignant to-day rings this description of our island fortress. It takes a great upheaval like that we are enduring to render obvious facts of great poetry evident to our senses.'[9]

This is the familiar method which today goes by the name of 'presentism',[10] a mode of historical analysis whereby concepts and perspectives developed in the present are surreptitiously and anachronistically projected onto the past in order to interpret it – a logical fallacy leading to the passing of moral judgements which can only be avoided through the slightly lesser evil of moral relativism.

Further exploration of the way presentism acts in the conflicting relations between individuals and the nation – Shakespeare's history plays here supply an impressive catalogue of examples – has been carried out in some more recent studies which have brilliantly investigated historically localized 'wartime Shakespeare' in order to discuss ideological conflicts: this is the case of the outcome of the researches carried out by Irena Makaryk and Marissa McHugh, Tina Krontiris and Zoltán Márkus over the last decade.[11]

A more recent example of the approach which turns to Shakespeare in order to stimulate new awareness and shed a stronger light on the 'conflict through Shakespeare' knot is David Greig's 2010 play,

Dunsinane.[12] In this sequel to Shakespeare's Scottish play, Lady Macbeth is reprieved from suicide and takes centre stage, sharing the action with a commander of the English troops who leads an army of invaders but also tries to act as a mediator. Greig's rewriting overturns Shakespeare's own rewriting: both history plays aim at laying bare the state of things between Scotland and England in their own time, but with opposing agendas. In the construction of the notion of Great Britain, the process of union between Scotland and England was imposed upon their people by two monarchs – Elizabeth and James – raising much concern and anxiety. The ultimate agreement of intent between the Scots and the English at the end of Shakespeare's tragedy resulted from the manipulation of the historical source on which it was based, Holinshed's chronicles, in which the complex mechanisms regulating succession to the Scottish throne had already been misunderstood, or at any rate misreported: in Scotland, the legitimacy of the succession allowed for the possibility of an alternation between the clans, whereas in England succession was legitimate only within the same family, because its main aim was the consolidation of the newly formed centralized nation-state. The 'indissoluble' union between the two countries separated by Hadrian's Wall is a concept that was fabricated and implemented through an act of power; and what we find in Shakespeare is the story of Macbeth as written by an Englishman.

Four hundred years later, Greig picks up the story from where it was left in Shakespeare and proceeds to excavate that initial sense of cultural alienation, opening it up to the possibility of actual political separation in the future. In *Dunsinane*, the tragic defeat of the play's hero is the defeat of a well-meaning man who genuinely tries to bring peace to a war-torn society, but in the process of enforcing this peace becomes a cruel tyrant himself. While British reviewers were quick to point to Afghanistan and Iraq as the historical situations of belligerence that the play was alluding to via Shakespeare, for a post-devolution audience Greig's critical revision also powerfully spotlights the issue of a possible independence for Scotland in the near future, exposing the indissoluble bond with England as a political construct of the Renaissance rather than a fact of nature. By uncovering the original conflict inside *Macbeth*, the playwright points to the difficulty and disagreement inherent in the concept of a United Kingdom from its very outset, and to Britishness as an embattled construct resulting from English political and cultural hegemony. In Greig's hands, *Macbeth* becomes a dynamic, formidable intertext wherein the formation of England as a nation-state may be questioned and challenged, and devolution, with its impulse towards the dissolution of a unified Britain, produces the same anxiety that the union of the two crowns had produced in Shakespeare's times: the sense of loss inherent in the legacy of union and empire which lies at the core of that very idea of Britishness recurrently invoked at times of crisis and conflict – often with the complicity, or perhaps even the connivance, of Shakespeare.

Notes

1. Terence Hawkes, *Meaning by Shakespeare* (London: Routledge, 1992). According to Bate, 'The history of appropriation may suggest that "Shakespeare" was not a man who lived from 1564 to 1616 but a body of work that is refashioned by each subsequent age in the image of itself.' See Jonathan Bate, *Shakespearean Constitutions* (Oxford: Clarendon Press, 1989), 3.
2. Harold Bloom, *A Map of Misreading* (Oxford: Oxford University Press, 1975).
3. Hawkes, 3.
4. Theodore Spencer, *Shakespeare and the Nature of Man* (Cambridge: Cambridge University Press, 1943).
5. See Marion Bodwell Smith, *Dualities in Shakespeare* (Toronto: Toronto University Press, 1966); Rosalie L. Coolie, *Paradoxia Epidemica* (Princeton: Princeton University Press, 1966); Norman Rabkin, *Shakespeare and the Common Understanding* (New York: Free Press, 1967).
6. Robert Grudin, *Mighty Opposites: Shakespeare and Renaissance Contrariety* (Berkeley and London: University of California Press, 1979). The same direction was subsequently taken by Colin N. Manlove in *The Gap in Shakespeare: The Motif of Division from* Richard II *to* The Tempest (London: Vision, 1981) and, a few years later, by Stanley C. Boorman in *Human Conflict in Shakespeare* (London and New York: Routledge and Kegan Paul, 1987).
7. Jennifer A. Bates, *Hegel and Shakespeare on Moral Imagination* (Albany: State University of New York Press, 2010).
8. Particularly representative of this approach, on Italian ground, are the following major critical studies: Fernando Ferrara, *Shakespeare e la commedia* (Bari: Adriatica, 1964); Paola Pugliatti, *I segni latenti* (Messina: D'Anna, 1976), particularly the part on the structuring of *King Lear;* Marcello Pagnini, *Il paradigma della specularità* (Pisa: Pacini, 1976), with specific reference to his reading of *A Midsummer Night's Dream*, where the Italian semiologist puts forth an interpretation of specularity in terms of binary structures both in the formal and in the semantic dimension, in a synchronic and contextual reading which constantly connects the play's formal qualities to its episteme.
9. G. Wilson Knight, *This Sceptred Isle: Shakespeare's Message for England at War*, (Folcroft, Pa.: Folcroft Library Editions, 1980), 5.
10. For a critique of Knight's 'presentist' stance see 'Conclusion: Speaking to You in English', in Terence Hawkes, *Shakespeare in the Present* (London: Routledge, 2002) 127–43 (129–31).
11. Irena R. Makaryk and Joseph G. Price (eds), *Shakespeare in the World of Communism and Socialism* (Toronto: University of Toronto Press, 2006);

Tina Krontiris, 'Shakespeare and Censorship during the Second World War: *Othello* in Occupied Greece', in *Shakespeare and the Second World War: Memory, Culture, Identity*, ed. by Irena R. Makaryk and Marissa McHugh (Toronto: University of Toronto Press, 2012); Zoltán Márkus (Vassar College, NY) is currently engaged in a research project entitled 'Shakespeares at War: Cultural Appropriations of Shakespeare in London and Berlin during World War II'.

12. David Greig, *Dunsinane* (London: Faber, 2010).

8
Translating Shakespeare in Sociolinguistic Conflicts: A Preliminary European Study

Jesús Tronch-Pérez

Defining conflicts

In the following pages, my engagement with the topic of Shakespeare and conflict from a European perspective will centre on aspects of translating Shakespeare into certain minority languages of Europe in those conflictive situations that sociolinguists call diglossia and language secessionism.[1]

Diglossia is a much-debated term, but I will use it in the extended sense of a situation in which varieties of a language or different languages coexist *hierarchically* in a given society, that is, when a high or dominant code is used by speakers in all or most domains of prestige (formal, official, governmental, administrative, educational, religious, in 'respected' literature), while a low or subordinate code is relegated to minor uses (informal, 'street', folk, private).[2] Interlingual diglossia (also called 'societal bilingualism') generally leads to the gradual disappearance ('language shift') of the minority or minorized language (usually the native one, often lacking official status) either by assimilation within, or replacement by, the predominant language (usually the language of the power elite). Linguistic secessionism is a recent label[3] for the claim that a given variety of language constitutes a linguistic system distinct and separate from the language to which it has been affiliated. Notable cases are the secession of Moldovan from Romanian in the present-day Republic of Moldova, and the splitting of Serbo-Croat into Croatian, Serbian and Bosniak.[4]

As Louis-Jean Calvet points out, diglossia conflicts arise 'for historical and sociological reasons which result from the form of power and the organization of society'.[5] This is also applicable to linguistic secessionism. Secessionist or integrationist claims are motivated by political agendas seeking to strengthen or diminish the symbolic force that the language exerts over the ethnic or national identity of the speakers of a territory, and therefore its force in the configuration of a given statehood.

I will discuss how Shakespeare translations and the translating of Shakespeare feature in some 'language wars' in Europe by considering how ideologies, social pressures and attitudes, and cultural values are stylistically negotiated by diglossic translators. First, I will explain the results of a preliminary survey of 'minority' Shakespeares in some minorized languages, and will deal with common aspects and problems of translating Shakespeare into these languages. Second, I will exemplify these observations in specific cases of translated Shakespeares in my native region of Valencia, in Spain, where Catalan (with the official, as well as traditional and popular name of Valencian) is the minorized language in a diglossic hierarchy with Spanish.

Surveying diglossic translations of Shakespeare

Of the approximately 60 minority languages in the European Union,[6] my survey centres on 13, mainly of Romance, Germanic and Celtic origin. These languages vary in their social and literary vitality, and have been categorized by UNESCO studies as constitutive of different degrees of endangerment.[7] The surveyed languages also vary as regards the number and chronology of translations and adaptations of Shakespeare's plays that have been made into them.[8] Comparing these two aspects in order to find out whether the relative strength of these 'minority' Shakespeares could be related to the social health of their respective languages, one can observe a general correlation as shown in Table 8.1 below.

As shown in the table, languages with higher degrees of vulnerability have fewer than ten Shakespeare translations, while relatively stable languages are, in general, those with the most translations. Two contrasting positions are represented by two geographically contiguous languages: Catalan and Aragonese. Catalan is a 'safe' language[9] and ranks at the top, having an established and flourishing tradition of Shakespeare translations with over 130 titles (including dubbed versions of the complete BBC series).[10] In contrast, Aragonese is definitely endangered and has no Shakespeare translation (not even of a sonnet).

The correlation is not exact in absolute terms. For instance, with 16 translations, Galician ranks higher as a 'safe' language than Western Frisian does with 54, and Breton shows five translations while ranking below others with fewer translations. This is because the UNESCO

Table 8.1 Correlation between Shakespeare translations, minority languages and UNESCO degrees of endangerment

Language*	Number of Shakespeare translations	Degree of endangerment (UNESCO *Atlas*)
Catalan-Valencian-Balear	over 130	Safe
Galician	16	
Western Frisian	54	Vulnerable
Basque	38	
Welsh	9	
Scots	3 and fragments	
Friulian	2	Definitely endangered
Romansch	1 and 4 performance versions	
Aragonese	0	
Asturian	2	
Occitan	2 and fragments of 2	Definitely endangered Severely endangered
Breton	5	Severely endangered
North Frisian	1 and fragments of 1	

Note: *For the name of the languages and their category as such – controversial issues – I have followed *Ethnologue: Languages of the World*, ed. by M. Paul Lewis (Dallas, Tex.: SIL International, 2009).

criteria[11] refer to the present-day situation while the number of Shakespeare translations is cumulative over time. The earliest West Frisian Shakespeare dates back to 1829 and the whole Shakespeare canon was translated by Douwe Kalma between the 1920s and his death in 1953.[12] Other factors should also be taken into account. The Breton translation of *Macbeth* was made in 1942 by Roparz Hemon, an important figure in the 'Breton movement', while analogous political support for Aragonese and Occitan is absent or weak.

However, for the rest of the languages in the table, the correlation holds. The scarcity of translations into Welsh and Scots can be related to the fact that speakers of these languages of Britain are also speakers of the language of Shakespeare. Friulian and Asturian have two relatively recent translations, which coincides with the fact that the standardization of these languages is recent, as is that of Romansch.[13] Romansch is an official language in Switzerland, and has a literary tradition dating back to the mid-sixteenth century (including translation of the New Testament), but its poor record with regard to translations of Shakespeare can be related to the very low number of speakers, calculated at around 35,000. In Occitan, a pattern emerges in which the less endangered variety, Gascon, is related to renderings of whole plays rather than of fragments. Interestingly, the upgrading of Galician to a 'safe' degree in 2009 from the 'potentially endangered' category in 1999[14] coincides with the fact that half of the translations appeared in this ten-year period.

Thus, the fortunes of Shakespeare translations can act as an approximate barometer for the social situation and vitality of a minorized language.[15]

Aspects and problems of diglossic translations[16]

Just as the 'vernaculars' in Renaissance Europe (English among them) raised their literary and political status with the help of translations and adaptations of classical texts (Plutarch or Plautus as rewritten, for instance, by Shakespeare), so low-prestige languages resort to translating and adapting a 'new' classical author such as Shakespeare as a strategy for social survival, promotion or legitimization, or for a linguistic and literary enrichment that may help reverse language shift.[17] For instance, Catalan translators in the early twentieth century, such as Josep Carner and Alfonso Par, claimed that their work was a means for the 'extolment' of Catalan and for the regeneration of its precarious social use and literature.[18] However, these motivations and attitudes are not present in all translations. The earliest 'Catalan Shakespeares' were theatrical parodies of *Othello* and *Hamlet* (1873, 1883) written in an Italianized Catalan or macaronic Italian that mocked the popularity of Shakespeare created by Italian companies performing in Barcelona rather than pursuing a prestige-seeking agenda.[19]

Often translations are embedded in literary revivalist movements[20] in which, as Buffery nicely puts it, 'a minority Shakespeare [is] employed to achieve cultural majority'.[21] The Frisian translators Teatse E. Holtrop and, more actively, Douwe Kalma were involved in movements such as the Christian Society for the Frisian Language and Literature (Kristlik Selskip foar Fryske Tael en Skriftennisse), created in 1908, and the Community of Young Frisians (Jongfryske Mienskip), created in 1918. Early Occitan translators Palay and Cubaynes were *majorals* of the Félibrige, the literary association for the promotion of Occitan founded in 1854. The two *Macbeth* translations into Scots in 1992 contributed, as McLure states, to 'the mood of cultural nationalism then (and still) prevalent in Scotland'.[22] Yet, this correlation between revivalist movements and Shakespeare translations does not always hold: the Rexurdimento movement for Galician, initiated in 1864, did not produce Shakespeare translations.

In general, these cultural movements are paralleled by political nationalism for which the preservation of the minorized language is a central tenet. Breton translator Roparz Hemon was a militant nationalist, and Frisian Douwe Kalma was politically involved during the Second World War. David Purves was a parliamentary candidate for the Scottish National Party in 1974, and has been involved in politics for a long time. For him, translating *Macbeth* into Scots was an 'aspect' of his political nationalism, as well as an act of repatriation of a play set in Scotland which would become more Scottish by expressing it in the native language. I must point out, however, that such an explicit activism is the exception rather than the rule in many of the translators I have studied and interviewed.

These political movements are seen as a response to the state nationalism that caused or fostered the diglossic situation. The rise of modern nation-states such as France, Spain and the UK in the sixteenth and seventeenth centuries is sustained by an ideology of cultural uniformism and linguistic homogenization that seeks to shape a single collective identity, as well as to reduce transaction costs and to achieve better control of social communication.[23] In France, Occitan and Breton translators such as Cubaynes and Hemon were called separatists and also anti-French since the use of any language other than French was perceived as a threat to French national identity.

Most language secessionisms and integrationisms are connected to ideological conflicts involving languages and national identities. Secessionisms are criticized as an instrument of state nationalism since they worsen diglossia and facilitate language shift in favour of the dominant official language. The mere fact of rendering Shakespeare into Scots is a statement of support for Scots as an independent language, a central claim of the Scottish Renaissance.[24]

Secessionism often resorts to using a different standard for spelling and grammar. Supporters of Galician as a language distinct from Portuguese use a standard that emphasizes their differences and accepts linguistic features derived from Castilianization.[25] This standard was made official in 1983 by the right-wing government. The opposing reintegrationist view, held by a social minority, claims that this 'isolationism' is an instrument of Spanish nationalism (endorsed by the regional conservative government) seeking to efface any ties with Portugal, ties that are emphasized by

Galician independentists and that question the unity of Spain. Galician Shakespeare translators are inevitably caught in these 'normative wars'. All Shakespeare translations appear in the official standard (mostly in government-funded publications), and while translating Shakespeare does not necessarily entail an explicit political stance on the part of the translator, the fact that such a cultural icon appears in the 'isolationist' standard offers strong support for the cause of Galician as a separate language.

In contrast, the unity of Occitan is implicit in all Shakespeare translations either through their translators' commitment to the Félibrige or through the acceptance of the classical norm proposed in 1935.[26] No translator has followed standards based on claims that Auvergnat and Provençal are different languages, claims that undermine the force of the threat that a unified Occitan covering most of southern France may carry for French national unity.

Another interesting aspect is the relationship between Shakespeare translations and the target literature. From the perspective of Even-Zohar's Polysystem Theory (in which translations are conceived as an integral and active system within the literary polysystem of the target culture),[27] translated Shakespeares can help to shape a modern native literature, to add to literary repertoires, or to renew literary models. The Basque translator Juan Garzia pointed out that his translation of Shakespeare's Sonnets (1995) in the three-quatrain-plus-couplet structure stimulated experiments in this form by Basque poets. Catalan dramatist and theatre entrepreneur Adrià Gual was a key figure in the renewal of Catalan theatre and was responsible for mainstream Shakespeare productions, which, as Buffery remarks, 'led to the identification of Shakespeare with projects to renew Catalan theatre'.[28]

Sometimes, the native tradition can pose difficulties, as when readers associate the minority language with literary uses that do not serve for Shakespeare. As Asturian translator Milio Rodríguez observed in a private communication, a woman began to laugh at the beginning of the performance of his version of *Henry V* – regardless of the fact that the scene was serious – because to her, Asturian was synonymous with the customary one-act farce.

At the specific level of translators' linguistic decisions, rendering Shakespeare into a minority language is often taken as a sort of test for the language, a way of showing that it can deal with texts endowed with such complexity of style and thought. Some problems are inherent to the limitations of the minorized language itself. David Purves warned in his preface that his rendering of *Macbeth* had to be read 'allowing for the constraints of the Scots language'.[29] Anfós Par pointed out that the dictionary available at that time did not help him with specific vocabulary, and that for greeting formulas he had to resort to his own creativity.[30]

When a standard is not well established, the use of a given linguistic model (often – as we have seen – with ideological connotations) can be problematic in terms of reaching a wide readership. The lack of an established model may lead translators to shape one of their own making. The Basque translator of the complete works published in 1974–76, Bedita Larrakoetxea, chose a dialectal model that is no longer used, a decision that makes his work difficult for generations of readers educated within the unified standard established in the late 1970s.

Some translators, in their attempt to dignify the language, opt for an archaic model. In the case of Catalan, as exemplified in Par's *Lear*, this norm is justified by the existence of a glorious literary past that is seen as an 'Edenic, pre-lapsarian'[31] state of the language one would like to bring back. Douwe Kalma, in his attempt to formulate a literary model of West Frisian free of Dutch influences, also opted for an archaic language, using an elevated and often obscure style, which has meant that his Shakespeare has been found 'unnatural and even incomprehensible'[32] and, consequently, new translations of some plays have been written for performance.[33] Catalan Josep Carner drew on French vocabulary and even prosody and was criticized for using archaisms and Gallicisms that the audience did not understand.[34] Yet these are not the predominant strategies. In general, translators reject archaisms and incline towards more present-day usages with a view to communicating more effectively with spectators and readers. This can also explain the predominance of translations aimed at theatre audiences, which is the case not only with early translations but also with recent renderings.

In languages such as Occitan, Breton, Frisian (especially North and East Frisian), Welsh, or Low Saxon, the absence or the interruption of a literary tradition has led to a situation in which registers other than the oral, informal and intimate are lacking or insufficiently developed. In these cases, diglossic translators struggle with a limited vocabulary and resort either to existing colloquial expressions (which do not help to match the literary status of the source and cause readers to judge the translation negatively), to archaisms or neologisms (which do not help to make the target audience feel more comfortable), or to foreign loans, usually from the dominant state language (which adulterates the genuine identity of the minority language). In any case, as Wolf points out, none of these strategies 'will enable them to produce an idiom that will appear normal, neutral and unmarked'[35] to readers.

Another key factor is the intended readership or audience and their attitude towards the language. A potential problem for diglossic translators – and for publishers and theatre entrepreneurs – is that specific choices in register, vocabulary and style seeking to match Shakespeare's artistry may alienate audiences, who may be illiterate even in their own mother tongue. Readers or spectators may reject a text that is difficult for them to understand and that is consequently perceived as not belonging to their own culture. However, if the cultural and political atmosphere favours the language, such attitudes of disregard are likely to change, as in the case of Scots audiences since the 1980s.[36]

Understandably, these limitations are more easily overcome when Shakespeare is rendered in dramaturgical adaptations or rewritings. For Galician director and playwright Manuel Guede, adapting Shakespeare for the stage made him feel less constrained by the shortcomings of the literary tradition and the limitations inherent in the language. This may also explain why free versions of Shakespeare for the stage or adaptations for children are quite common.

The 'language wars' in the Valencia region of Spain

The diglossic situation in which Catalan tends to shift towards Spanish in all domains is a situation which the Valencian region historically shares with other Catalan-speaking communities in Spain.[37] From being a dominant language, even enjoying a literary Golden Age in the fifteenth century, Catalan started to decline as a vehicle of the political and cultural elites in the sixteenth century. The remaining Arabic speakers of the Moorish minority were expelled in 1609. Diglossia became a *de jure* situation in the early eighteenth century when the Bourbon monarchy initiated a state centralization involving cultural homogenization in favour of the language of Castile: decrees and acts were passed enforcing Spanish as the only language in administrative and juridical functions (1714), in education (1768, 1837, 1854), and in cultural manifestations such as printed folk literature and theatre performances (1799). The nineteenth-century revivalist movement, the Renaixença, renewed some literary usage, but did not prove as culturally and politically effective for the recovery of the language as in Catalonia. With the advent of Spanish-speaking immigration and mass media from the mid-twentieth century, both diglossia and the Castilianization of the language (especially in lexis) worsened. The 1982 Statute of Autonomy granting Valencian official status[38] and the 1984 law on the 'Use and Teaching of Valencian' revitalized hopes for the social betterment of the language.

The origins of linguistic secessionism can be traced back to descriptions of the language from the seventeenth century but its political and cultural impact started in the 1970s.[39] The Valencian Renaixença brought about debates over its relationship to Catalan and Majorcan as well as to Occitan, and over orthographic and grammatical standards. In 1932 cultural associations and writers agreed to follow a standard based on the one already consolidated in Catalonia but adapted to Valencian peculiarities, thus implicitly acknowledging that Valencians and Catalans spoke the same language. This was questioned in the 1970s by secessionist voices that, with the advent of democracy, were promoted by the Right and extreme Right as a strategy to oppose the leftist aspirations of Valencian nationalists, which were akin to Catalanism. In 1978, when a pre-autonomous regional government started to use the generally agreed standard in its official gazette, secessionists promoted an alternative standard with spelling forms closer to Castilian and grammatical features peculiar to Valencian idiosyncrasies. In a strong, populist campaign they succeeded in spreading social prejudice against unitary views of the language and the official standard, which was denounced as serving a Catalan imperialism that sought the annexation of Valencia. This was a period of social and political tension, dubbed by the media 'The Battle of Valencia', which created a still-existing fracture among Valencians. Even now, some do not welcome the compulsory teaching of Valencian, still regarded as of little use even amongst native speakers, and object to the use of the official standard, stigmatized as 'Catalan' and therefore anti-Valencian, despite the fact that it has been gradually adopting more and more Valencian peculiarities.

As sociolinguists have observed, this secessionist conflict helps to hide the more serious diglossic conflict, and ultimately serves the agenda of a Spanish nationalism that by severing any ties between Valencia and Catalonia, which are at the basis of independentist positions, continues to pursue linguistic homogenization as the basis of Spain's identity.[40]

Four Shakespeare-related productions in Valencian

The earliest production dates from 1983: *Antoni i Cleopatra*, a free adaptation of *Antony and Cleopatra* by Manuel Molins, a prominent dramatist of the so-called 'Independent Theatre', which in the 1970s pushed forward the normalization of the language in playwriting and the opening up to new genres differing from the traditional ones in which Valencian had been used; Molins is still an indefatigable cultural activist in the promotion of the language. Molins and other key figures in this movement, such as Rodolf Sirera and Juli Leal, made the translation and adaptation of world playwrights a 'normal' theatre practice.[41] *Antoni i Cleopatra* was the brainchild of Molins himself, who proposed it to Rodolf Sirera, general manager of Teatres de la Diputació. In 1980 this public institution had financed the first significant large-scale theatre production in Valencian, Ibsen's *The Lady of the Sea*, in a version by Sirera himself, which rendered tangible his commitment to making Valencian a normal language for theatre.

All these elements might suggest that this adaptation aimed to appropriate the prestige associated with Shakespeare in order to dignify drama written in Catalan in Valencia and, by extension, to overcome the diglossia conflict by upgrading the use of Catalan to respectable, artistic functions. I asked Molins himself this question and he appeared to confirm – though not explicitly – that this was so. The choice of Shakespeare was also influenced by the convergence of several other factors. The first was a strong personal infatuation with the author of *Hamlet*. The second was an indirect critique of the situation in Valencia, where Shakespeare was perceived as being monopolized by the university project of Manuel Ángel Conejero and his team Instituto Shakespeare, a project thanks to which by 1983 Shakespeare was being translated into Spanish, and not into Catalan. And finally, *Antony and Cleopatra* could allow for a rethinking of some of the premises of the leftist nationalist movement: the character of the mature and decadent Cleopatra, no longer able to use her seductive beauty as a strategy for the survival of her people against the rising power of the ambitious Octavius, can be read as an allegory of the helpless state of Valencian nationalism, unable to seduce the politicians of the new democracy and properly address a citizenship that is ignorant of its own history. This political reading, however, was not materialized as the result of specific decisions on the part of the director (José Luis Sáiz), as Molins complained. The text remains unpublished.

As for the issue of the linguistic model, Molins employed the official standard and a highbrow, literary model, resorting to the then canonical Shakespeare translation into Catalan by Josep Maria Sagarra, even borrowing whole passages from it. He made one concession to spectators who would not be so literate in Catalan by introducing a low-register-speaking messenger. He used blank decasyllabic verse, akin to iambic pentameter and to the prosodic pattern of fifteenth-century classical poets Ausiàs March and Jordi de Sant Jordi.

This contrasts with the 2001 production of *Somni d'una nit d'estiu* (*A Midsummer Night's Dream*), which used a new 'canonical' translation, by

Salvador Oliva, with Oliva himself and director Joan Peris adapting the text to Valencian features. As Peris privately explained, the verse was retained by combining alexandrines and decasyllables, but the main purpose was to get the text across and reach the audience. It was not a translation for scholars, but for the average theatregoer who would go to a play to identify with the characters, and therefore the language should not be an obstacle. This is not to say that the whole text was popularized. Varieties were allowed depending on the character and situation: the Duke was given more unfamiliar and elevated expressions, but the 'mechanicals', clearly impersonating local Valencian craftsmen as amateur actors, spoke in the real dialect of the rural small towns around the city of Valencia.

This production bears a certain relevance in terms of the 'language wars' also on account of its producers. The company Teatre Micalet, created in 1995, was related to the Societat el Micalet, one of the few private cultural institutions vocally to endorse a defence of Valencian. A rare example of a theatre enterprise committed to producing only shows in Valencian, it managed to survive economically until May 2011, when the conservative regional government stopped its subsidies. *Somni d'una nit d'estiu* was their only Shakespeare, and was part of a repertoire that included Molière and Goldoni, and modern classics such as Priestley, Brecht, Brian Friel and Dario Fo. The text is unpublished.

Further back in time, in 1987, Teatres de la Diputació produced *La comèdia de les equivocacions* (*The Comedy of Errors*), directed by Juli Leal, both in Catalan and in Spanish. The Catalan text, in the official standard, was the result of negotiations between the translators Sara Mañero and Julia McLucas, intent on keeping a literary level of language, and the director who insisted that the language should be as close as possible to real Valencian, and therefore include its Castilianisms. The printed version reads as a mixture of these two positions, but Mañero told me that the text spoken on the stage more closely reflected the director's intentions.

Again, one could hypothesize that this production was another instance of appropriation of Shakespeare's prestige for the promotion of Valencian. However, when I interviewed the director he explicitly denied this: he had been commissioned to stage a classic and he chose *The Comedy of Errors* because he had enjoyed the 1976 musical version directed by Trevor Nunn for the Royal Shakespeare Company. In keeping with his intention to reach the audience, Leal's Nunn-inspired version domesticated the story by giving it a Mediterranean, and even possibly Valencian, setting: the town square with its palm trees was strikingly reminiscent of the emblematic Valencian city of Elche. The costumes also mixed Hellenism, local Valencian and present-day features.

The last theatre production on which I will comment also involved negotiations with regard to the standard, but in this case they were carried out between the translators and external agents in the context of heated local politics in 1991. Some members of the Instituto Shakespeare had translated *Macbeth* in 1990–91, under the direction of Manuel Ángel Conejero, with a view to initiating a parallel project of translating Shakespeare's plays into Catalan along the principles established for the Spanish series. The aim was a 'theatrical translation' using free verse to render Shakespeare's blank verse.[42] The translation, which employed official spelling and grammar, was thus an experiment to test the resources of a Valencian standard that might prove adequate for the players' delivery, as well as for theatregoers with varying degrees of literacy in Valencian. Besides being aimed at finding its place within the tradition of previous Catalan translations, this *Macbeth*, like Molins's *Antoni i Cleopatra*, was intended to prove Valencian suitable not only for popular and traditional theatre, but also for drama with a classical stature.

By joining forces with the conservative People's Party in the spring local elections, the right-wing regionalists (both advocating Valencian as a separate language) seized municipal power in the city of Valencia for the first time since the restoration of democracy. Once they took charge of culture and educational services and declared that they would use the secessionist standard, the 'language war' was reopened[43] – and a Shakespeare translation caught up in the conflict. Conejero, who had given support to the regionalists during the electoral campaign and was to become director of the Palau de la Música, announced that this venue – the city's cultural icon – would host a production of *Macbeth* in Valencian. Would Shakespeare be exploited in order to confer cultural prestige and dignity to the secessionists' linguistic option? When the conservative mayoress nominated a cultural advisory board that would decide which Valencian the town council was to use, Conejero (who was also on the board) stated that the Palau de la Música would use the official standard. This political move was perceived as a 'cultural pact' to put an end to the war[44] and raised expectations that Shakespeare could mediate in this endemic conflict between Valencians.

The translation was revised through careful negotiation with members of the cultural advisory board in order to limit the possible offence that certain words and expressions might give to secessionist sensitivities. This *Macbeth* was printed (in a limited and poorly distributed edition) shortly before its premiere on 17 December.[45] The use of the official standard in the performance and publication of *Macbeth*, as well as in the concert programmes, under the auspices of the regionalist-governed institution, was a politically significant act.[46] It was a confirmation of the 'cultural pact' proposed in the summer and an obstacle to secessionists who wished to use Shakespeare to prove the viability of their Valencian and thereby strengthen their political beliefs and their hold on the general public. Would this Shakespeare production be the first step towards acknowledging the need to abandon sterile confrontation? Any hope of mediation proved to be illusory. The regionalists went on to enforce their peculiar Valencian upon the areas they were in charge of, and the issue of the identity of the language and its standard continues to be instrumentalized for political purposes (especially before and during electoral campaigns).

On this occasion Shakespeare failed as a mediator in sociolinguistic conflicts and the translation of his work into a minorized language did not help to heal any rifts. I asked some European translators whether they thought Shakespeare could mediate in the 'language wars', and their answer was invariably 'no'. The translators I interviewed were pessimistic about the future of their language but they remained loyal to it and continued writing and translating. While this might lead some to think that a discussion of Shakespeare in forgotten languages is pointless, it should be observed that around 55 million people in Europe speak a minority language, and that with the exception of Iceland, all European countries host regional or minority languages.[47] One of the significant characteristics of our ongoing definition of Europe is diversity. The Council of Europe is committed to protecting linguistic diversity and multilingualism. Unless all the languages and cultures of this region of the world are taken into account, a European perspective on Shakespeare Studies will never be completely and truly European.

Notes

1. This study results from Research Project FFI2008-01969/FILO, financed by the Ministerio de Ciencia e Innovación.
2. Harold F. Schiffman, 'Diglossia as a Sociolinguistic Situation', in *The Handbook of Sociolinguistics*, ed. by Florian Coulmas (Oxford: Blackwell, 1997), 205–16.
3. Among others, Miquel Strubell, 'Catalan in Valencia: The Story of an Attempted Secession', in *Sprachstandardisierung = Standardisation des langues = Standardization of languages*, ed. by Georges Lüdi (Freiburg: Universitätsverlag Freiburg, 1994), 229–55.
4. Charles King, *The Moldovans: Romania, Russia and the Politics of Culture* (Stanford: Hoover Institution Press, 2000); Robert Greenberg, *Language and*

Identity in the Balkans: Serbo-Croatian and its Disintegration (Oxford: Oxford University Press, 2004).

5. Louis-Jean Calvet, *Language Wars and Linguistic Politics* (Oxford: Oxford University Press, 1998), 29.

6. 'Minority Languages: Facts & Figures', *Mercator European Research Centre on Multilingualism and Language Learning*, online at http://www.mercator-research.eu/minority-languages/facts-figures (accessed 5 May 2011), which further states that 'There are however many more, for example, the German minorities which are widely spread around Europe.'

7. *Atlas of the World's Languages in Danger*, ed. by Christopher Moseley (Paris, UNESCO, 2010), online version: http://www.unesco.org/culture/en/endangeredlanguages/atlas (first consulted 1 October 2009; last accessed 5 May 2011); Tapani Salminen, *UNESCO Red Book on Endangered Languages: Europe*, 1999, online at http://www.helsinki.fi/~tasalmin/europe_index.html (accessed 5 May 2011).

8. For a list of the Shakespeare translations in my survey, see http://www.uv.es/shaxpere/min/minority_shakespeares_2009_european_survey.html.

9. The 'safe' category, observed in October 2009, is no longer used in the *Atlas*, where Catalan only appears as 'definitely endangered' in the Sardinian town of Alghero. Catalan could be judged as vulnerable in areas of the Valencia region, concerning which the *Atlas* is silent.

10. Helena Buffery, *Shakespeare in Catalan: Translating Imperialism* (Cardiff: University of Wales, 2007). The BBC series was produced between 1979 and 1984; the Catalan-dubbed versions of the 37 plays were shown between April 1984 and December 1991.

11. 'A Methodology for Assessing Language Vitality and Endangerment', UNESCO, http://www.unesco.org/new/en/culture/themes/cultural-diversity/languages-and-multilingualism/endangered-languages/language-vitality/ (accessed 5 May 2011).

12. Eric Hoekstra, 'Shakespeare's Sonnets in West Frisian', in *William Shakespeare's Sonnets for the First Time Globally Reprinted. A Quatercentenary Anthology 1609–2009*, ed. by Manfred Pfister and Jürgen Gutsch (Dozwil: SIGNAThUR, 2009), 249–53 (250).

13. Romansch in 1985 (Manfred Gross, *Romansh: Facts & Figures* (Chur: Lia Rumantscha, 2004), 92); Friulian in 1996 (Paolo Coluzzi, 'Regional and Minority Languages in Italy', *Working Papers*, 14 (2004), 1–38 (21)); the Academy of Asturian Language was created in 1981, a grammar issued in 1998 and a dictionary in 2000 (Roberto González-Quevedo, 'Normativización de la lengua asturiana', in *La configuració social de la norma lingüística a l'Europa llatina*, ed. by Antoni Ferrando and Miquel Nicolás (Alacant: Institut Interuniversitari de Filologia Valenciana, 2006), 355–74).

14. Salminen.

15. Similarly, reception studies of Greek and Roman classics also show that the translations of classical authors constitute an index 'for the analysis of change in scholarly, educational and artistic conventions': see Lorna Hardwick, *Translating Worlds, Translating Cultures* (London: Duckworth, 2000), 34. The comparability of the two situations confirms Shakespeare's status as a classic from a sociolinguistic perspective.

16. Information for this section comes from published material and personal interviews with translators. I would like to thank Chusé Inazio Nabarro (Aragonese), Milio Rodríguez (Asturian), Juan Garzia (Basque), Salvador Oliva, Manuel Molins, Sara Mañero (Catalan), David Purves (Scots), Gwyn Thomas (Welsh) for allowing me to discuss translation problems with them.

17. This comparison is inspired by Roshni Mooneeram's *From Creole to Standard: Shakespeare, Language, and Literature in a Postcolonial Context* (Amsterdam: Rodopi, 2009), Chapters 4 and 5.

18. See Dídac Pujol, *Traduir Shakespeare: Les reflexions dels traductors Catalans* ((?): Punctum & Trilcat, 2007), 75–80 and 101–12.

19. For a full discussion, see Jesús Tronch-Pérez, 'Non-Catalyst and Marginal Shakespeares in the Nineteenth-Century Revival of Catalan-Speaking Cultures', *Shakespeare Survey*, 64 (2011), 188–98.

20. See Joan-Lluís Marfany, 'Minority Languages and Literary Revivals', *Past and Present*, 184 (2004), 137–67.

21. Buffery, 1.

22. J. Derrick McLure, 'Scots for Shakespeare', in *Shakespeare and the Language of Translation*, ed. by Ton Hoenselaars (London: Thomson Learning, 2004), 217–39 (219).

23. Karl W. Deutsch, 'The Trend of European Nationalism', in *Readings in the Sociology of Language*, ed. by J. Fishman (The Hague: Mouton, 1968), 598–606; David D. Laitin, 'Language and States', *Estudio/Working Paper*, 1990/3 (Madrid: Inst. Juan March, 1990).

24. McLure, 218.

25. Màrio J. Herreiro Valeiro, 'The Discourse of Language in Galiza: Normalisation, Diglossia and Conflict', *Estudios de Sociolingüística*, 3 (2003), 289–320; Jaine E. Beswick, *Regional Nationalism in Spain: Language Use and Ethnic Identity in Galicia* (Clevedon: Multilingual Matters, 2007), 84–90, 125–34.

26. Derived from the work of Loïs Alibert, *Gramatica occitana segón los parlars lengadocians* (Tolosa: Societat d'Estudis Occitans, 1935) and institutionalized by the Institut d'Estudis Occitans (founded in 1945) and Conselh de Lenga Occitana (1997).

27. Itamar Even-Zohar, 'The Position of Translated Literature within the Literary Polysystem', in *Literature and Translation: New Perspectives in Literary Studies*, ed. by James S. Holmes, José Lambert and Raymond van den Broeck (Leuven: Acco, 1978), 117–27.

28. Buffery, 32.

29. McLure, 231.

30. Pujol, 108–9.

31. Leanore Lieblein, '"Cette belle langue": the "Tradaptation" of Shakespeare in Quebec', in Hoenselaars, *Shakespeare*, 255–69 (266).

32. Henk Wolf, 'Copying Mona Lisa with a Paint Roller – Stylistic Aspects of Shakespeare Translation in North Frisian', in *Shakespeare's Sonnets Globally Reprinted*, 243–8 (244).

33. Jelle Krol, 'West Frisian Literature in Translation', in *Handbuch des Friesischen / Handbook of Frisian Studies*, ed. by Horst H. Munske, with N. Arhammar (Tübingen: Max Niemeyer, 2001), 232–44 (238).

34. Buffery, 154.

35. Wolf, 244.
36. John Corbett, *Written in the Language of the Scottish Nation: A History of Literary Translation into Scots* (Clevedon: Multilingual Matters, 1999), 173.
37. For accounts in English, see Miquel Angel Pradilla, 'The Catalan-speaking Communities', in *Multilingualism in Spain*, ed. by M. Teresa Turell (Clevedon: Multilingual Matters, 2001), 58–90; Francisco Giménez-Menéndez and José Ramón Gómez-Molina, 'Spanish and Catalan in the Community of Valencia', *International Journal of the Sociology of Language*, 184 (2007), 95–107; and Miguel Siguan, *Multilingual Spain* (Amsterdam: Swets and Zeitlinger, 1993).
38. However the official status is not on a par with Spanish: while Valencian citizens have the duty to know Spanish, they only have the right to use Valencian.
39. M. Sanchis Guarner, *La llengua dels valencians* (Valencia: Tres i Quatre, 1980), 39–64, 183–202. For accounts in English, see Strubell 'Catalan in Valencia', and Vicent Climent-Ferrando, 'The Origins and Evolution of Language Secessionism in Valencia: An Analysis from the Transition Period until Today', *Working Papers*, 18 (2005), 1–53.
40. Rafael L. Ninyoles, *Conflicte Lingüístic Valencià* (Valencia: Tres i Quatre, 1985), 108–16.
41. Josep Lluís Sirera, 'Els espectacles i l'ús del valencià', in *Llibre blanc de l'ús del valencià II*, coord. by Honorat Ros (València: Publicacions de l'Acadèmia Valenciana de la Llengua, 2007), 313–25 (314).
42. Manuel Ángel Conejero, Vicent Montalt and Jesús Tronch, 'Traduir Shakespeare al català: un esforç retòric i teatral', in *Actes del Primer Congrés Internacional sobre Traducció*, ed. by Miquel Edo (Barcelona: Universitat Autònoma de Barcelona, 1997), 899–906.
43. 'CC OO condena la "reapertura de la guerra lingüística" por parte de UV', *Levante*, 18 July 1991, 27.
44. José R. Seguí, 'Rita Barberá nombra un consejo asesor para poner fin a la "guerra cultural"', *Levante*, 2 August 1991, 44.
45. William Shakespeare, *Macbeth: Còpia d'actors*, trans. by Manuel Ángel Conejero, Vicent Montalt and Jesús Tronch (Valencia: Palau de la Música de València, 1991). The production, by theatre company TeatreJove, was directed by Jaime Pujol, following a previous production directed by Edward Wilson but with a different cast of young players.
46. There were no theatre reviews in the main newspapers and cultural magazines, but the newspaper supporting the socialist opposition referred to this production in the context of a criticism of the regionalists' use of the Palau de la Música for theatre purposes and the ambivalence displayed in using the official model of Valencian at the Palau and the secessionist model in other areas (*Levante*, 18 December 1991, 61). Theatregoers welcomed or criticized the linguistic model according to their respective positions.
47. As stated in 'Minority Languages: Facts & Figures'.

9
Shakespeare and the Continental Avant-Garde through García Lorca's *El público* (1930)

Juan F. Cerdá

El público (*The Public*) emerged in the context of Federico García Lorca's productive trip to America (1929–30). Probably conceived in New York, then written primarily in Cuba, and completed in Spain in the summer of 1930, this experimental play, crafted by Lorca through the theatrical languages of the avant-garde, constructs an elusive exploration of patriarchy and homophobia. The influence of Pirandello, Jarry and the Surrealists is palpable in what constituted a radical turn in Lorca's dramatic style, yet it is Shakespeare's *Romeo and Juliet* that provided Lorca with a visible intertext through which to voice his challenge to the boundaries of gender identity and his critique of socially-established gender roles and sexual practices in the 1930s. Shakespeare's *Romeo and Juliet* will be performed as a transgressively innovatory piece of drama by the metatheatrical characters at the end of *El público*. However, before postulating a new conception of its action, character, dialogue and visuals, *Romeo and Juliet* is first presented at the beginning of the play as an example of the fossilization of theatre. Lorca's experimental work first treats Shakespeare as an emblem of outdated drama, and then transforms one of his works into a source for theatrical renewal.

In parallel to Lorca's ambivalent understanding of Shakespearean drama, which situates the English playwright at the centre of both theatrical conservatism and theatrical innovation, *El público* provides an opportunity to examine the continental avant-garde's take on Shakespeare. Thus, from the metatheatrics of Pirandello, to Jarry's explicit absurdism, to Artaud's Theatre of Cruelty, Lorca's appropriative dramaturgy borrows elements from the foundations of the Dada and Surrealist movements to construct an experimental spectacle that puts Shakespeare's *Romeo and Juliet* through the blender of European experimental theatre. Because of its controversial subject matter, Lorca's play was never performed during his lifetime. The manuscript, unpublished until the late 1970s, was only known to a few intimate acquaintances of the Spanish poet. However, Lorca's obscure text testifies to an understanding of experimental drama in which Shakespeare functions as a conflictively reversible paradigm of theatrical practice.

'How did Romeo urinate?': Lorca's explicit metadrama

Although Lorca overtly denied his work's affiliations with any artistic group, many of the theatrical elements through which *El público* is constructed combine to provide a unique opportunity to observe Shakespearean dramaturgy as it dialogues with early twentieth-century experimental and avant-garde theatre from continental Europe:

> SERVANT: Sir.
> DIRECTOR: What?
> SERVANT: There is the public.
> DIRECTOR: Show them in.[1]

Right from the opening lines of the first scene, *El público* inscribes itself in a tradition of self-referential drama which may, in a sense, be traced back to Shakespeare's own early modern context. However, this new mode of sustained metatheatricality erupts at the beginning of the twentieth century, as a response against naturalistic drama, through the 1920s plays of Luigi Pirandello.[2] In Lorca's case, interest in Pirandello is closely related to the innovatory aspirations of his own experimental theatre. In this way, *El público*'s metatheatrics react against the expectations of mainstream Spanish theatregoers to counteract what Vitale has referred to as the 'tranquilizing effect' that reassured the regular theatregoer of the 1930s commercial stage.[3]

The dialogue between the Director and his Servant at the beginning of *El público*, which mirrors the opening scene of *Sei personaggi in cerca d'autore*, provides the Pirandellian metatheatrical frame that holds the play together and formally allows Lorca to revise Shakespeare's *Romeo and Juliet*. García Lorca's difficult, fragmented, highly abstract piece includes three Shakespearean passages:

(1) The play opens with the discussion of the 'Open Air Theatre' production of *Romeo and Juliet*, a conventional rendition of Shakespeare's play for which the Director – the main character in the play – is heavily criticized by the threatening Man 1, Man 2 and Man 3.

(2) In Scene Three, around the middle of this short play, the Three White Horses attempt to rape Juliet, who will eventually take action against her assailants, and the scene develops into an exploration of the idea of submission and domination. In the process, the passive features ascribed by the play to Shakespeare's Juliet are reversed into sexually active (even sadistic) attributes which expand the play's exploration of gender and sex. In Lorca's Freudian investigation of sexual repression, Juliet will ultimately be restored to her initial passive condition by following what *El público* seems to establish as an inevitable return to her submissive heterosexual iconicity.

(3) At the end of the play, the characters' network of hetero and homo-sexual relations eventually resolves in the report of the enactment of the sepulchre scene in *Romeo and Juliet* – the so-called 'beneath the sand' (*bajo la arena*) performance, Lorca's metaphor for a new kind of theatrical practice. In the tragic finale, this time re-performed by a male Romeo and a male Juliet, the play's homophobic metatheatrical audience is reported to rise up against and kill the Shakespearean characters.

Hardly ever performed on the stage,[4] at the time when Lorca was writing *El público*, *Romeo and Juliet* circulated in Spanish popular culture as the iconic representation of romantic love. Ostensibly stripped of much of its subversive potential, and in continuity with a typically nineteenth-century understanding of the play, *Romeo and Juliet* is initially linked in *El público* to a set of culturally inherited connotations – heteronormativity, feminine passivity, conventional theatrical practice – which the metatheatrical framework then helps to deconstruct. Through Pirandellian metatheatricality, then, *Romeo and Juliet* sheds its conservative attributes and the Shakespearean characters are opened up to new signification. In an early dialogue, where Man 1 and the Director discuss the 'Open Air Theatre' production of *Romeo and Juliet*, the characters argue:

> MAN 1: Romeo could be a bird and Juliet could be a stone. Romeo could be a grain of salt and Juliet could be a map.
> DIRECTOR: But they'll never stop being Romeo and Juliet.
>
> (*EP*, 119)

Yet, despite the Director's words, through the play's metatheatrical mechanisms the Shakespearean characters in *El público* do stop being Romeo and Juliet. Thus, the play manages to dismantle the accumulated cultural connotations of Shakespeare's tragedy and subverts them through the redemptive all-male re-enacting of the Shakespearean play. However, Lorca's play closes with the heteronormative play-within-the-play audience violently rejecting the new staging.

This problematic rewriting of *Romeo and Juliet* presents a conflict in which Shakespearean drama is depicted as either artistically conventional or as incapable of satisfying the audience's limited tolerance. Lorca's treatment of Shakespearean drama thus intersects with the innovatory ideas of other contemporary practitioners of continental experimental drama, such as the work of French proto-Surrealist playwright Alfred Jarry. Parallels with Lorca's play include the compressed poetic prose of Jarry's characters, an anti-realist reconception of stage semiotics, a 'reaction to drawing-room comedy', which the French writer described as 'an aesthetically false lesson of false sentimentalism',[5] and an anticipation of the Theatre of the Absurd. For example, Jarry's idea that 'an original work will, at least on the first night, be greeted by a public that remains bemused and, consequently, numb'[6] resonates, in *El público*, with some of the characters' reluctance to let the audience interact with the theatrical event, as when the students criticize the audience's violent reaction to *Romeo and Juliet*:

> STUDENT 1: There's everyone's big mistake and for that reason the theater's in the throes of death. The audience shouldn't try to penetrate the silk and cardboard that the poet erects in the bedroom.
> STUDENT 2: [...] The audience is to fall asleep upon the words and they must not see through the column to the sheep bleating and the clouds traveling across the sky.
>
> (*EP*, 119)

But the most visible link between Jarry's dramaturgy and Lorca's treatment of Shakespearean drama in *El público* is what Perry, following Bakhtin, has described as the 'emphasis on lower bodily appetites and functions' and the 'obsessively scatological' language of *Ubu roi* (1896),[7] and the way these connect with Man 2's explicit inquiry about Romeo's private necessities ('How did Romeo urinate, Mr. Director? Isn't it nice seeing Romeo urinate?'; *EP*, 107). Here, Man 2 readdresses Jarry's concern about the need for drama to incorporate elements that are proscribed on the mainstream stage. Among others, concrete examples of the assimilation of Jarry's provocative theatrical etiquette in *El público* include Man 1's explicit denunciation of the audience's inability to cope with uncomfortable material ('There are people who vomit when an octopus is turned inside out, and others who turn pale if they hear the word cancer pronounced with the right intonation'; *EP*, 108), or Man 2's demands that the Director provide a scatological rendition of *Romeo and Juliet*.

Here, *El público* seems to suggest that Shakespeare's tragedy, what it has come to represent, and how it has come to be performed are insufficient to inspire a renewal of theatrical practice. Ultimately, together with Jarry's inclusion of irreverent content and the assimilation of Pirandellian self-referentiality, the play suggests that in order for Shakespeare's *Romeo and Juliet* to become a medium for cultural and social renovation, the play needs to be queered back to its same-sex configuration where the main characters would have been played by male actors. In this way, *El público* aims at challenging not only the boundaries of the audience's linguistic decorum but, ultimately, its tolerance towards homosexuality, for which Shakespeare's play is initially shown as an insufficiently progressive theatrical source and, finally, as too radical a solution.

Against Shakespeare: Dada and Surrealism

Together with Pirandello and Jarry, *El público* also allows a contextualization of Lorca's play – and, by extension, of Shakespearean drama – within the larger scope of the continental avant-garde and, especially, of Dada and Surrealism. Ultimately, it is through the iconoclasm of these groups that Shakespeare's *Romeo and Juliet* comes to be both questioned and reclaimed as a dramatic model. Around 1926, Lorca had declared himself an outsider to the 'beautiful and bitter battle of abstract art' that his friends Salvador Dalí and Luis Buñuel were fighting out in Paris with the rest of the Surrealist group.[8] Yet, in October 1927, Salvador Dalí wrote a letter to García Lorca expressing his desire to see him crowned as the main poet of the Surrealist movement.[9] Also, in 1928, Dalí included Lorca in the dedication of his *Manifiesto amarillo* (*Yellow Manifesto*) together with other recognizable Surrealist figures such as De Chirico, Arp, Eluard, Aragon, Miró, Desnos and Breton.[10] Still, although *El público*, with much of García Lorca's work from 1929 on, can be said to conform 'to Lorca's second mode, in which, having detached himself from neo-popularist aesthetics, the poet feels in his element within the domains of Surrealism',[11] Lorca and his dramaturgy were never actually a part of the Surrealist movement itself.

The relationship between Surrealism and theatre is, in fact, a problematic one. While strictly literary genres like poetry or prose lend themselves to the automatic writing advocated by Breton as the key to the representation of the oneiric unconscious, drama – an almost necessarily premeditated practice – was in a way formally unsuitable for the Surrealist project. By 1926–27, the group's think tank (Breton, Aragon, Eluard, Péret and Unik) had signed off playwrights like Artaud, Vitrac and Soupault, who were deemed incompatible with the movement's objectives. Together with this, these playwrights were accused of 'granting value to literary activity', yet another incongruence with respect to the Surrealist agenda.[12] Bearing in mind the affinities between *El público* and some of the theatrical proposals included in Artaud's Theatre of Cruelty, had Lorca – very much a literary activist – ever belonged to the Surrealist project, he would have been excluded together with Artaud and the others.

However, the Dada group, as predecessor to Breton's Surrealism, is related to Lorca's re-evaluation of theatrical practice in the same way as *El público* can be seen to partake of what has been described as the Dadaist movement's 'double direction': on the one hand, its 'nihilist and violent attack against art' – 'MAN 1: I'll have to shoot myself in order to inaugurate the true theater' (*EP*, 121) – and, on the other, the 'games, masks and buffooneries' which, through a game of folding screens and identity changes, are central to *El público* as an antidote to the conventions of the Spanish mainstream stage.[13] This 'double direction' is at the core of Lorca's attack on Shakespearean drama.

In 1933, Lorca commented on the situation of Spanish theatrical culture through typically Dadaist, aggressive and confrontational language: 'Right now, generally speaking, [Spanish theatre] is theatre for pigs, by pigs. It's theatre made by pigs, aimed at pigs.'[14] In this way, Lorca's rethinking of theatrical practice in *El público* participates in the Dadaist rejection of bourgeois art and theatre, which, as Ades notes, aimed to take 'a step towards the destruction of its conventional means of understanding the world and of dealing with its own experiences according to pre-established patterns' through the 'disorientation of the audience'.[15] As Tristan Tzara, founding father of Dada, points out regarding the first Dadaist spectacle performed in Zurich in 1917, Oscar Kokoschka's *Sphinx und Strohmann* 'decided our theatre's role, which will lead theatre direction towards the invention of an exploding wind; the stage in the audience; a visible direction in grotesque terms; Dada Theatre. Above all, masks, shotguns, the effigy of the director.'[16]

In *El público*, Lorca metatheatrically stages such a spectacle. The Director's 'beneath the sand' production of Shakespeare's *Romeo and*

Juliet symbolizes the kind of theatre advocated by Dada, which implies a violent reaction against traditional theatrical practice:

> DIRECTOR (*irritated*): But that's deception! That's theater! If I spent three days battling the roots and the pounding waves, it was to destroy the theater.
> [...] One's got to destroy the theater or live in the theater! Hissing from the windows won't work!
>
> (*EP*, 122)

Together with some of the especially aggressive elements in *El público*, possibly closer to the hostile gestures of Dada, Lorca's play is formally grounded in the aesthetics of the Surrealist movement. As Ades notes, 'both movements were similar enough for many ex-Dada members such as Ernst, Man Ray and Arp to subscribe to the Surrealists without making radical changes to their work';[17] so, in a way, Lorca's play partakes in those shared values that Surrealism inherited from the Dadaists, and which produce Lorca's problematic view of Shakespeare's tragedy.

The liberal academic institution (Residencia de Estudiantes) that Lorca attended as a student held several conferences on Freud only a year after his works were translated into Spanish in 1922. Then, in 1925 and 1926, Surrealist figures like Aragon, Eluard, Claudel, Cendrars and Max Jacobs also visited the Residencia. As Huélamo Kosma explains, the arrival of these French influences triggered the interest of Lorca, Dalí and other members of the Residencia in Freud's psychoanalytical theory and in Surrealist aesthetics.[18] These new aesthetics are palpable in *El público*'s 'combination of non-verbal signs; costume design, wigs, objects, movement and character transformation',[19] as well as in its scenery. For example, the stage direction for the last scene in the play reads:

> *The same set as in the First Scene [The Director's room {...} Blue set. A large imprinted hand on the wall. The windows are X-rays]. To the left, a large horse's head placed on the floor. To the right, a huge eye and a group of trees with clouds leaning against the wall.*
>
> (*EP*, 106, 122)

In this way, Shakespeare's characters are relocated from the stage of Elizabethan Verona into Lorca's Surrealist environment. Thus, when Juliet's realistic sepulchre is taken out on stage and offset against a '*wall of sand. On the left, and painted on the wall, a transparent moon, almost like gelatin. In the center, an immense green, lanceolate leaf*' (*EP*, 111), *El público* is appropriating Shakespeare's play through the language of Surrealism to oppose the conventional aesthetics of the mainstream stage.

The play's apparently incoherent and densely metaphorical language at times borders on the automatic writings of the Surrealists, as in Juliet's description of her sepulchre's visitors:

> Yesterday there were forty and I was asleep. The spiders came, then came the little girls, and the young woman raped by the dog, who covered her face with geraniums, and yet I still kept calm. When nymphs talk about cheese it could be that of siren's milk or that of clover. But now they are four, they are four boys who wanted to fit me with a little clay phallus, and they were determined to paint an ink moustache on me.
>
> (*EP*, 114)

Thus, through Surrealist imagery, *El público* creates a theatrical hiatus in *Romeo and Juliet*, a moment for the Shakespeare-based character to be recast as a dramatic representation of abused femininity. In this inset speech, Shakespeare's blank verse is replaced by the verbal images of Surrealism, and Shakespeare's Juliet is brought back to the conventional sexual politics of the 'Open Air Theatre'. In parallel to Juliet's masculinization, the White Horses' assault also reminds one of the iconoclasm of Marcel Duchamp's *L.H.O.O.Q.* (1919), where another icon of Western culture is given an ink moustache. Here Lorca, following Duchamp, partakes of the avant-garde's paradoxical practice of using the masterpiece to articulate its debunking.

No more masterpieces: Shakespeare meets Artaud

As Antonin Artaud suggested, 'it is not a question of suppressing the spoken language but of giving words approximately the importance they have in dreams'.[20] Thus, in the way *El público* agglutinates formal features of Surrealism at the same time as it participates in a larger spectrum of modern experimentation and in the iconoclasm of the avant-garde, Lorca's play ultimately appears to be attuned to many of the theatrical precepts of Antonin Artaud who, after his expulsion from the Surrealist group around 1926, and his work as co-director of the Alfred Jarry Theatre in Paris (1926–28) with fellow Surrealist exile Roger

Vitrac, laid the foundations of his Theatre of Cruelty around the time Lorca produced his experimental writings. Theatre, Artaud thought,

> must organize [dramatic language] into veritable hieroglyphs, with the help of characters and objects, and make use of their symbolism and interconnections in relation to all organs and all levels. [...] The question, then, for the theatre, is to create a metaphysics of speech, gesture, and expression, in order to rescue it from its servitude to psychology and 'human interest'. [...] It is not, moreover, a question of bringing metaphysical ideas directly onto the stage, but of creating what you might call temptations, indraughts of air around these ideas. And humor with its anarchy, poetry with its symbolism and its images, furnish a basic notion of ways to channel the temptation of these ideas.[21]

Through the interaction of its hieroglyphic characters, costumes and objects, its oneiric, associative language and its Surrealist visuals, *El público* can be said to provide an Artaudian Juliet.

Lorca's *El público* was written around two years before Artaud published his manifesto, yet both Lorca's experimental dramas and Artaud's ideas about theatre belong to the larger project by the early twentieth-century European avant-garde to violently subvert the course of artistic expression. In his 'Premier manifeste' ('First Manifesto'), Artaud gave precise indications for the plays that should be staged in such theatres, and García Lorca's *El público* seems to answer two of these remarks directly:

> *We shall stage, without taking account of the text:*
> *1. An adaptation of a work from the time of Shakespeare, a work entirely consistent with our present troubled state of mind [...]*
> *9. Works from the Elizabethan theater stripped of their text and retaining only the accouterments of period, situations, characters, and action.[22]*

As Artaud prescribes, Shakespeare's text is manifestly absent from Lorca's rewriting of *Romeo and Juliet*. The only linguistic resonances with Shakespeare's play are Man 3 and Juliet's vague references to the nightingale and a speech, also by Man 3, where the character is intended to speak lines from Shakespeare's play, although Lorca's manuscript does not specify which lines (*EP*, 164–5). Lorca's *El público* is not literally interested in Shakespeare's play, or in the original resonances of its dramatic language. Following, as it were, Artaud's suggestion, *El público* only retains the trappings of the period or, rather, what its situations, characters and plots have come to signify at the beginning of the twentieth century. In this way, *Romeo and Juliet* starts off in *El público* as an iconic symbol of the kind of theatre that both Lorca and Artaud are trying to counteract through their experimental dramaturgy. It is precisely this detachment from Shakespeare's play text that allows Lorca to transform *Romeo and Juliet* into a valid theatrical artefact by the end of *El público*. In Lorca's play, the chaos provoked by the inner audience's violent response to the 'beneath the sand' performance of *Romeo and Juliet* can be related to Artaud's description of the 'present troubled state of mind':

> STUDENT 4: What's inadmissible is that they murdered them.
> STUDENT 1: And that they also murdered the true Juliet, who was moaning underneath the seats.
> STUDENT 4: Out of pure curiosity, just to see what they had inside of them.
> STUDENT 3: And what have they brought to light? A cluster of wounds and an absolute disorientation.
>
> (*EP*, 120)

Lorca's use of Shakespeare can perhaps be best described through Artaud's advice on adapting classical theatre: 'Instead of continuing to rely upon texts considered definitive and sacred', he suggests, 'it is essential to put an end to the subjugation of the theater to the text, and to recover the notion of a kind of language half-way between gesture and thought.'[23] Thus, *Romeo and Juliet* is central in Lorca's attempt to construct a radically new theatrical spectacle and to address a set of social concerns, although, in order to accomplish this, Lorca has to liberate *El público* from the Shakespearean text and adapt Shakespeare's tragedy to his specific theatrical and ideological interests. These specific theatrical and ideological concerns of course emerge from the concrete problems of the Spanish theatrical and cultural context of the late 1920s and 1930s. Yet, Lorca's play is at the same time connected to a wider creative flux that sweeps across continental Europe in the shape of the artistic avant-gardes and experimental theatre. Thus, by inserting Shakespeare's *Romeo and Juliet* in a tradition of theatrical experimentation and of the confrontational continental avant-garde, Lorca's *El público* testifies to some of the roles played by Shakespearean drama in the first decades of the twentieth century within European culture.

Hugh Grady has suggested that 'given the modernist desire to overcome tradition and the past, it seems something of an anomaly [...] to realize that in both the theatre and in literary criticism [...] Shakespeare was an important component of the modernist revolution'.[24] Indeed, Shakespeare may be part of Grady's idea of a 'modernist revolution'; yet, given the strongly Anglo-centred nature of 'modernism' as a cultural label and of Grady's point of view as a specialist in Shakespeare's *British* reception, cultural artefacts such as García Lorca's *El público* raise uncertainty as to whether Shakespeare can still be described in such an optimistic manner in a wider European context.

Shakespeare may have stood as an unproblematically inspirational source in previous work by Lorca – such as his youthful poems, the farcical *La zapatera prodigiosa* (*The Shoemaker's Prodigious Wife*), or even his *Mariana Pineda* – yet, in *El público*, Shakespearean drama seems to trigger a kind of negative productivity where *Romeo and Juliet* is represented as an oppositional, or at least problematic, model. In a way, Lorca's play raises questions regarding the extent to which Shakespeare should also be considered as an opponent or, at least, as a less amicable figure for the ideological and creative changes of the cultural revolution of the continental avant-garde. Lorca's use of *Romeo and Juliet* in *El público* reinforces the idea of Shakespeare's centrality in the developments of European culture inasmuch as any appropriation of Shakespearean drama includes a certain level of homage or cultural recognition, regardless of the intensity of parody or distortion of the source. Still, the uses to which Shakespeare's *Romeo and Juliet* is put in Lorca's play are worth careful consideration, as their conflicting features invite a reconsideration of exclusively positive or optimistically productive accounts of Shakespearean appropriation in European modernity.

Grady concedes that 'Already, in the 1890s, George Bernard Shaw had campaigned against Shakespeare's high status in *fin-de-siècle* cultural life, arguing tirelessly that after Ibsen, Shakespeare's dramaturgy was obsolete and only the strength of traditionalism in antiquarian Britain prevented this from being generally acknowledged.' 'Of course', Grady adds, 'the overthrow never came. Instead Shakespeare was refunctioned as a modernist poet and playwright of multiple dimensions for the twentieth century, and it was Shaw and his version of literary history that came to seem dated and quaint.'[25] My point here is that, once Shakespeare is extirpated from the Anglo-American sphere and viewed in a wider European context, those 'multiple dimensions' include instances where Shakespeare is not refashioned but, rather, questioned as a model for modernity. In this way, Shaw's perspective is not defeated but, rather, it anticipates a number of concerns that would be soon picked up by experimental theatre practitioners throughout the Continent. In contrast to the British modernist movement, the amount of attention paid to Shakespeare by the continental avant-garde produces quite a different picture of Shakespeare's supposed centrality. Revealingly, moreover, when experimental practitioners like Antonin Artaud reflect on the matter, it is Shakespeare's apocrypha and not his actual dramas that are prescribed: 'one of the apocryphal plays of Shakespeare, such as *Arden of Feversham*, or an entirely different play from the same period'.[26] It seems as if both Artaud's and Lorca's reactions to Shakespeare respond to a similar discontent with the masterpiece which triggers a necessity to replace it with a falsification, in the case of Artaud, or, in the case of this late Lorca, with a representation of the original that stands in for the original itself, in what might even be seen as a prefiguration of postmodern aesthetics. This is a perspective that exceeds the optimistic view of British modernism. In a genuinely confrontational manner, then, the avant-garde's challenge to Shakespeare's cultural iconicity constitutes a central feature in the critical assessment of Shakespeare's conflict-ridden European reception.

Notes

This work was produced within the research project FFI-2011-24160, financed by the Ministerio de Economía y Competitividad and Feder.

1. Federico García Lorca, *The Public*, in *Adaptations of Shakespeare: A Critical Anthology of Plays from the Seventeenth Century to the Present*, ed. by Daniel Fischlin and Mark Fortier (London and New York: Routledge, 2000), 103–24 (106). All further quotations from *El público*, abbreviated as *EP*, will be taken from this edition and noted parenthetically in the text. For a Spanish edition of the play, see Federico García Lorca, *El público*, ed. by Javier Huerta Calvo (Madrid: Espasa Calpe, 2006).
2. *Sei personaggi in cerca d'autore* (*Six Characters in Search of an Author*, 1921); *Ciascuno a suo modo* (*Each in His Own Way*, 1924); and *Questa sera si recita a soggetto* (*Tonight We Improvise*, 1930).
3. Rosanna Vitale, *El metateatro en la obra de García Lorca* (Madrid: Lieges, 1991), 35. Unless otherwise specified, all translations from Spanish are mine.
4. As an example, in Madrid, the first performance of the play in Spanish in the twentieth century dates from 1943 (see the 'Shakespearean Performances in Spain SHAKREP' on www.um.es/shakespeare (accessed 10 October 2012)).
5. Jarry quoted in John Fletcher, *Forces in Modern French Drama* (London: University of London Press, 1972), 190.
6. Alfred Jarry, *Selected Works of Alfred Jarry*, ed. by Roger Shattuck and Simon Watson Taylor (London: Jonathan Cape, 1969), 69.
7. Curtis Perry, 'Vaulting Ambitions and Killing Machines: Shakespeare, Jarry, Ionesco, and the Senecan Absurd', in *Shakespeare Without Class: Misappropriations of Cultural Capital*, ed. by Donald Hedrick and Bryan Reynolds (New York: Palgrave, 2000), 85–106 (87).

8. Federico García Lorca, *Obras completas*, 2 vols, ed. by Arturo del Hoyo (Madrid: Aguilar, 1980), I, 1172–4.

9. Ricard Salvat i Ferrer, 'Federico García Lorca y las vanguardias catalanas', *Boletín de la Fundación Federico García Lorca*, 19–20 (1996), 175–86 (180).

10. Mary Ann Caws, *Manifesto: A Century of Isms* (Lincoln: University of Nebraska Press, 2001), 367–71.

11. Huerta Calvo in *El público*, 68.

12. Maurice Nadeau, *Historia del surrealismo* (Barcelona: Ariel, 1972), 137.

13. Dawn Ades, *El Dada y el Surrealismo* (Barcelona: Labor, 1975), 5.

14. Lorca quoted in Jose Antonio Sánchez, 'The Impossible Theatre: The Spanish Stage at the Time of the Avant-Garde', *Contemporary Theatre Review*, 7 (1998), 7–30 (7).

15. Ades, 32.

16. Ángel Berenguer, 'Teatro y subteatro en Federico García Lorca', in *Federico García Lorca: Perfiles críticos*, ed. by Kurt Reichenberger and Alfredo Rodríguez López-Vázquez (Kassel: Reichenberger, 1992), 1–18 (14).

17. Ades, 57.

18. Julio Huélamo Kosma, 'La influencia de Freud en el teatro de García Lorca', *Boletín de la Fundación Federico García Lorca*, 6 (1989), 59–83 (59).

19. Miriam Balboa Echeverría, *Lorca: el espacio de la representation* (Barcelona: Ediciones Del Mall, 1986), 108.

20. Antonin Artaud, *The Theater and its Double* (New York: Grove Press, 1958), 94.

21. Artaud, 90.

22. Artaud, 99–100.

23. Artaud, 89.

24. Hugh Grady, 'Modernity, Modernism and Postmodernism in the Twentieth-Century's Shakespeare', in *Shakespeare and Modern Theatre: the Performance of Modernity*, ed. by Michael D. Bristol and Kathleen McLuskie (London: Routledge, 2001), 20–33 (21).

25. Grady, 21.

26. Artaud, 99.

10
Negotiating the Memory of the 'People's War': *Hamlet* and the Ghosts of Welfare in *A Diary for Timothy* by Humphrey Jennings (1944–45)

Alessandra Marzola

An excerpt from the 1944 *Hamlet* performed at the Haymarket Theatre in London featuring John Gielgud appears for about six minutes right in the middle of Humphrey Jennings's 1945 war documentary *A Diary for Timothy*.[1] Although announced as an embedded quotation, Jennings's brief live footage of the graveyard scene disappoints the viewers' expectations: crosscut with offstage live dialogues, the quotations from Shakespeare are unpacked and broken into fragments. That Jennings should employ this avant-garde Eisensteinian technique comes as no surprise given his credentials as a bold, versatile intellectual engaging in Surrealist experiments since the 1930s, and committed not only to film directing, but also to painting, photography and poetry. What is more striking is that he should choose to disrupt the compactness of what had been conceived as an uplifting patriotic narrative with this Shakespearean outburst. In spite of its brevity, Jennings's six-minute *Hamlet* works crucially and subversively upon the 40-minute long *A Diary for Timothy* and affects the viewers' response both to previous and subsequent sequences which become 'Hamletized' in the process. In its turn, the discursive context of Jennings's 1945 end-of-the-war film brings about the dismantling of the traditional Shakespearean embedment and therefore points to late twentieth-century Shakespearean remediations.

In what follows I am going to retrace the symptomatic ways in which Jennings's documentary challenges the memory both of the People's War and of Shakespeare's epitomic tragedy of modernity. A short description of the why and when of *A Diary*, and a brief review of this highly popular and sentimental documentary will pave the way to my extended discussion of Jennings's use of Gielgud's *Hamlet.*

A Diary for Timothy[2]

Humphrey Jennings, at the time a renowned director, had, like so many other liberal or leftist intellectuals, trained at Grierson's sociological documentary school. Far more experimental than his 'uncompromisingly serious teacher',[3] he had paid his tribute to the People's War by documenting its climactic stages in highly acclaimed films which still stand out as the visual landmarks of Englishness at war.[4] In the wake of such prestigious war service, and with the end of the war in sight, Jennings was asked not only to shoot its final events but also to point to its future rewards through a sort of bridging narrative. He was expected to tie up the end with the beginning, the extinguishing of warfare with the nascence of Welfare, in ways that would be ideologically consistent with the rhetoric of the People's War. Given these requirements, Jennings's decision to record the early days of Timothy Jenkins, an ordinary middle-class baby, born on the fifth anniversary of the outbreak of war, appears definitely appropriate. Singled out as the symbolically overcharged representative of the postwar generation, Timothy features as the real protagonist, even if the prominence of his role soon appears to be ironically deflated. From the very first shot, the camera actually appears to pin him down rather than just frame him. Not only is he exposed as the unknowing addressee of the narrative of surrounding events: in the course of the film, and at regular intervals, he is also warned, preached at, and even threateningly questioned.

Within the time span of four months – from September 1944 to January 1945 – shots of Timothy's early progress into life are made to fit into the frame of a national patriotic narrative recording England's contemporary transition from war to peace. E.M. Forster's script, voiced by Michael Redgrave in a mournful tone, pieces together Jennings's montage of edifying selected *tranches de vie*, designed to highlight the regenerating power of Englishness in a time of war by smoothly blending sight and sound, people and places. A miner, a farmer, a wounded pilot and an engine driver are seen to perform their daily duties with a militant zeal that is tinged with a heroic flavour by the relentlessness of the 'worst war ever known';[5] a conflict whose presence is at intervals conjured up by radio broadcasts of news bulletins. While dwelling on the healing power of the People's War, Jennings shows the signs of rebuilding, regeneration and survival: roofs are repaired, landmines are cleared from beaches, people are protected from bombing in the Underground air raid shelters, prefabs are built, the wounded pilot gets back to dancing, and, in addition to all this, just before Christmas, Tim is baptized. As life is seen to go on communally, in private and public interiors (cosy homes, concert halls and theatres), allusions to the social gains of war and to the emerging Welfare revolution add gleams of hope for the future. The alternation between invigorating episodes, allusions and events on the one hand, and recurrent hints to the persistence of war on the other, is masterfully rendered, as is typical of Jennings at his best, through overcharged symbolical patterns: sequences of excavations, of mines taken up, of underground shelters, are studiously juxtaposed to the lingering presence of a purifying rain. This sets up an impressive visual counterpart of the threshold between war and peace, earth and sky, burial and rebirth; a counterpart that oversteps the boundaries of the social documentary style with its added emotional overtones.

Supported by Forster's script and by Redgrave's interpretation, Jennings's skilful editing 'betters the instructions' of the Crown Film Unit and of the Ministry of Information with contradictory and symptomatic results. *A Diary* goes one step further than its title and takes the shape of a forcible indoctrination, an overwhelmingly authoritative memorial record laden with warnings and ominous forebodings, and offering neither encouragement nor support. In spite of its laboured emphasis on rebirth and new democracy, and indeed contrary to its declared purposes, Jennings's film dooms Timothy and the war babies to the impotence of doubt, ushering them into a future ridden with uncertain prospects and unresolved interrogatives:

> Up to now we've done the talking, but before long you'll sit up and take notice. What are you going to say about it and what are you going to do? [...] Are you going to have greed for money and power ousting decency from the world as they have in the past? Or are you going to make the world a different place – you and all the other babes?

Actually, the diary's imperiousness does not subjugate Timothy alone. Combining description with blunt interpretation, Redgrave's voicing of Forster's patronizing script muffles and backgrounds the sparse comments of all the characters, no matter how important their roles, leaving no space for the disclosure of individual voices. Conversely, major emphasis falls on deep silence and awestruck listening. Close-ups of families gathered around the wireless listening in religious silence to the BBC news, and of the Covent Garden audience mesmerized by Myra Hess's uplifting performance of Beethoven's 'Appassionata', point to hypnotized listening as a form of choral subjugation to the frozen version of history fed by patriotic discourses ranging from war bulletins to lunchtime musical entertainment. Jennings's close-up shots of listening people also catch sullenly hallucinated gazes whose mournfulness matches a pervasive sense of melancholy. Adding to Redgrave's glum delivery, and to frequent allusions to absent fathers and friends, these sorrowful gazes come to infect even the most joyous epiphanies with a sense of loss verging on nostalgia for what is dead and forfeited, including the war itself. Unable to resist the arresting power of the war, *A Diary* belies its auspicious predicaments by envisaging the endless repetition of violence in an increasingly risky and haphazard world, where evil and good are dangerously mixed up. It is as if the prospect of enduring emergency were the only way to keep alive the winning power of social cohesion. Rather than the new freedom won at the price of so many sacrifices, what the future is shown to have in store for humans is blind fate. Ultimately, in a sharp ideological about-turn, the freezing of history into myth is made to serve nihilistic, rather than constructive purposes.

Timothy in the graveyard: crosscuts

In the light of *A Diary*'s mournful memorial address, Jennings's decision to include footage of the graveyard scene from Shakespeare's quintessential tragedy of memory comes as no surprise. Apart from the obvious contextual appropriateness of Shakespeare's best-known *memento mori*, what stands out in *Hamlet* as strikingly coincidental with the threatening mode of address of *A Diary* is the commanding narrative of an absent and ghostly father-king, who has cursed the prince of Denmark with the task of remembering things which it would be easier to forget, and of setting right times that are out of joint. Moreover, when halfway through the film the November 1944 Haymarket production of *Hamlet* cuts in, the nostalgically mournful aura of *A Diary* is already firmly established in the viewers' minds and the tone is set for them to develop gloomy associations between their own memory of *Hamlet* and Jennings's report of the final stages of the war. Jennings's interpolated *Hamlet*, however, does more than just trigger subliminal associations for, as is proper in a documentary of ideas, we have already been told what to look for. Rather than explaining what is going to happen,

Redgrave's introductory comment 'sets the key to the kind of thinking the spectator will be expected to do in the next few minutes'.[6] Spectators are reminded that what follows will have to stand as the counterproof of *A Diary*'s glum forebodings, the evidence for unpredictability and uncertainty, with – as the film puts it – 'the bad so mixed up with the good you never know what's coming'.

'What's coming' could not be more unpredictable. Although the initial close-up of the Haymarket Theatre marquee raises expectations of a regular embedded performance, the canonical aura of theatrical *Hamlet* is seen rapidly to dissolve as fragmented quotations, crosscut with an ARP men's discussion in a military canteen about the mechanics of V1 rockets, are literally thrown offstage, and made to fit into and play in a ghostlike manner against the grain of the film's visual and narrative mosaic. Unlike Myra Hess's Covent Garden concert, here there are no audience shots, no lingering on the cohesive effects of great art upon hypnotized listeners, but just gales of laughter (surprisingly enough, the only amusing moment in the documentary) in response to the Clown's clue on Hamlet's madness which will not be seen in England for 'there the men are as mad as he' (5.1.153).[7] Openly reverting to his most daring Surrealist experimentalism, Jennings effaces the boundary lines between stage and screen, quotation and script, through a recontextualization that turns *Hamlet* into a catalyst for *A Diary*'s gloomiest clues, while eliciting disturbingly contemporary, historically located responses to the Haymarket production.

From the very first shot of the *Hamlet* sequence, when the voice of the Gravedigger slowly fades in, uttering the lines about the coincidental birth date of Shakespeare's protagonist (5.1.141–50), Tim and the prince of Denmark become superimposed: Tim's similarly coincidental birth date reverberates on the unknowing Suffolk baby, and as a result Shakespeare's entire play is pinpointed as the subtext of *A Diary*. Any intuitive or subliminal association the viewer might have developed so far with the narrative mode of Hamlet's ghost is at this point given evidential confirmation but, as a short description of Jennings's editing will show, the crosscutting adds more specifically disquieting resonances, given that *Hamlet*'s explosiveness is sparked off by the end-of-the-war context of *A Diary*.

Jennings's sudden cutaway to the military canteen plunges the play into war planning. We never learn whether the purpose of the wardens' meticulous calculations is going to be aggressive or defensive, for the brief, decontextualized exchange comes to a sudden halt, when a question on trajectories ending with 'you know?' prompts, as it were, the terse, bathetic answer 'I know not' (5.1.174) from the Clown at the Haymarket. A new cut back to the canteen surprises us with a terrifying blast which abruptly ends the ARP men's conversation. At the same time, Gielgud's subsequent musing on Yorick's chopfallen skull (5.1.187–92) works as an apt, albeit cynically dispirited, comment both on the previous blast, and on the following shot of men vainly digging in the rubble for survivors. There is no signal whatsoever of any termination to the *Hamlet* sequence. Unlike the beginning, emphatically highlighted through Redgrave's introductory announcement, the end of Jennings's crosscut is blurred by the overflowing of the play into the script. It is as if *Hamlet* had dissolved into the infective aura of the documentary. Rather than generically reminding Tim of the mixture of good and evil, or of the risks of chance, as predicted, Jennings's cuts from Shakespeare's graveyard scene short-circuit to the thwarted technical discussion, unveiling the analogy between the Gravedigger's jovial indifference to death, and the wardens' equal obliviousness of impending mortal threats. And while the absorption of the wardens in calculations echoes the Clown's operative zeal, the digging through the rubble in search of survivors is sinisterly paralleled by the digging of graves. In the play, much as in the film, the emphasis is laid not on chance in general, but on the chance that death may come at any time, no matter how keen the attempt to divert it from its predictable course through calculating thought. More threateningly than Shakespeare's *memento mori*, the live shot of the bombing actually backfires, chastising diversion, repression and aggressiveness. Exposed as vain sublimations of the fear of death, war calculations are made into symptoms of the death drive which – as argued in one of Jennings's favourite books, Sigmund Freud's *Civilization and its Discontents*[8] – is constitutive of the West's ineradicable thrust towards aggressiveness and guilt. But what looks even more desecrating is the juxtaposition of what will be Hamlet's unceremonious disposal of Yorick's skull with the bombed site's absent casualties. Jennings cuts the scene from the play just before we get to Hamlet's disgusted 'Pah!' at the idea that Alexander might have smelled like Yorick now does (5.1.194–5). This gap, unequivocally if disturbingly, is made to stand in for the Danish Prince's feelings about the inhabitants of the bombed-out military canteen. Conversely, the wardens' scenes bring to the fore the connection between war and peace, Shakespeare's past and Timothy's present, albeit in ways that seem dangerously contradictory to the ideological predicates of both the documentary and the highly canonical Haymarket production. As shown in Reisz's close reading of this sequence, the 'two scenes are knit together so closely as to come over to the spectator as a complex but homogeneous continuity'. As a result, '[Jennings's] cuts do not so much make points themselves; they switch the argument about, and keep it going at different levels'.[9] Feeding upon each other, screen and play are made to elicit a symptomatic vision, as if the film were now to be reeled back in the light of its central sequence, and as if Shakespeare's graveyard scene were to be reconsidered, along with the whole play, in the light of this film documenting the end of the war.

While infecting *The Diary*'s regenerative thrust with shadows of impending death, Jennings's *Hamlet* also implicitly redeploys the dispirited gazes of women caught grappling with thoughts of absence and death as symptoms of a general disease, with the native hue of their resolution sicklied over with the pale cast of thought. More poignantly, the concept of death as retribution, heralded through Jennings's intercutting of *Hamlet*'s lines on Yorick with the bomb-shelled canteen, spreads a plague of penalizing guilt not only on the men absorbed in ballistics, but also on all of the *Diary*'s characters, including Timothy's frequently-evoked absent father.

Conversely, Jennings's crosscut backfires onto Gielgud's *Hamlet*, which, in November 1945, at the time of Jennings's footage, was being enthusiastically praised as a flawless contribution to the national fantasy. Backed by the West End management and by the Arts Council, an ideal combination of the commercial and the state-aided Shakespeare, the production, whose patriotic flavour was enhanced by daily bombings overhead, was said to 'give food for hope of a Shakespearean revival'.[10] In the general opinion it stood as a signpost to the surviving power of art and to the universal, transcendental appeal of Shakespeare's play.

More than simply disrupting the theatrical status of *Hamlet*, Jennings's montage makes a clean sweep of the highly-charged patriotic aura of this production. As a matter of fact his editing opens up the play's power to expose and deflagrate the wishful threads of the very fantasy of warfare/Welfare to which *A Diary* was meant to subscribe. With its abrupt raid into the homogeneously flat narrative of the film, the *Hamlet* sequence not only relentlessly chastises the death drive inherent in the vanity of war predictions, and of ballistic calculations; it also works as a highlighting of and retribution for the coalescence of the lingering mournfulness, hypnotized inertia, and subjugation looming large upon the whole film. Reeled back against the grain of its central scene, these resurface as what Slavoj Žižek, in his Lacanian interpretation of democracy, has described as 'the inert stains resisting communication and interpretation, and smearing the blankness of democracy'[11] or as 'the leftover to which formal democracy clings [...] the pathological fact of a nation-state'.[12] What Jennings's film also highlights, however, is that in so far as it is 'the only point that gives consistency to the subjects and to their being in the world',[13] this pathological stain is the very condition both of warfare patriotism and of Welfare democracy.

In the light of the end-of-the-war cultural anxieties about the dangers of Bolshevized Welfare, it is not surprising that in *A Diary* the stain that smears the blank of democracy should show itself as the totalitarian unconscious of the Welfare State, whose constitutive binding power had been both enhanced and authorized by the war emergency. Now that the end of the war is in sight, however, Jennings proves less concerned about the Bolshevization of Welfare than worried about the democratization of patriotic Bolshevism, for we are made to feel and fear that without the defensive screen of the war, the ghostly imprint of *Hamlet* will freeze all possibility of freedom and choice. It is not by chance that at the end of the film Tim should be gloomily warned precisely against the risks of freedom and choice, and unsupportively ushered into a world where exercising 'the right to criticize and to grumble' is envisaged as no easy job:

> Life is going to become more dangerous than before, oddly enough, more dangerous, because now we have the power to choose and the right to criticize and even to grumble. We are free men. We have to decide for ourselves. And part of your bother, Tim, will be learning to grow up free.

In Jennings's dispiriting conclusion, *Hamlet* becomes remediated as the lingering symptomatic aura of *A Diary*, imprinted in the postwar generation as the totalitarian substance of warfare and Welfare.[14]

Jennings the Observer

Breaking as it does into the linear, sentimental narrative of *A Diary*, the *Hamlet* sequence marks the abrupt resurgence of Jennings's idiosyncratically Anglicized version of Surrealism, which, far from committing itself to pure aesthetics, had from the start been steeped in politics. The disruptive crosscut of film and play echoes the shockingly unpredictable juxtaposition of different objects, people and scenes of English daily life which feature as Jennings's dominant stylistic trait in the photographs, collages and paintings he produced during the 1930s. Like the ghostly version of warfare-Welfare surfacing in *A Diary*, the glimpses of revolutionary truth granted by these works upset received versions of Englishness and show how Jennings brilliantly puts his homemade Surrealism to subtle political ends.[15]

Still, it was Jennings's experience as a Mass Observer that really sharpened his insight into mass rituals, and allowed him to bridge the gap between Surrealism and the People's War, feeding the disconcerting visuals of *A Diary for Timothy*. The revolutionary purpose of the Mass Observation project, launched by Jennings in 1936 along with two poets and an amateur anthropologist, was to daily scrutinize mass behaviours through a method which combined new psychology and anthropology with a daring aesthetics of social life grounded in Surrealism. Jennings's aim was to build up 'a science of ourselves for ourselves'[16] in order to drastically democratize observation and effectively counter the biased policies of market research and Malinowskian anthropology.[17] In the light of *A Diary*, what is most revealing about the project is that the radicalism of its democratic intentions should drift dangerously towards totalitarianism. Enlisted to report daily on the minute details of their own practices, the observers in fact also scrutinized and put on the record the activities of their close neighbours, giving way to an inquiry system which disquietingly echoed panoptical surveillance. The revolutionary thrust of the project, flawed by such inherent ambiguity, was doomed to failure. And fail it did, thwarted, amongst other things, by inner disputes and the coming war. And yet, however short-lived, the Mass Observation project, whose documents are now available at the University of Sussex, still exposes totalitarianism both as the symptomatic leftover of democracy, and as its very condition. Boldly combining Surrealist suggestions, nationalistic concerns, voyeuristic drifts, and democratic ambitions, Mass Observation works as the fuel of Jennings's peculiar war patriotism in general, but, more specifically, of the postwar narrative deployed in *A Diary*. From the Mass Observation headquarters at Bolton not only did Jennings daily get in touch with the living bodies of the English 'mass', much in the same way as Orwell was doing at Wigan Pier;[18] as a Mass Observer/observed, he also experienced the duplicity of gaze democracy, the point where scrutiny verges on spying, and where inquiry fades into coercion. It is this crucial fault line of democracy that the *Hamlet* sequence, acting as a trigger to the Surrealist potential of *A Diary*, captures, highlights and redeploys in the light of the ending war.

Responses

Although ostensibly Shakespeare-eccentric, that is to say not focused on what happens to the play *Hamlet*,[19] *A Diary* is, at the same time, imperiously *Hamlet*-centric. In so far as the memory of the war handed down to Timothy as a legacy bears the imprints of Shakespeare's play, with its peculiar problematics of memory, *A Diary* is crucially focused on *Hamlet*. This, however, has gone largely unnoticed. Except for studies on film editing, the *Hamlet* sequence has received no special attention whatsoever, and its cutting edge has been dulled, neutralized by and incorporated into the unreserved praise of Jennings's tribute to the mood of the nation. Eulogized as one of Jennings's masterpieces,[20] *A Diary* has stood the test of time mainly on account of its overflowing emotional appeal against which even its technical flaws, only sporadically mentioned, have proved irrelevant. What has struck British viewers – especially those born around the same time as Timothy – as irresistibly moving is precisely its aura of lingering mournfulness, which, coupled with the misgivings about the future, has been acknowledged as the truthful record of a deeply ingrained communal engrossment with the very notion of England, and as an accurate premonition of future failures.[21]

Rather than the target of critical review or popular appraisal, the film has therefore become the object of self-recognition. Like the 'suet puddings and the red pillar boxes, the solid breakfasts and the gloomy Sundays' pinpointed by Orwell as the icons of an England that stretches both into the future and the past, Jennings's *Hamlet* has also 'entered into [the] soul'[22] of the nation and contributed to the mythologizing memory of the People's War. In a sense, this kind of response doubles the hypnotic allegiance to patriotic discourses highlighted in the film, and proves the virtual continuity between the end-of-the-war and the postwar democratic Englishness. That this should have happened is not surprising, nor is it a matter of wonder that the chastising potential of the graveyard scene and of the whole narrative addressed to Timothy should have been enjoyed. Turned into a fantasy by the very historical circumstances of its reception, the film has lost its status as a war documentary to take on an emotional appeal that equals the enchanting power of children's fairy tales. The fantasy provided by *A Diary* does not resemble a symptomatic narrative, a 'signifying formation overtaking itself towards its interpretation'.[23] Rather, it takes the shape of daydreaming formation, where the subject 'can enjoy his symptom more than himself', and inertly cling to its persistence, lingering in *jouissance*.[24]

Outside Britain, however, and especially overseas, there have been signs pointing to an entirely different mood of response. A fierce rebuttal, in stark contrast with unanimous popular commendation, came from Canadian film scholar Andrew Britton in 1986. In an essay entitled 'Their Finest Hour: Humphrey Jennings and the British Imperial Myth of World War II', Britton vehemently attacks the imperialist bias of Jennings's war films in general. Jennings's socialist convictions and artistic credentials are seen to be belied, indeed 'debilitated', by his endorsement of the official British war mythology, whose content is exposed as 'the nostalgia for a classless society' or for the idealized body of the organic community.[25] *A Diary for Timothy* is targeted as a case in point. Far from being interpreted as a symptom, the dejected aura of the film is taken at face value and chastised as incongruous with what would be expected of 'an artist with socialist sympathies'. Jennings in his turn is mercilessly accused of 'a shocking lack of emotional energy'.[26] As shown in the following outraged comment, however, it is Jennings's treatment of *Hamlet* that really cuts to the quick, provoking the harshness:

> What Jennings thought that he was doing in this sequence it is impossible to tell: the enacted meaning is distressingly clear, but one cannot imagine it to have been fully conscious [...] the British character becomes the object of a querulous and cynical irony which culminates in the juxtaposition [...] of Yorick's skull [...] and the absent bomb-site victim.[27]

Obviously enough, it is not for Britton to 'enjoy the symptoms' of a nation which is not his own. And yet, it is striking that they should be so vehemently resented. The emotionality of Britton's objection to the *Hamlet* sequence, where the disruptiveness of the symptoms of warfare is enhanced, shows that a raw nerve has been touched. Apparently, the point is not so much that Jennings has betrayed Britton's political expectations. Rather, it seems to me, he stands accused of outrageously disgracing the North American memory of the war. Once unprotected by the dreamlike formation of the English fantasy, and exposed to Britton's North American sanguineness, the inertia looming in *A Diary* surfaces as an intolerable reversal of the 'animal spirits' whose vital thrust John Maynard Keynes famously recognized as the driving force of Protestant capitalism.[28] Jennings's challenge to the very foundations of Puritan Britain and North America alike, brought about by the deflagrating remediation of *Hamlet*, strikes the Canadian critic as incompatible with the memorial narrative of the war and, consequently, as aesthetically and culturally unacceptable.

No matter how emotionally charged, however, Britton's rebuttal of *A Diary* serves to bring the film out of the shelter of national fantasy and into the open. By identifying the central sequence as the fault line of the war memory handed on to Timothy and to the postwar babies, Britton's rereading shows how crucially Jennings's remediation of *Hamlet* can affect, challenge and problematize the frozen memory of the war. Thus the way is paved for Jennings's *Hamlet* to take leave of the fantasy, and circulate freely, as happens in the video clip in Michael Almereyda's film *Hamlet 2000*, which briefly features the Gielgud shot by Jennings as part of the stored technological memory of the main character.[29] The way is also paved for alternative readings of Jennings's remediation of Shakespeare, which, transcending competing national allegiances and incompatible war mythologies, may newly assess how the overcharged memorial aura of *A Diary* continues to affect our own perceptions of the war.

Notes

The phrase 'The People's War' as applied to the British Home Front in World War II probably originated with Angus Calder's *The People's War: Britain 1939–1945*, first published in 1969 (London: Pimlico, 2008). It is also used by the BBC for the title of their World War II archive.

1. Humphrey Jennings, *A Diary for Timothy*, UK, 1946. Although released in 1946, *A Diary for Timothy* was completed in 1945 and shot between 1944 and early 1945. The film is freely available from the *Internet Archive* website, www.archive.org/details/DiaryForTimothy (accessed 9 October 2012).
2. For a close reading of the film in the light of the end-of-the-war context see Alessandra Marzola, '"A Diary for Timothy" di Humphrey Jennings (1944–1945): La fine della guerra e gli spettri della democrazia', *Dintorni*, 2 (2007), 185–200.
3. Kevin Jackson, *Humphrey Jennings* (London: Picador, 2004), 133.
4. As shown by the list that follows, Jennings's war documentaries, commissioned by the Ministry of War Information and mostly produced by the Crown Film Unit, mark the progress of the People's War: *Spring Offensive* (1940), *London Can Take It* (1940), *This is England* (1941), *Words for Battle* (1941), *Listen to Britain* (1942), *Fires Were Started* (1943), *The True Story of Lili Marlene* (1944), *The 80 Days* (1944), *V1* (1944), *A Defeated People* (1945).
5. To my knowledge, the screenplay of *A Diary for Timothy* is not currently available. All the quotations are therefore my own transcript of the film dialogues.
6. Karel Reisz and Gavin Millar, *On the Technique of Film Editing* (London: Focal Press, 2003), 161.
7. Quotations from *Hamlet* are from the Cambridge University Press edition which was presumably the reference text for the Haymarket production: William Shakespeare, *Hamlet*, ed. by J. Dover Wilson (Cambridge: Cambridge University Press, 2003).
8. Sigmund Freud, *Civilization and its Discontents* (London: Hogarth Press, 1930). Originally published in Vienna in the same year as *Das Unbehagen in der Kultur* ['The uneasiness of culture'].

9. Reisz and Millar, 162.
10. See Muriel St Claire Byrne, 'Fifty Years of Shakespeare Production: 1898–1948', *Shakespeare Survey*, 2 (1949), 1–20 (16).
11. Slavoj Žižek, *The Sublime Object of Ideology* (London: Verso, 1989), 75.
12. Slavoj Žižek, *Looking Awry: An Introduction to Jacques Lacan through Popular Culture* (Cambridge, Mass.: MIT Press, 1992), 164–5.
13. Žižek, *Looking Awry*, 165.
14. For a discussion of the totalitarian substance of warfare and Welfare fantasies see Alessandra Marzola, 'Fantasie di Guerra: *Warfare e Welfare*', in *Maschere dell'impero: percorsi coloniali della letteratura inglese*, ed. by Elio Di Piazza, Daniela Corona and Marcella Romeo (Pisa: ETS, 2005), 51–69.
15. For a guide to Jennings's life and works see Jackson, *Humphrey Jennings* and *The Humphrey Jennings Film Reader*, ed. by Kevin Jackson (London: Carcanet, 1993).
16. The phrase was coined by Charles Madge, the London poet who was also a member of the MO project, and was later appropriated by the MO Group including Jennings himself. In a letter to *The New Statesman and Nation* dated 2 January 1937, Madge had announced that the project would develop what he called 'a science of ourselves for ourselves'.
17. For an accurate survey of the Mass Observation project see Ben Highmore, *Everyday Life and Cultural Theory: An Introduction* (London: Routledge, 2002), 75–112.
18. Anthony Aldgate and Jeffrey Weeks, *Britain Can Take It. The British Cinema in the 2nd World War* (New York: Taurig, 2007), 225–6.
19. See Richard Burt, 'Introduction: Shakespeare, More or Less? From Shakespearecentricity to Shakespeareccentricity and Back', in *Shakespeares after Shakespeare: An Encyclopedia of the Bard in Mass Media and Popular Culture*, 2 vols, ed. by Richard Burt (Westport, Conn. and London: Greenwood Press, 2007), I, 1–9; Thomas Cartelli and Catherine Rowe, *New Wave Shakespeare on Screen* (Cambridge: Polity, 2007).
20. See Jack C. Ellis and Betsy A. McLane, *A New History of the Documentary Film* (London: Continuum, 2005).
21. Jackson, *Humphrey Jennings*, 302.
22. George Orwell, 'England your England' (1941), in *A Patriot after All, 1940–1941*, ed. by Peter Davison (London: Secker & Warburg, 1998), 392–409 (393).
23. Žižek, *Ideology*, 74.
24. Žižek, *Ideology*, 75.
25. Andrew Britton, 'Their Finest Hour: Humphrey Jennings and the British Imperial Myth of World War II', in *Britton on Film: The Complete Film Criticism of Andrew Britton*, ed. by Barry K. Grant (Detroit, Mich.: Wayne State University Press, 2009), 302–13 (306). Originally published in *CineACTION!*, 18 (1989), 37–44.
26. Britton, 311, 309.
27. Britton, 311.
28. John Maynard Keynes, *The General Theory of Employment, Interest and Money* (London: Macmillan, 1973), 161–2.
29. See Cartelli and Rowe, 60–8.

11

'IN THE FEARFUL ARMOUR': Shakespeare, Heiner Müller and the Wall

Miguel Ramalhete Gomes

Hamletmaschine (1977), Heiner Müller's second major rewriting of Shakespeare, was banned in the former GDR, a fate shared by many of his other dramatic works.[1] In this play, German history is revisited through the lens of the equally historical engagement of German culture with Shakespeare. This chapter focuses on one of the motifs from the play, that of the prison which also functions as a safe haven. To do so, I concentrate on what is probably Müller's specific material source for this image: the Berlin Wall, which in *Hamletmaschine*, I argue, takes the double function of prison and armour.

This imagery and its uses in the play will be the centre around which a consideration of Müller's troubled relation with the GDR revolves, since, rather than becoming a dissident and an exile like many other East German intellectuals, Müller insisted on working inside the GDR and within certain bounds. Both the construction and the demolition of the Berlin Wall had an impact on Müller's activity as a playwright and these two moments can be said to frame his peculiar dramatization of the relations between state politics and literature, a dramatization that, in some instances, was strongly mediated by the work and the imagined figure of William Shakespeare.

Prison state

When, in *Surveiller et punir* (1975), Michel Foucault claimed that the prison was a paradigmatic place for the exercise of a mechanism supposedly organizing Western society ever since the nineteenth century, he seemed almost to be trying to gloss Hamlet's famous dictum, 'Denmark's a prison' (2.2.239).[2] Even more than the school or the hospital, it was the prison that most clearly exemplified what Foucault called the 'panopticism' characteristic of modern disciplinary society. In the last sentence of the book, this genealogy was made explicit: 'At this point I end a book that must serve as a historical background to various studies of the power of normalization and the formation of knowledge in modern society.'[3] Foucault's proposal became fashionable during the 1980s, and the metaphor of the panopticon acquired a life of its own, as the prison was boldly made to prefigure a particular form of society. However, the likening of democratic states from the second half of the twentieth century to prisons was a common enough *topos*. In his critique of the May '68 generation, Theodor W. Adorno had described the desperate impotence felt by students when facing what he called an 'administered society'; it was the feeling, he said, that you get finding 'the exits blocked'.[4]

A prison is normally and normatively thought of as an unpleasant place. Literary prisons, however, have not always or not systematically been described as disagreeable. Consider, in *The Two Noble Kinsmen*, Arcite's and Palamon's mutual encouragement during their imprisonment:

> Arcite: Whilst Palamon is with me, let me perish
> If I think this our prison.
> [...]
> Palamon: You have made me –
> I thank you, cousin Arcite – almost wanton
> With my captivity. What a misery
> It is to live abroad, and everywhere!
>
> (*TNK*, 2.2.61–2 and 95–8)

Another prison-related inversion of behaviour is briefly mentioned in *Measure for Measure*, where prison life is said to have wrought its effects on Barnardine, of whom the Provost says: 'He hath evermore had the liberty of the prison. Give him leave to escape hence, he would not' (4.2.137–8). Of course, Barnardine is no example of merriness in jail; it is rather that prison has so thoroughly broken him as to make him incapable of wanting to go out into the world again. And both Palamon and Arcite only console each other for as long as they do not see Emilia. Shortly after she appears, Palamon comments: 'Never till now was I in prison, Arcite' (*TNK*, 2.2.132).

The phenomenology of the prison allows for this double valuation: the enclosed space can be experienced as both stifling and potentially invigorating, even if only temporarily. The wall separating inside from outside is both a restriction and a stimulus for the creation of forms.

Furthermore, from a more existential perspective, it is simultaneously a blocked exit and a protection from the outside.

Behind the wall

One of the clearest examples of such a double function was the notorious Berlin Wall, built in 1961 as an 'anti-Fascist defensive wall' (*antifaschistischer Schutzwall*), an expression coined by Horst Sindermann for East German propaganda purposes. As defence, it protected East Germany from the perilous influence of Western Europe; as a prison wall, it kept East Germans from fleeing.

The construction of the Berlin Wall and the change in East German politics that came with it were partly responsible for Heiner Müller's fall from grace in 1961. Before 1961, Müller was the promising, though internationally unknown, author of a small number of plays, of which *Der Lohndrücker* (*The Wage Dumper*, 1957) was probably the most accomplished. In 1959, Müller won the Heinrich Mann award (attributed by the Academy of the Arts of the GDR) for both this play and *Die Korrektur* (*The Correction*, 1957–58). The risk of writing about contemporary GDR affairs eventually had its consequences and the 1961 play *Die Umsiedlerin oder Das Leben auf dem Lande* (*The Resettler Woman or Life in the Country*), a raucous peasant comedy, became a theatrical event marked by its untimely quality.

Müller's *Die Umsiedlerin* had been written and rehearsed in parallel since 1959, and, if Müller's account of the production in his autobiography is to be believed, the play was throughout this period taken to be truly socialist.[5] On 13 August, East Germany closed the borders. The premiere of the play was on 30 September, the rehearsals having taken place as the wall was being built. During the premiere party, Müller recounts, some of the guests were heard to say that those involved in the play could 'now open for the Bautzen prison festival'.[6] Bautzen was notorious for its penitentiaries for political prisoners. Things soon became serious, imprisonment was mentioned and, rumour has it, the play was finally said to be 'not a case for literary criticism but for State security'.[7] The play was characterized as counterrevolutionary, which remained open to either a subjective or objective reading. Subjective meant imprisonment, while objective meant stupidity, and Müller managed to get away with the second. Müller had to write and deliver a humiliating self-criticism.[8] He was eventually expelled from the Writers' Association and told to go and work in the fields to get to know the reality supposedly distorted in his play. The consequence of this process was two years of isolation and serious financial strain.

At this point Müller may be said to have followed Hans Eisler's humorous advice: 'Think of Schiller. An Austrian tyrant is murdered in Switzerland. This is the sort of play you must write in Germany.'[9] There followed a string of plays on mythological subjects – Philoctetes, Hercules, Oedipus, Prometheus – and, simultaneously, the first important encounters with Shakespeare. This first group of plays included a translation of *As You Like It* (1967); *Waldstück* (*Forest Play*, 1968–69), a rewriting of Gerhard Winterlich's very loose adaptation of *A Midsummer Night's Dream*, called *Horizonte* (*Horizons*); and *Macbeth, nach Shakespeare* (*Macbeth, after Shakespeare*, 1972), a violent rewriting which attracted its own share of scandal. Müller's turn to Shakespeare in the late 1960s was far from accidental. In the GDR, as Lawrence Guntner explains, from 1964 onwards 'Shakespeare was officially declared the normative standard for theatre, a classical monument to be emulated by playwrights and directors but not to be questioned.'[10] Such a conspicuous sequence of dramatic dealings with Shakespeare suggests that Müller capitalized on Shakespeare's canonical status as a way to get back into the literary and theatrical milieus. The use of literary models from Ancient Greece or from early modern England also allowed Müller to continue writing political drama at a time when a direct engagement with political subjects had become particularly dangerous.[11]

Heiner Müller's dramatic production was characterized by a stance which was critical of the GDR (and for that matter of the FRG), yet did not include the possibility of dissidence.[12] Dissatisfaction found its most desperate expression in the sarcastic description of a protective prison wall in the play *Der Bau* (*The Construction Site*, 1965): 'BARKA: Congratulations for the defensive wall. [...] Had I known that I was building my own prison here, I would have packed each side of it with dynamite.'[13] According to Müller's autobiography, the awareness of imprisonment was, however, *not* accompanied by a desire to escape and this complicates the notion of a wall announced as defensive, revealed to be oppressive, and eventually proved to be productive: 'A dictatorship is of course more colourful for a playwright than a democracy. Shakespeare is unthinkable in a democracy.'[14] In Müller's case, it must be granted, the possibility of dissidence was strongly attenuated by increasing journey privileges from the late 1960s onwards, an advantage that strongly contributed towards making borders more elastic. Müller could no longer be said to be staying in the GDR against his own will.[15] The Berlin Wall, in his particular case, was no longer a physical wall. Its *symbolic* ramifications, of course, were another matter. The possibility of looking at the GDR from the outside gave Müller a uniqueness of vision which put an admittedly Janus-faced wall to use in disrupting any simple opposition between inside and outside.[16]

Armouring up

This unique situation of voluntary entrapment finds its most intense and thorough exploration in Müller's *Hamletmaschine* (1977). The basic idea, a wall that is simultaneously a prison and an armour, or, in other words, a stifling environment that is nevertheless instrumental in triggering dramatic production, is repeated with several variations during this brief nine-page play.[17]

The first mention of prisons in the text is a rare direct translation from Shakespeare's play: 'Denmark is a prison, a wall is growing between the two of us.'[18] The initial notion of a national territory likened to a prison is immediately appropriated for the East German case, once the reference is made to a dividing wall.[19] It is worth quoting in full the Folio-only section in *Hamlet* where this phrase appears. Hamlet greets the newly-arrived Rosencrantz and Guildenstern and shortly after asks them:

HAMLET: [...] What have you, my good friends, deserved at the hands of Fortune that she sends you to prison hither?
GUILDENSTERN: Prison, my lord?
HAMLET: Denmark's a prison.
ROSENCRANTZ: Then is the world one.
HAMLET: A goodly one, in which there are many confines, wards, and dungeons, Denmark being one o'th' worst.
ROSENCRANTZ: We think not so, my lord.
HAMLET: Why, then 'tis none to you; for there is nothing either good or bad but thinking makes it so. To me it is a prison.
(*Ham.*, 2.2.235–45)

Prison is not simply a physical space but also an emotional category, a material thing which, as I briefly tried to show at the beginning of this chapter, can carry more than one form of symbolic investment. In Müller's play, a prison is a different thing depending on whether the speaker is Hamlet or Ophelia. Ophelia's prison is much more aggressively dealt with than Hamlet's. In the play, Ophelia is associated with the late twentieth-century German activist Ulrike Meinhof, believed to have committed suicide in Stammheim prison in May 1976. In Ophelia's first monologue, prison means the captivity of bourgeois life, whose instruments she then destroys: 'I smash the tools of my captivity, the chair the table the bed. I destroy the battlefield that was my home. [...] I set fire to my prison' (547–8). The excerpt alludes to Ulrike Meinhof's symbolic and dramatic exit from bourgeois life and simultaneous entry into illegality. In his autobiography, Müller narrates this episode, recounting how Meinhof and the group that had formed around Andreas Baader met in her apartment after an attempt against the office of *Der Spiegel* and threw the furniture out of the window.[20]

Ophelia appears again at the end of the play, tied with white gauze to a chair, physically trapped, motionless, but nonetheless promising, in the name of all the victims, that there will be uprisings. This is the section whose heading is partly quoted in this chapter's title: 'FIERCELY ENDURING / MILLENNIA / IN THE FEARFUL ARMOUR' (*HM*, 553). It is a quotation from Friedrich Hölderlin, namely from Fragment No. Seven. This should be read along with Fragment No. Six, which simply says 'SHAKESPEAR'.[21] The editorial order of the fragments in editions of Hölderlin might seem to suggest that it is Shakespeare who fiercely waits within the armour. In his famous speech delivered in 1988 to the East German Shakespeare Society, Müller made this exact point:

> A fragment by Hölderlin describes the unreleased Shakespeare: FIERCELY ENDURING / IN THE FEARFUL ARMOUR / MILLENNIA. Shakespeare's wilderness. What does he wait for, why in armour and for how long yet.[22]

In *Hamletmaschine*, the armour is the ghost's body armour which is so frequently mentioned in *Hamlet*. In the context of Ophelia's scene, however, it looks as if it is she who is trapped in the armour of her white gauze, exposed, that is, to the customary and disabling insinuation of madness, a suggestion which was made, in 2002, in the case of Ulrike Meinhof. While arguably a fierce endurance is indeed expressed in Ophelia's last scene, the reference to the armour demands that one go back to the previous scene for a complete identification between prison and armour.

Scene Four opens with an empty suit of armour on stage, an axe stuck in the helmet. The Hamlet Performer removes mask and costume and refuses to play his role. He then fantasizes what his role could have been had it been performed, and this leads to a description of a violent uprising, modelled upon the 1956 Budapest uprising, in which his place, the position he occupies, is multiple to say the least: 'My place, were my drama yet to take place, would be on both sides of the front, between the frontlines, over and above them' (*HM*, 550). This multiple position-taking, not simply a non-position or a refusal to take a position, is what leads to the final paradox of describing the GDR as a prison surrounded by a giant wall, a wall that Müller in another text aptly described as 'an image of the actual situation in armed concrete'.[23] The split subjectivity leads the Hamlet Performer to declare: 'I am my own prisoner' (*HM*, 551). Comfort and privileges are proved to have a tighter grip over this figure of the intellectual than any prison wall: 'How do you spell COMPLACENCY' (*HM*, 551). The situation is eventually spelled out:

> In the solitude of airports
> I breathe again I am
> A privileged person My nausea
> Is a privilege
> Protected by wall
> Barbed wire prison

(*HM*, 552)

The wall and the barbed wire, the distinctive components of a carceral space, are also the instruments of protection, the physical marks of an opponent, the East German state, which justified the continuous criticism from within that so distinctively characterized Müller's texts. The prison thus becomes the armour into which Hamlet steps at the end of the scene, after which he uses the axe to split the heads of three naked women masked as Marx, Lenin and Mao. The following indication, 'Snow. Ice Age' (*HM*, 553), which has been interpreted as referring to capitalism in Müller-cipher,[24] also alludes to the petrifaction and abandonment of all hope in the notion of 'really existing socialism', with which intellectuals, represented in this play by Hamlet, compromise: 'the real, effectual revolution must enter suspended animation for an eon or so.'[25] To enter the armour, to paralyse oneself in the carapace so characteristic of artists in the Socialist bloc, is equivalent to the ultimate compromise.[26] It means voluntary imprisonment behind the defensive wall and a fierce wait, for millennia if need be, for another chance of hope.[27]

In the same year as *Hamletmaschine*, Müller wrote a famous letter to Reiner Steinweg about the Brechtian didactic play, in which Müller declared he no longer knew his addressees, his plays being now theatrical experiments detached from any possibility of having an impact or an effect.[28] This is certainly related to the fact that, up to the moment when he received the National Prize of the GDR in 1986, an event that made him within the following year the most performed author in East Germany,[29] a great number of Müller's plays had been prohibited in the GDR both on the stage and in print. These texts that by 1977, for historical reasons, had ceased to have any critical potential he called 'isolated texts waiting for history'.[30]

Emptying the prison

The wait was not long. History (or, according to some wishful-thinking late-Hegelians, its end) came twelve years later, as Müller was rehearsing both *Hamlet* and *Hamletmaschine* at the Deutsches Theater. The five-hour (excluding the intervals) *Hamlet/Maschine* was presented on 24 March 1990 in a city without a wall.[31] During a mass demonstration in Alexanderplatz on 4 November 1989, Müller had been given the chance to make a speech, an opportunity that he used to read a pamphlet demanding independent unions.[32] The unexpected text was booed and whistled, there being an evident lack of understanding between the demonstrators and the critical voice of the rapidly decaying regime.[33] As the ghost in the *Hamlet/Maschine* production went from representing Stalin to also representing the Deutsche Bank,[34] Müller confessed his discomfort at finding himself without an opponent.[35] Müller's participation in that historical moment had been awkward and confused, and could be compared to that of Brecht during the 1953 uprising.[36] In what could be read as an irresistible parallel with Günter Grass's *Die Plebejer proben den Aufstand* (*The Plebeians Rehearse the Uprising*, 1966), a play that fantasized a painful encounter between a Brecht figure rehearsing a version of *Coriolanus* and the workers from the June 1953 uprising, Müller described 'the uncomfortable feeling', during the demonstration of 4 November, 'that a theatre was being staged there',[37] that this uprising too had a peculiar relation to the theatre which was at odds with his own political hopes.[38]

The wall was demolished, the prison was temporarily emptied and Müller took to writing poems and giving interviews. In the period following 1989 he completed only one play, *Germania 3 Gespenster am toten Mann* (*Germania 3 Ghosts at the Dead Man*), which was published posthumously in 1996. Interestingly, *Germania 3* returns to the connection between *Hamlet* and the Berlin Wall. The play begins with the following stage direction: '*Night. The Berlin Wall. THÄLMANN and ULBRICHT keep sentry.*'[39] The obvious reference is *Hamlet*, which begins with two armed sentinels guarding the battlements at night. In *Germania 3*, the battlements become the Berlin Wall, while its two sentinels are icons from the history of the German Communist Party. As in Hamlet's comparison between Denmark and a prison, the entire East German territory is presented as one giant prison – houses are called 'fuck cells' (*Fickzellen*) by Ulbricht.[40] Unlike its depiction in *Hamletmaschine*, however, the wall is now nothing but a fortification made to incarcerate its own builders.

Conflict on ice

Heiner Müller's engagement with Shakespeare is a classic case of a lifelong interest in both his work and imagined figure. Shakespeare provided Müller with a powerful mediation in dealing with conflicted political and aesthetic issues in a German context which, as is well known, had already made Shakespeare into a figure of authority to back a considerable number of different and contradictory positions. Müller's appropriation of this tradition in *Hamletmaschine* combined a significant revision of Brechtian aesthetics with a paradoxical view of the GDR as both a prison and an armour. The play was probably Müller's most extreme reaction to GDR politics; its prohibition in his own country led to its being staged and published abroad, a contingency which bypassed open internal conflict. Being cut off from GDR audiences, Müller could not help but contend that, in this case, history, meaning conflict, was being put on ice and postponed. Müller's dramatization of conflict through Shakespeare, a previously successful strategy in *Macbeth, nach Shakespeare*, had found its most acute point in *Hamletmaschine*. Although robbed of an immediate impact in the GDR, the play did considerable damage in the theatrical and political climate of the FRG, and has continued to do so in a reunited Germany and abroad, ensuring that its oblique use of Shakespeare remains as bewildering and confrontational as ever.

Notes

1. This study has taken shape in the margins of a larger ongoing doctoral project, called *Texts Waiting for History: William Shakespeare Rewritten by Heiner Müller*, which focuses on Heiner Müller's reception of the work and figure of William Shakespeare, with a specific focus on dramatic rewritings.
2. All quotations from Shakespeare are from *The Norton Shakespeare*, ed. by Stephen Greenblatt et al. (New York and London: Norton, 2008).
3. Michel Foucault, *Discipline and Punish: The Birth of the Prison*, trans. by Alan Sheridan (Harmondsworth and New York: Penguin, 1991), 308.
4. Theodor W. Adorno, *Critical Models: Interventions and Catchwords*, trans. by Henry W. Pickford (New York: Columbia University Press, 2005), 265.

154 Shakespeare and Conflict

5. This paragraph roughly tracks Müller's partly unreliable narrative of the events in his autobiography. For a biographical account of the same events, see Jan-Christoph Hauschild, *Heiner Müller oder Das Prinzip Zweifel. Eine Biographie* (Berlin: Aufbau Taschenbuch, 2003), 186–219. For a more thorough and academic account of the so-called *Resettler* affair, as well as for a collection of documents pertaining to these events, see Matthias Braun, *Drama um eine Komödie: Das Ensemble von SED und Staatssicherheit, FDJ und Ministerium der Kultur gegen Heiner Müllers* Die Umsiedlerin oder Das Leben auf dem Lande *im Oktober 1961* (Berlin: Chistoph Links, 1995).

6. Heiner Müller, *Werke 9 – Eine Autobiographie*, ed. by Frank Hörnigk (Frankfurt am Main: Suhrkamp, 2005), 131. Unless otherwise stated, all translations are my own.

7. Müller, *Werke 9*, 132–3.

8. Heiner Müller, *Werke 8 – Die Schriften*, ed. by Frank Hörnigk (Frankfurt am Main: Suhrkamp, 2005), 150–2.

9. Müller, *Werke 9*, 139.

10. Lawrence Guntner, 'Brecht and Beyond: Shakespeare on the East German Stage', in *Foreign Shakespeare: Contemporary Performance*, ed. by Dennis Kennedy (Cambridge: Cambridge University Press, 1995), 109–39 (114).

11. See Heiner Müller, *Werke 10 – Gespräche 1*, ed. by Frank Hörnigk (Frankfurt am Main: Suhrkamp, 2008), 212.

12. See Müller, *Werke 9*, 141; Manfred Pfister, 'Hamlets Made in Germany, East and West', in *Shakespeare in the New Europe*, ed. by Michael Hattaway et al. (Sheffield: Sheffield Academic Press, 1994), 76–91 (90–1); Florence Baillet, *Heiner Müller* (Paris: Belin, 2003), 186.

13. Heiner Müller, *Werke 3 – Die Stücke 1*, ed. by Frank Hörnigk (Frankfurt am Main: Suhrkamp, 2000), 349. For a slightly ambivalent justification of the wall by Müller in 1985, see Müller, *Werke 10*, 393.

14. Müller, *Werke 9*, 87. Müller even went so far as saying that 'Germany was a good material for drama up to the reunification. I fear that, with the end of the GDR, Shakespeare reception in Germany may have come to an end.' Müller, *Werke 9*, 209–10.

15. Müller often deconstructed discourses of dissidence as well as Western criticisms of the GDR. In a group discussion from 1985, when asked why he opted to stay in the GDR, when he could easily leave, Müller answered: 'Yes, to begin with I would return the question. You live here [in the FRG] and you must certainly have a lot against the Federal Republic, but you still live here, and you prefer to live here. And I consider it somewhat odd that one always asks to people who come here from the GDR why it is that they live in the GDR in the first place.' Müller, *Werke 10*, 406.

16. 'I like to stand with a leg on both sides of the Wall. It may perhaps be a schizophrenic position, but no other seems real enough for me.' Müller, *Werke 10*, 196.

17. This coincidence of prison and armour was made explicit by Müller in an interview led by Alexander Kluge. In it, Müller compared revolution with a column of tanks, whose main characteristic was 'protection in prison. That is, prison as protection and protection as prison.' Heiner Müller, *Werke 11 – Gespräche 2*, ed. by Frank Hörnigk (Frankfurt am Main: Suhrkamp, 2008), 643.

18. Heiner Müller, *Werke 4 – Die Stücke 2*, ed. by Frank Hörnigk (Frankfurt am Main: Suhrkamp, 2001), 546. Quotations are taken from Carl Weber's translation, with occasional silent modifications: Heiner Müller, *Hamletmachine and Other Texts for the Stage*, ed. and trans. by Carl Weber (New York: Performing Arts Journal Publications, 1984). For this reason, in further quotations (noted parenthetically in the text with the abbreviation *HM*) the page numbers in brackets will refer to the German text.

19. The comparison was common in such contexts, so Ann Thompson and Neil Taylor tell us: 'The concept of the whole state as a prison dominated a number of productions of *Hamlet* in the former Soviet Union and eastern Europe during communist rule, most notably exemplified by the "Iron Curtain *Hamlet*" directed by Nikolai Okhlopkov in Moscow in 1954.' Ann Thompson and Neil Taylor, 'Appendix 1: Folio-Only Passages', in *Hamlet*, by William Shakespeare, ed. by Ann Thompson and Neil Taylor (London: Thomson Learning, 2006), 465–73 (466n).

20. Müller, *Werke 9*, 230–1.

21. Friedrich Hölderlin, *Sämtliche Gedichte und Hyperion*, ed. by Jochen Schmidt (Frankfurt am Main and Leipzig: Insel, 2001), 425–6.

22. Müller, *Werke 8*, 335.

23. Müller, *Werke 9*, 286. Lawrence Guntner has made use of the same image: 'The "material" Wall of bricks, concrete, and barbed wire soon became a "cultural wall" to keep unwanted cultural developments out and dissidents in line.' Lawrence Guntner, 'In Search of a Socialist Shakespeare: *Hamlet* on East German Stages', in *Shakespeare in the Worlds of Communism and Socialism*, ed. by Irena R. Makaryk and Joseph G. Price (Toronto: University of Toronto Press, 2006), 177–204 (181).

24. Müller, *Werke 10*, 20.

25. Jonathan Kalb, *The Theatre of Heiner Müller* (Cambridge: Cambridge University Press, 1998), 119.

26. Roland Petersohn, *Heiner Müllers Shakespeare-Rezeption* (Frankfurt am Main: Peter Lang, 1993), 93.

27. Müller's abandonment of hope in this text is, despite what some authors say (see Guntner, 'Brecht', 130), and notwithstanding Müller's customary scepticism, a matter of historical circumstance. The petrifaction of hope in *Hamletmaschine* is followed, for instance, by the new power relations of *Anatomie Titus Fall of Rome ein Shakespearekommentar* (*Anatomy Titus Fall of Rome A Shakespeare Commentary*, 1985), in which a new hope comes from the Third World, represented by the Goths of *Titus Andronicus*. Given Müller's heterodox Marxism, it should be added that this does not refer to a new hope of humanist reconcilement, but to a new chance for class struggle in Europe. See Müller, *Werke 10*, 172.

28. Müller, *Werke 8*, 187.

29. Müller, *Werke 9*, 279–80.

30. Müller, *Werke 8*, 187.

31. For an account of this production, see Wilhelm Hortmann, *Shakespeare on the German Stage: The Twentieth Century. With a Section on Shakespeare on Stage in the German Democratic Republic by Maik Hamburger* (Cambridge and New York: Cambridge University Press, 1998), 428–34; Guntner, 'Brecht', 130–4; Guntner, 'In Search of', 193–6.

32. Müller, *Werke 8*, 359–60.
33. Müller, *Werke 9*, 279.
34. Müller, *Werke 11*, 620, 701.
35. Müller, *Werke 9*, 276.
36. In response to the uprising in East Berlin on 17 June 1953, Brecht sent an open letter to Walter Ulbricht, the General Secretary of the SED (the Socialist Unity Party), in which he first referred to the reasons for the uprising, which he thought were just, after which he expressed his solidarity with the SED. On 21 June 1953, the government had the letter published in the party newspaper *Neues Deutschland*, but included only the complimentary declaration of solidarity. Brecht's intended strategy apart, this produced very negative effects, and his plays were for some time dropped from West German theatres.
37. Müller, *Werke 9*, 278.
38. See Baillet, 190 and Pfister, 76–7. Müller says that this demonstration had actually been registered with the police and therefore, of course, with the STASI, so that 'it was basically theatre, with a calculated outcome'. Heiner Müller, *Werke 12 – Gespräche 3*, ed. by Frank Hörnigk (Frankfurt am Main: Suhrkamp, 2008), 486.
39. Heiner Müller, *Werke 5 – Die Stücke 3*, ed. by Frank Hörnigk (Frankfurt am Main: Suhrkamp, 2002), 255. Quotations in English are taken from Heiner Müller, *A Heiner Müller Reader*, ed. and trans. by Carl Weber (Baltimore and London: Johns Hopkins University Press, 2001).
40. Müller, *Werke 5*, 255.

12

From Individual Conflict to Interlocking Conflicts: Performing *The Merchant of Venice* for New European Audiences

Francesca Rayner

Imagining a New Europe

Writing in 1994, after the fall of the Berlin Wall and the Eastern European revolutions that came in its wake, Michael Hattaway, Boika Sokolova and Derek Roper noted that at their 1991 conference on 'Shakespeare in the New Europe', 'there were still euphoric feelings of liberation, visions of a dream come true, glimpses of a redeemed "New Europe" whose proud citizens we were ready to become'; however, they observed, by 1994 this euphoria had already begun to dissipate in the face of the resurgence of nationalism as well as conflicts between regional, national and local interests. Such processes would accelerate in the next few years as 'the fictional communities of the nation were replaced by even more destructive communities of the tribe'.[1]

Ten years after the 'Shakespeare in the New Europe' conference, Janelle Reinelt envisaged the New Europe as a shadowy presence emerging from the contours of the old as both its complement and its critique. From a North American perspective, Reinelt justifies her interest in the possibilities of such a formation in terms of its potential contrast with the United States, arguing that the New Europe represented at the time 'an unfilled signifier, an almost-empty term capable of endless mutations and transformations, an open and elusive term of great/little significance and power'. Reinelt is more interested in the supranational structure that came to be known as 'Fortress Europe' than in the post-revolutionary transformations in Eastern Europe, and her analysis of contemporary British drama's engagement with the theme of Europe is framed by this context, since she discusses plays which 'take up issues of displacement and belonging, interrogate what constitutes membership in any "European community", and raise issues of territoriality, historical memory and social justice'.[2]

Writing in 2011 amid a worldwide economic crisis that has thrown into relief the fragilities of this extended New Europe, with the further destabilizing factor of the recent waves of migration from Northern Africa following the uprisings and regime changes of the so-called Arab Spring, Reinelt's vision of this extended Europe as 'a liminal concept, fluid and indeterminate, and most importantly, a site of possible struggle' which 'could signal a call for an inclusive, socially responsible super-democracy' seems indeed remote.[3] Yet what this briefest of overviews of critical responses to the New Europe makes clear is not only how history very quickly overtakes theory, but also how limited the appeal of thinking through questions related to the New Europe appears in comparison with the plethora of nationally-based analytical frameworks for Shakespeare and performance. Evidently, there are valid reasons for this, as countries have distinct histories and performance traditions, not to mention intracultural specificities. Totalizing narratives across these divergent realities are not only impossible tasks but also politically undesirable. Yet the performance of a play like *The Merchant of Venice* seems to demand consideration within the shifting histories of Europe as well as within national frameworks, both because the politicized history of Jewishness has itself extended across national borders, and because similar questions related to the contemporary reception of the play have been raised in a variety of national contexts.[4] Consequently, the following analysis of a 2008 production of the play in Portugal takes full account of the local and national factors which shaped these performances, but it also sees itself as a contribution towards a wider cartography of New European performances of the play and of the ways in which 'Shakespeare' and 'conflict' have been (re)created within them. As such, it prefaces discussion of the Portuguese performances with that of three performances from other national contexts that, in their different ways, illustrate issues which create a frame of reference for the production that is the focus of this chapter.

The Merchant of Venice in the New Europe

Taking place as it did one year before the fall of the Berlin Wall, Peter Zadek's 1988 production of *The Merchant of Venice* at the Vienna Burgtheater, with Gert Voss in the role of Shylock, can be seen as a turning point in the transition from Old to New European frameworks for the play. Staged at the time of the Kurt Waldheim controversy, the production necessarily invoked the legacy of Nazism, but it also functioned as a contemporary critique of international capitalism and the violence of the State of Israel against Palestinians. In this multipoliticized setting, the play's vexed question, 'Which is the Merchant here, and which the Jew?' (4.1.174),[5] was complicated by a performance context where, as Sabine Schülting has observed, 'Christian society cannot ward off the "foreigners", since the boundary between the self and its others has become blurred.'[6] Zadek's production challenged what had become the orthodoxies of postwar performances of the play. It changed the narrative of victimized Jews into a more compromised view of recent Jewish history, and it moved away from an exclusive focus on the figure of Shylock, opening up instead to a social and political setting which dehumanized both Jews and Christians. It was, as a result, an important step in the transition from what Schülting, following Wilhelm Hortmann, has referred to as 'expiation Shylocks'[7] towards more multidimensional representations of the character, and from a primary focus on an individualized conflict between Christian and Jew towards an emphasis on interlocking conflicts which placed religious antagonism within a wider nexus of power relations.

Emblematic of such shifts in a context neighbouring Portugal was the Centro Dramático Nacional of Spain's 1992 performance of *The Merchant of Venice*, after a thirty-year absence from the stage. The production took place against a background of political demonstrations concerned with immigration and the murder of a Latin American woman that had occurred the day before the production opened. Keith Gregor notes that the performances were 'intended as a forthright engagement with Spanish socio-political reality' and quotes the director José Carlos Plaza on his reasons for staging the play:

[The play] has a close relation to the preoccupations, obsessions and extremisms of a society like ours in which money has become a fundamental value for distinguishing between one social class and another. Other problems don't seem to be of so much interest or, at least, there is a certain insensitivity towards them, as with what is happening now with the problems of North Africans who are trying to escape their poverty and who are drowning in order to reach the promised land. In the *Merchant of Venice* I take sides and join the band of the pariahs – in this case, the Jews.[8]

Despite this clear sense of the performances as a committed social intervention, Gregor's analysis suggests that their political impetus was undermined by 'glitz and glamour',[9] as seen in the casting of the singer and actress Ana Belén as Portia, and a degree of opportunistic gesturing towards the provocative in the explicitly gay relationship between Bassanio and Antonio. What the performances illustrate more clearly, however, is the way in which the play was being used less to tell a story about the history of the Jews than to debate contemporary multiculturalism within Spain, with the nexus of interlocking power relations still centred on religion, but also encompassing questions of race and sexuality. This prompts the question, however, as to what extent the experiences of Shakespeare's Jews can be made to stand in for contemporary society's various others in ways that do not simply conflate different religious and racial identities.

Whilst questions of fragmentation within the New Europe have tended to be more thematic than stylistic, the new millennium has witnessed occasional attempts to link concerns with multiple and often conflicting identity formations with a more postmodern aesthetics. An example of such an approach is the 2009 *Merchant of Venice* directed by Edward Hall for his all-male Propeller company in the United Kingdom. Boika Sokolova has discussed this production in terms of a Britain 'engulfed by massive social problems [...] a country in conflict with itself'. Venice here became a literal prison characterized by 'racial tensions, gang turf wars and the links between crime, money and sex', while renderings of 'Onward, Christian Soldiers' and 'Stand Up for Jesus' reinforced the religious tribalism governing the prison.[10] In such a context, the gender and sexual crossings prompted by the all-male cast were more often connected with exploitation and survival than with playful incursions into otherness, and Shylock's brutality was indistinguishable from that of the other inmates and indeed of the institution itself. In a moment of exemplary black humour, for example, the production's Shylock (Richard Clothier) assaulted Salerio (Sam Swainsbury) and gouged out his left eye, before proclaiming 'Hath not a Jew eyes?' The channelling of the production's aesthetics of disintegration through the body created a highly experiential performance where the marks of violence on the performing bodies inscribed gender, sexual and religious difference across a continuum of brutalized selves.

Portuguese theatre history and *The Merchant of Venice*

Political conflicts involving Jews and Jewishness have marked key periods of theatre history in Portugal. In the eighteenth century, the dramatist António José da Silva (1705–39), who is even now referred to in critical editions as 'The Jew' (*O Judeu*), wrote a series of comic operas which were performed at the popular Teatro do Bairro Alto in Lisbon during the 1730s. Although these performances were highly successful with audiences, their satire of an unscrupulous church and a lascivious monarch brought the dramatist into conflict with the Inquisition and after a particularly malevolent trial involving a number of forced testimonies, he was burnt at an *auto-da-fé*, despite his continuing insistence that he was a Christian.

Two centuries later, the dramatist Bernardo Santareno wrote *O Judeu* (1966), a play which drew parallels between da Silva's persecution and contemporary Portugal under the Fascist 'New State' (Estado Novo, 1933–74). Using a range of Brechtian devices, including a narrator and excerpts from da Silva's operas, Santareno linked the regime of fear surrounding the eighteenth-century dramatist to the political detention and torture of opponents under Salazar's dictatorship. Santareno, who himself came from a Jewish background, included in the play a dream where da Silva has a vision of the Nazi concentration camps; and in the scene where the eighteenth-century Jew is burnt at the stake, Santareno challenges contemporary audiences never to forget this episode and to protest against the hatred and intolerance of their own time. Santareno knew as he was writing the play that it would not be staged, and his predictions proved true: it was censored immediately and only performed on a Portuguese stage much later, in 1981. This production added yet another layer of theatre history, for the performances took place at Portugal's main national theatre, the Dona Maria II in Lisbon, a nineteenth-century building erected on what had been the site of the Palace of the Inquisition.

These traces of a rich, though discontinuous national tradition may go some way towards explaining why Shakespeare's *The Merchant of Venice* has been performed infrequently in Portugal. The Italians Ermete Novelli and Emmanuel Rossi brought the play to Portugal in the nineteenth century as a vehicle for their own performances as Shylock and, in the twentieth century, it was subject to a variety of adaptations and textual additions that suggest that this play, which resists performance as a straightforward comedy, elicits continuing discomfort.[11] Within this context, the staging of the play by Ricardo Pais at Porto's Teatro Nacional São João in 2008, with a specially commissioned new translation, had all the makings of a significant theatrical event. This sense of exceptionality was heightened by the fact that, by representing yet another instance of conflicted Portuguese theatrical engagements with Jewishness, marked this time by economics and politics, *The Merchant of Venice* was Pais's last major production at the São João before he resigned as its Artistic Director. In the 'Reading Manual' that accompanied the performances, Pais justified his decision to audiences by stating that 'Theatre, as an institution and artistic practice, no longer has any particular space or place in public sector administration, which is increasingly authoritarian, secretive and abusive of its best practitioners.'[12] *The Merchant of Venice* might seem a curious choice for a swansong, but given that Pais had established much of his reputation on the basis of his postmodern stagings of Shakespeare, and within a political context where his theatre work had been compromised by continuous wrangling with the government over funding, a Shakespeare comedy with such a central focus on money might sum up both the achievements and the frustrations that led to his resignation.

Contextualizing the play

Each new performance of *The Merchant of Venice* necessarily becomes an intervention in its politicized performance history, whether this was the intention of the director and the performers or not. For this reason, recent performances of *The Merchant of Venice* have often felt the need to contextualize the play and its representations of Jewishness, either by providing a historical background or through attention to performance setting. As with Pais's other performances of Shakespeare, contemporary critical theory played an important role in the thinking behind the Porto performances. Pais openly acknowledged his debt to the North American critic, Janet Adelman's *Blood Relations: Christian and Jew in the Merchant of Venice* (2008) and invited her to Porto to take part in a series of public sessions organized by the theatre to provide a historical background on the experience of the Jews in Portugal and to discuss critical perspectives on *The Merchant of Venice*. Among the speakers were historians, novelists, academics, translators and prominent members of the Jewish community in Lisbon, representing therefore a broad variety of perspectives both on the cultural issues in general and, specifically, those showcased by the play. During one of the sessions, the audience were challenged to date representations of Jews from different historical periods, and were surprised to find out how complex this task turned out to be. What the sessions did not, however, in any manner discuss was the contemporary place of Jewishness within Portugal.[13] Janet Adelman herself, who had been invited to talk about the ideas outlined in her book, in fact spent much of her talk praising Pais's production for the insights it had afforded *her*. Moreover, although the sessions were well-attended and some of the individual contributions were included within the production programme, both the sessions and these contributions were essentially performance adjuncts and the majority of the audience would have relied exclusively on the performances for their understanding of the play. Esther Mucznik, the Vice-President of the Jewish Community in Lisbon and one of the speakers at the sessions, did, however, later comment in an article for the national newspaper *O Público* that the risks the staging of the play involved had been worthwhile, 'because debate is always preferable to censorship'.[14]

The text as image: Antonio and Shylock's common bond

For the performances, Pais regrouped the textual scenes set in Venice in the first half and those set in Belmont in the second. His decision to separate the Venice and Belmont scenes stemmed from a desire to create new moments of suspense (who are the two 'men' in the trial scene, for example, and how do they know Antonio and Bassanio?) which would only be resolved in the second half of the play. Such major reconfigurations of Shakespearean texts have been rare in contemporary Portuguese productions and Pais himself referred to the performance as a 'free version'[15] of the play. Such a radical alteration might be viewed within the wider context of Pais's impending resignation, where this bold move would have confirmed his authority as a director of Shakespeare and contributed towards his theatrical legacy. The negative corollary of this decision, though, was that it created a first half full of action followed by a rather dull second half. Indeed, many in the audience commented that little would have been lost if they had left during the interval.

One of the key questions raised by postmodern performances of Shakespeare is the status of the image within a visually saturated culture. Pais's staging explored the power of individual images to substantiate a theatrical and social viewpoint on the play. He did so through a particularly potent stage image that strategically came just after the interval – its positioning in a liminal space between the two halves of the play conditioned its impact, for it was one of the few moments where the darker hues of Venice momentarily challenged the artificial light of Belmont. The image was referred to by cast, director and translator as 'Antonio's reverie' and was explained by the translator Daniel Jonas in terms of a psychic doubling between Antonio and Shylock:

> It seemed to us at a certain stage that there might be a psychological reading of Antonio, a nightmare that could suggest a doubling or an

equivalence between the two heavyweights of the play. This led to the idea of Antonio appropriating the words of Shylock to express a great weight, a major psychic pressure, a traumatic episode. He speaks lines that are not his, including one of Aragon's lines.[16]

This notion of the interdependency of Antonio and Shylock is indebted to Pais's and Jonas's reading of Adelman's *Blood Relations*, particularly its exploration of the anxieties resulting from Christianity's roots in Judaism and subsequent attempts to supersede these Jewish roots by distancing the Jew as 'other'. Adelman argues that this denied consanguinity between Christian and Jew frames the conflicts of the play, constructing Shylock as a figment of Antonio's desire and a 'figure for the disowned other within the self'.[17]

The onstage embodiment of this interdependency emphasized the physicality of their bond. Out of the dark at the back of the stage, lighting revealed the bodies of the actor playing Shylock (António Durães) lying on top of the actor playing Antonio (Albano Jerónimo), both partially hidden by smoke (see Figure 12.1). As Durães is significantly larger than Jerónimo, this was something of a physical feat, especially as Jerónimo continued to recite lines from the play while pinned down by Durães's considerable bulk. There is no doubt as to the image's

Figure 12.1   Shylock (António Durães) lying on top of Antonio (Albano Jerónimo) in Ricardo Pais's production of *The Merchant of Venice*. Porto, Teatro Nacional São João, 2008. Courtesy of the photographer, João Tuna

unsettling power. It starkly conveyed Antonio's perception of the very little that separated him from Shylock and made Shylock embody, in physical as well as moral terms, a 'thing of darkness' which Antonio refused to acknowledge as his own. However, although it carried a dramatic force that condensed within it a particular understanding of the relationship between the 'two heavyweights of the play', this psychological view of Christian and Jew framed their relationship in essentially individual terms. While the performances hinted elsewhere at a rather superficial link between Antonio's self-hatred and his homosexuality, the projection of this self-hatred onto Shylock was cast here as a personal rather than a political failing. Indeed, the image effectively *evacuated* the social and the political, allowing the individual and the theatrical to come more fully to the fore. Within such a setting, critical reviews of the performances found it difficult to locate António Durães's mercurial Shylock, with his long black tunic and yellow star. Valdemar Cruz in *O Expresso* wondered whether this Jew was 'the one who stifles the camps of Sabra and Shatila in Palestine [*sic*] or the one who carries with him the memory of the Holocaust',[18] while Jorge Louraço Figueira in *O Público* argued that the smoke surrounding Antonio and Shylock simultaneously evoked 'an *auto-da-fé* and the gas chambers'.[19]

Belonging and displacement: Jessica's New European citizenship

In a move reminiscent of the ending of Michael Radford's 2004 film version of *The Merchant of Venice*, Pais's performances ended with Jessica's story. However, while Radford's ending challenged Shylock's patriarchal view of Jessica's callousness and emphasized instead the transmission of a maternal Jewish heritage through her mother's ring, Pais gave the final word to Jessica (Sara Carinhas, Figure 12.2) and Lorenzo (José Eduardo Silva) with their ambiguously-toned exchanges on music. This relocation sidelined the two Christian couples and their emphasis on marriage and instead placed centre stage an interfaith couple who actually voice the possibility that their future together might not be a happy one.[20]

In *Blood Relations*, Adelman devotes a whole chapter to the figure of Jessica and her transgression of boundaries that are religious (Jew-Christian), protoracial (Hebrew-Gentile), and national (stranger-citizen). However, Adelman points out that Jessica retains her Jewish blood, which is potentially passed on to any of her children with Lorenzo, meaning that she will continue to be seen as an outsider in Belmont.[21]

Figure 12.2   Jessica (Sara Carinhas) in Ricardo Pais's production of *The Merchant of Venice*. Porto, Teatro Nacional São João, 2008. Courtesy of the photographer, João Tuna

For Ricardo Pais, such intersections also gave Jessica an important role in performance, since 'Jessica embodies something that is, for me, central to the play – ambivalence'.[22] This ambivalence was connected in particular with her doubled Christian and Jewish identity, but also with the ways in which her gender further complicates her religious and racial identity. It is an ambivalence that leads not to anger or violence as with Antonio and Shylock, but to sadness and stasis. Commenting on Jessica's melancholy at hearing 'sweet music' (5.1.69), Pais noted that 'music suggests to Jessica [...] melancholy because it is equivalent in some sense to the recuperation of what she has lost',[23] while Daniel Jonas suggested that 'this melancholy, which marks Shylock and Antonio, reappears at the end – in Jessica'.[24] As such, this final, halting exchange linked Shylock's fate in the first half with Jessica's sadness in the second. It also linked the performative with the social as, keying into a particularly New European form of ambivalence, the figure of the Jewish daughter in an overwhelmingly Christian society came to crystallize the contradictions which surround religious belief for young women straddling two religious cultures or accommodating a religious background within a secular state. The recognition of ambivalence, however, seemed only to promote stasis, as Jessica and Lorenzo remained at opposite ends of the stage until the very close of the play. The performances presented no solution to these contemporary double binds and ended instead on a poignant note as Lorenzo's verbal evocation of the music of the spheres evanesced into haunting violin music before fading into darkness and silence.

Pais's staging of the play can thus be viewed as a challenging artistic intervention into an increasingly multifaith, multiethnic Europe, with the parallel between a defeated Shylock and an uncertain Jessica linking Old and New European readings of the play. It was certainly a success since it sold out each night and continued to be staged after the December break well into the new year, attracting in particular a younger audience. Just as with the Propeller performances, the production's search for new narratives in which to frame the play also encompassed a reaching out towards new ways of staging those narratives. Within its aesthetics of fragmentation, for example, a memorable image was used to narrate a moral fable about the psychology of hatred, and a fragmentary verbal exchange was deployed to give voice to the multiplicity at the heart of contemporary New European identities. What the performances lost in linearity, they tended to regain in immediacy, although there is always a risk, partially realized in the less accomplished second half, that the pursuit of immediacy will impact negatively on the performance as a whole. However, it is precisely this continuing insistence on taking risks, even when the results are not entirely successful, that has distinguished Ricardo Pais's work with Shakespeare at the São João and which will be greatly missed in the redrawn contours of an austere and penny-pinching New Europe.

Notes

1. Michael Hattaway, Boika Sokolova and Derek Roper, 'Introduction', in *Shakespeare in the New Europe*, ed. by Michael Hattaway, Boika Sokolova and Derek Roper (Sheffield: Sheffield Academic Press, 1994), 15–21 (15–16).
2. Janelle Reinelt, 'Performing Europe: Identity Formation for a "New" Europe', in *Theatre, History and National Identities*, ed. by Helka Makinen, S.E. Wilmer and W.B. Worthen (Helsinki: Helsinki University Press, 2001), 227–55 (227, 237).
3. Reinelt, 227.

4. I would like to thank Masolino D'Amico, Juan Cerdá, Nicoleta Cinpoes, Nancy Isenberg, Ludwig Schnauder, Sara Soncini and Mariangela Tempera for their information on stagings of the play in different national contexts.
5. All quotations are taken from the New Cambridge Shakespeare edition (Cambridge: Cambridge University Press, 2003).
6. Sabine Schülting, '"I am not bound to please thee with my answers": *The Merchant of Venice* on the Post-War German stage', in *World-Wide Shakespeare: Local Appropriations in Film and Performance*, ed. by Sonia Massai (London and New York: Routledge, 2005), 65–71 (69). Schülting and Zeno Ackermann lead a research project at the Freie Universität Berlin, entitled 'Shylock und der (neue) deutsche Geist: Shakespeares *Der Kaufmann von Venedig* nach 1945', which looks at postwar representations of Shylock. See http://www.geisteswissenschaften.fu-berlin.de/v/shylock/index.html (accessed 4 November 2011).
7. Schülting, 68.
8. Quoted in Keith Gregor, *Shakespeare in the Spanish Theatre 1772 to the Present* (London and New York: Continuum, 2010), 115–16.
9. Gregor, 116.
10. Boika Sokolova, 'Broken Britain: *Othello, King Lear* and *The Merchant of Venice*', paper presented in the performance seminar at 'Shakespeare and Conflict: A European Perspective', Eighth International ESRA Conference, Pisa, November 2009. My thanks to Boika Sokolova for allowing me to quote from her unpublished text.
11. These have included the addition of prologues as well as complete rewritings of the play. Gareth Armstrong's solo *Shylock* (1998), for instance, which contextualizes its focus on Tubal within a history of the Jews 'from Moses to Barbra Streisand' has been performed twice in Portugal, once by the author himself in 2001 as part of the PoNTI Festival in Porto, and the second time in a Catalan performance directed by Luca Valentino, which premiered in Barcelona in 2000 and was then performed in Portugal during the Almada Theatre Festival in 2002 and 2003, in Barcelona in 2010 and at the Centro Universitario Teatrale (now the Centro Shylock) in Venice in 2011. Although not staged in Portugal, Arnold Wesker's politicized rewriting of the play, *Shylock*, has been staged within a variety of European countries. It premiered in Stockholm in 1976, in the UK at the Birmingham REP in 1978 and was later performed by the Jewish State Theatre in Bucharest in 2002. A stimulating essay by Maria Jones comparing performances of *The Merchant of Venice* with Wesker's *Shylock* can be found in Massai, *World-Wide Shakespeares*, 122–32.
12. Ricardo Pais, *O Mercador de Veneza: Manual de Leitura* (Porto: Teatro Nacional São João, 2008), 3; all translations from Portuguese sources, here and elsewhere, are mine.
13. This may have been because there is little organized anti-Semitism in contemporary Portugal. It also explains why in Portugal, as in Spain, the appropriation of the play as a forum for debate around multiculturalism often involves racial and religious conflations or a distance between the historical context of the text and the contemporary framework of its reception.
14. Esther Mucznik, 'Shakespeare 400 depois', *O Público*, 20 November 2008, 41. It is worth noting that this article appeared in the main newspaper, while other reviews appeared in newspaper supplements. This suggests that the

readership for this article may have been greater than for the reviews. Mucznik's words also indicate that in the aftermath of theatrical censorship, Portugal vigorously opposes prohibition.

15. Pais, *Manual*, 3.
16. Daniel Jonas quoted in Pedro Sobrado, 'Quarente e nove degraus: Extractos dos ensaios de mesa', in *Manual de Leitura*, 10–13 (10).
17. Janet Adelman, *Blood Relations: Christian and Jew in the Merchant of Venice* (Chicago: Chicago University Press, 2008), 12.
18. Valdemar Cruz, 'A Cena do Ódio', *O Público*, 15 November 2008, 28.
19. Jorge Louraço Figueira, 'O Sonho do Judeu e o pesadelo do cristão', *O Público*, 25 November 2008, 13.
20. Jorge Louraço Figueira was the only reviewer to note this relocation and its connection with the earlier image of Antonio and Shylock. In his four-star review of the performances, he also remarked the continuity with the nineteenth-century practice of joining together the scenes from the two locations of the play.
21. A similar argument is advanced by Stephen Orgel in *Imagining Shakespeare* (Basingstoke and New York: Palgrave Macmillan, 2003), 144–62, where the author points out that in Jewish law, identity passes through the mother. Orgel's chapter also includes a fascinating rereading of the Roderigo Lopez case, which emphasizes the anti-papist context of the trial.
22. Pais quoted in Sobrado, 12.
23. Pais quoted in Sobrado, 13.
24. Jonas quoted in Sobrado, 13.

13
Cut'n'mix *King Lear*: *Second Generation* and Asian-British Identities

Alessandra Marino

Travelling cultures: in and beyond Europe

In the panorama of Shakespeare's reception, performance and criticism in India, *King Lear* has a very important role. Even though it does not deal with the discovery of the Indies or produce any iconic image of the Orient, *King Lear* is widely regarded as a play presenting human and family relationships in *masala* fashion. Amitava Roy deals extensively with the encounter between *King Lear* and the Asian subcontinent, underlining the ways in which the family dynamics that emerge in the play echo traditional Indian lifestyle:

> The familial organization of Lear's and Gloucester's households (grown-up daughters and sons staying with parents and within an extended family) is obsolete now in England (and the West) whereas it's still the norm in India. [...] Let me put it to you in a rather aggressive and polemical way: how can an English girl of 18 and above studying *King Lear* in college or university feel the agony of Lear vis-a-vis his daughters or appreciate Cordelia's self-sacrificing commitment to and life-giving care for her 'four score and more' year old father, when that student has already left home at sixteen plus and probably gets to meet her parents only once or twice annually at Christmas or similar get-togethers?[1]

Although the form and content of Roy's question can be problematic as well as disturbing for a Western audience, they interestingly reveal the existence of a culturalist side of contemporary Shakespeare Studies which reads Shakespeare with the accent on social relations, both within the plays and in the context of their reception. Roy suggests that in India the contemporariness of Lear is triggered by the surfacing correspondence between the aged king's family and the actual order of the Bengali/Indian domestic sphere, as 'the power-struggle between parents and children for property that we see in Lear's household is a not unfamiliar day-to-day experience for [us] Indians'.[2] What the critic means by 'household' is not merely the representation of an extended family; as the argument of his essay moves on to show how Shakespeare is undoubtedly a 'contemporary' in South Asia, it is the issue of property and the struggle for its division that becomes central.

As in Roy's account, Lear's splitting of the reign is central in K.R. Srinivasa Iyengar's *Shakespeare: His World and His Art* (originally published in 1964), which underscores how any audience in India will be captured by the play from this very act of dividing the land, a decision that foreshadows the tragic epilogue. Speaking from his own subjective point of view, Srinivasa Iyengar maintains that Lear's project to partition the kingdom 'sends a thrill of horror through us, and for a second chronology abdicates its function, history and legend mingle, the past invades the present, and we wonder whether it isn't the Partition of India that is being talked about'.[3]

The partition in *King Lear* recalls the division of India and Pakistan in 1947. This moment, which gave birth to the modern nations, for millions of people meant the loss of their land, house and family. From India to Pakistan and vice versa, Muslims and Hindus were forced to migrate to comply with the new order established after Independence. It is after this epochal change that a wave of migrants left the subcontinent to reach the centre of the former empire, where their recognized status of citizens ended up in conflict with a sense of foreignness within the newly inhabited country. Srinivasa Iyengar's comment thus indirectly raises the point that in narratives of partition and subsequent migration, the bond with the land is as central as it is in *King Lear*.

Property is indeed a major theme in Shakespeare's play, a fact highlighted by Joseph Warton who, in his classical analysis of *Lear* in *The Adventurer* (1753), shows that Lear's madness is implicit in the decision of dividing his reign.[4] This act, already in itself foolish, in combination with his daughters' greed transforms the family drama into a political power struggle.

The elements of family (dis)order and the relation with one's land exert a transversal grip on audiences, reverberating differently in space and time. Against the backdrop of the associations with Indian history suggested by Roy and Srinivasa Iyengar, this chapter shows how property and familial tensions can also be employed as central keys for analysing *Second Generation*, a TV serial remake of *King Lear* written by Neil Biswas, produced and broadcast in the UK by Channel 4 in 2003.[5]

Set between England and India in the 1990s, *Second Generation* is the story of Mr Sharma (King Lear), a businessman who left Calcutta in the 1960s to settle in south-east London. Here he experiences a controversial relationship with the country that is at one and the same time the agent responsible for splitting his motherland and the 'stepmother' to which he turns, and faces the difficulties involved in raising his children in such a culturally different environment. The story quickly turns into a reflection on cultural contamination which recalls the plot of *King Lear*: in a nuclear family with a dying father, three daughters struggle to decide about his life and the destiny of his 'empire', an Indian food factory.

The various conflicts arising are both inter- and intragenerational: all the subjects present different ways of performing cultural belonging and hybridity, but the serial does not promote a reduction of difference to any neatly drawn and homogeneous representation of successive waves of migrant identities. The contradictory sides of cultural change and national identification in the context of migration shape the main framework of this family drama; by exploring them together with the king's madness and its connection with patriarchy, this chapter examines the way in which *King Lear* is both quoted and reimagined in Neil Biswas's script.

Conflicting wor(l)ds

When the serial opens Mr Sharma is in a coma and Heere, his youngest daughter, is trying to rejoin the family she has left to follow her dreams and her love. At the hospital she finds out that her sisters want to turn off their father's life-support and take control of the family business. Their plan is not successful: Mr Sharma unexpectedly recovers and his blind rage turns against Heere and her English boyfriend. In the meantime, Priya and Reena, the Goneril-and-Regan-like sisters, secretly try to carry out their plan to sell the factory. A twist in the plot occurs when Heere falls in love with an old flame, Sam, the son of Mr Khan, a Muslim family friend. Sam and his brother Firoz can be considered the doubles of Edgar and Edmund in *King Lear*: the 'evil' Firoz, Reena's secret lover, betrays both his father and Mr Sharma in order to pursue his own interest and become the manager of Sharma's factory; Sam, on the other hand, attempts a reconciliation with his father until he finds him hanged in his own house. When Mr Kahn dies, this Gloucester-like figure goes on living in Sharma's madness. The nostalgia for a mythic origin and for a sense of rootedness eventually becomes the common thread binding together the obsessed old man, Heere and Sam. Sam/ Edgar rescues Heere/Cordelia and Sharma/King Lear to start a new life with them in Calcutta, while the two other daughters are left to deal with the destruction of their marriages and family life.

In *Second Generation*, the worlds of India and England are separate and yet inextricably intertwined. The passage from home, or family life, to the social context is a process that enables cultural crossings: the twofold nature of Asian-British identity becomes manifest in the language shift (Bengali/English) and in the intersecting and clashing traditions. Presenting a small-screen version of the successful characters in Gurinder Chadha's movies, Heere and Sam live in a 'third space',[6] between the inherited family culture and the outer world. They embody the main conflict of the TV serial and, as Biswas points out,

> This conflict between cultures is as much part of their identity as their bilingualness. What is difficult for (non-Asian) people to understand is that this is not only a negative force, but also a positive one. This conflict shapes us, makes us who we are – we can't just be British, we can't just be Asian. We have grown up as both. Our choices in life – love, marriage, career, location, religion – are continually influenced by at least two cultures.[7]

Heere, the youngest daughter, is a Cordelia figure: her independent spirit leads her to escape the code of behaviour imposed by the Hindu tradition and opt for exile from her family. Even when she tries to make things up with them, she is accused of being a runaway and of sleeping around. Once Mr Sharma learns of Heere's socially unacceptable relationship with an Englishman, he declares that she is 'no longer part of the family'; she is then cruelly driven away by the eldest sister Priya, who blames her for crossing the 'barriers of race, religion, infidelity'.[8]

Sam is a DJ and producer working in the fashionable world of the London music industry who, despite being an British-Indian born in London, declares he believes in mixing cultures 'only in music'. As he tries to seduce Heere, he states in Bengali that her white boyfriend will never be able to know her the way he does and, with this politically incorrect opinion, he raises the issue of intercultural and interracial relationships.

Between East and West: madness and the crisis of patriarchy

In Biswas's script, *King Lear* is reduced to the essential core of a family conflict, where the intimate bond between the characters catalyses the tragic effects. One of the reasons why Biswas chooses a Lear-like pattern is probably that the Shakespearean story belongs to the Indian imaginary as a widely-known fairytale. Amitava Roy summarizes it as follows:

> In the Eastern version the two evil daughters tell the foolish king that they love him as or like the sky and the Himalayas, while the youngest daughter tells him that she loves him like, and as much as, salt. The stupid old king does not realize that it is salt that gives a taste to all food, and allows us to relish all that we eat, and foolishly kicks out the good daughter.[9]

The Eastern tale mirrors the first act of Shakespeare's tragedy in which characters and power relations are already exposed.

In the fairytale as well as in *King Lear*, what causes the third child's banishment is a misunderstanding of the (un)professed love for her father. In the tragedy Cordelia's lines express the failure of her very ability to speak: 'Unhappy that I am, I cannot have / My heart into my mouth: I love your majesty / According to my bond; no more, nor less' (1.1.93–5).[10] In the parallel popular story, the Indian Cordelia experiences a similar lack of the 'glib and oily art / To speak and purpose not' (1.1.227). Looking at *King Lear* through the lens of South Asian popular culture, it appears as a story connecting East and West. Its accent on parent–child relationships paves the way for an exploration of the conflicting communication between two generations of migrants and the reconfiguration of authority in a new social environment.

In *Second Generation*, the original plot of *King Lear* is accelerated and Mr Sharma's madness surfaces from the very first scenes. The serial opens with the old man recovering from a four-month coma; waking up, he falls prey to hallucinations and fits of anger. When he is still in hospital and struggling between life and death, a fool-like friend asks him: 'How does it feel to come back from the dead?' The question hints at Sharma's position between past and present, ghosts and the living, and anticipates the state of madness, or identity crisis, that is linked to this traumatic experience.

In 'Madness in *King Lear*' (1982), Kenneth Muir analyses the tragedy and underlines the subsequent steps driving Lear towards madness.

According to him, 'Lear is driven insane by a series of shocks. First, there is the attack by Goneril (1.4). This makes him angrily pretend not to know her, or to know himself, but at this point it is still pretence.'[11] But the moment when Lear denies having any daughter coincides with the emergence of his first doubts about his own beliefs. Lear asks: 'Doth any here know me? This is not Lear. / Doth Lear walk thus? Speak thus? Where are his eyes? / [...] Who is it that can tell me who I am?' (1.4.220–4). The recognition of his foolishness in banishing Cordelia starts to shake the integrity of the king, who confesses: 'I did her wrong' (1.5.24).

The second shock comes from facing Regan's ingratitude; this causes a premonition of madness and Lear finds himself praying: 'O, let me not be mad, not mad sweet heaven! / Keep me in temper. I will not be mad' (1.5.44–5). But the final step causing Lear's breakdown is the face-to-face encounter with Poor Tom, 'both a living embodiment of naked poverty and one who is apparently what Lear has feared to become'.[12]

Second Generation presents a parallel development of the story. Sharma/Lear's awakening from his long sleep is just the first of a series of shocking events and is promptly followed by Mr Khan's hanging himself, a more tragic rendition of blind Gloucester's failed attempt to jump off a cliff. Sharma, who had fired Khan from the factory and instead supported his own deceitful daughters, is finally forced by a 'fool' to acknowledge the plan they are pursuing. The fool, a drunkard establishing a connection with Shakespeare's tragedy, yells at the householder: 'They want to sell the factory. Are you blind as well as fool?' By pairing blindness and folly as Sharma's attributes, the mysterious character proposes an uncanny identification of Sharma with both Gloucester and the king. His words produce a carnivalesque effect of power inversion which anticipates Lear's progressive collapse; then with the line 'You produced some real poison here, you deserve each other', the fool provides an answer to the king's question in Shakespeare's text: 'Is there any cause in nature that makes these hard hearts?' Here Sharma is forced to recognize that he is in part responsible for his daughters' cruelty.

After the two women confine Sharma to a mental hospital and manage to sell the factory, Sharma understands he has been betrayed and starts looking for Heere again. But a final shock drives him mad: the old man is haunted by sudden visions of the ghost of his dead wife, Sonali. The truth about her absence, the great absence in *King Lear*, is a secret Sharma has kept during his whole life: she had committed suicide.

Sonali, who suffered from depression, had killed herself in the ultimate attempt to escape the unhappiness caused by the patriarchal order of her house and community. Her rebel spirit has been inherited by Heere/Cordelia, who resembles her mother so much that they appear like the same person in Sharma's hallucinations; mother and daughter become (con)fused in the eye of patriarchy.[13] While Heere fights her mother's struggle to affirm her own identity, the presence of Sonali's ghost transforms the other daughters' disrespect for their father into revenge for their mother's death.

Coppelia Kahn has underlined how the play can be read in relation to this absence and how Lear's repressed identification with the mother becomes the epitome of the collapse of patriarchy. When the king asks his daughters for a public statement of their love on the day of their engagement, his gesture reveals both anxiety for power over their lives and – Kahn argues – a dependence on the female figures. The father's act of self-assertion fails in imposing the patriarchal order since it exposes the vulnerability of the male subject:

> What the play depicts, of course, is the failure of that presence: the failure of a father's power to command love in a patriarchal world and the emotional penalty he pays for wielding power. Lear's very insistence on paternal power, in fact, belies its shakiness; similarly, the absence of the mother points to her hidden presence, as the lines with which I began might indicate.[14]

In the lines from the second act Coppelia Kahn refers to, the king defines his emotional state of torment as hysteria: 'O! How this mother swells upward toward my heart! / Hysterica passio! Down, thou climbing sorrow! / Thy element's below' (2.4.56–8). The hysteric King Lear thus recognizes the closeness to a 'mother' who lives inside him, and his body appears to be governed by a feminine repressed power haunting his 'womb'.[15]

In his afterlife condition, once he has come out of the coma, Sharma shows glimpses of awareness of the connection he has with his wife: his madness develops into a form of depression that creates an identification with Sonali. He does not just see her in visions, he can feel the pain she carried and the memory of her tears makes him burst into sighs. Sharma's troubled relation with Heere then emerges as a transposition of the intimate and conflicting dialogue the man has with Sonali during his illness. Sonali's ghost appears as a typical Freudian *revenant*: it is a sign of the repressed past haunting the present and threatening the linearity of history.[16] Different times and places coexist, showing a superimposition of youth and old age, Calcutta and London. The characteristics of Sharma's madness recall the folly of Lear. In the play, the king's derangement seems to take him back to his childhood. Cordelia describes her father's illness as a regression; the journey back in time is transformed by Biswas into a trip back to the place of Sharma's childhood: Calcutta. Once the old factory, which proves to be the symbol of Sharma's bond with England, is sold, his daughters' revenge is complete and, paradoxically, the householder is set free. Both in England and India Heere, like Cordelia, looks after her father in the days of his illness, but their new dwelling place brings about a change in their relationship.

In *King Lear* the time spent in prison brings father and child together: the intimacy and the contiguity between the characters, like two birds in a cage singing together, exposes the collapse of patriarchal authority and portrays a reversed power asymmetry (5.3.8–11). In *Second Generation*, the closeness between Mr Sharma and Heere is reinforced during their voluntary exile. In a parallel move to *King Lear*, the young woman subverts the power relation, by taking care of her childlike dad as if he were a child and satisfying his need to be mothered. Again, mother and daughter appear to be aligned in pursuing the same tasks;[17] but in India and with Sam, Heere gives birth to a nuclear family centred on the woman's freedom to assert her desire and on the empowering act of mothering. With the girl's last words affirming love for her partner, the return to the former colony exceeds mere compliance with the old patriarchal order, and the sense of familiarity with India mingles with the construction of a family centred on the female character.

This final twist implicitly challenges the possibility of describing and representing the essential features of both British and Indian families, and ultimately questions Roy's statement, quoted at the beginning of this chapter, in which he establishes a distinctively continuous relation between Lear's world and contemporary India.

Hybrid identities as cut'n'mix

In suggesting an exploration of the conflicts faced by second generations, the title of the TV series has a double meaning: on the one hand, it refers to the complex relation of Asian-British citizens with their origins; on the other, the work is a 'second-generation tape' which dilutes the purity of the original *King Lear* in order to promote its circulation as a work of popular culture. Biswas himself explains the duality in these terms:

> [The ambiguous title] Second Generation not only describes the children of immigrants, but also a copy of a videotape. Looked at positively, a second-generation tape is a useful way of promoting and spreading culture, making it available to a wider and more varied cross-section of people. Yet its quality is usually poorer, and some would say that the purity of the original master tape has been eroded. It's precisely this conflict between concentration or expansion, purity or dilution that animates the parents of the rebellious kids.[18]

Although in the final scenes Heere and Sam seem to be trapped in the impossibility of escaping their origin, no sense of cultural purity is provided and *Second Generation* remains a manifesto of hybridity. The serial exposes the bankruptcy of the multiculturalist discourse of assimilation, and portrays the Asian community in London as having weak relations with other groups and keeping its own distinctive culture and traditions, but it never invokes cultural 'purity'. All the characters define themselves as a mix of many sounds: at the end, Pryia, Reena and the rapper Uzi will continue to live in south-east London, where they were born, and they will carry on building their everyday hybrid world.

The aim of *Second Generation*, as the scriptwriter declares, is to create a truthful miniseries by recalling his own experience as a second-generation Indian in London, and by mingling autobiography with Shakespearean references. Biswas's choice of Shakespeare as a vehicle through which to portray the problems and conflicts faced by different generations of migrants and citizens in the UK stimulates a reflection on the very status and circulation of 'Shakespeare': rather than performing an act of appropriation of this quintessential icon of Englishness, Biswas reveals the blurring of the boundaries of cultural traditions and questions the possibility of identifying the Bard with a static image of national belonging.

Since *King Lear* provides a channel through which to portray family tensions both in the Indian subcontinent and in London, Shakespeare emerges as a hybrid sign that can be used, recycled and endlessly recirculated in an interconnected, post-colonial world. The appropriation enacted by Biswas's popular-culture take on the tragedy highlights Shakespeare's plural and planetary existence and, to borrow Richard Burt's remarks about contemporary screen adaptations, it successfully 'blur[s] if not fully deconstruct[s] distinctions between local and global, original and copy, pure and hybrid, indigenous and foreign, high and low, authentic and inauthentic, hermeneutic and post-hermeneutic'.[19]

Second Generation is a copy and a 'remake' of its early modern source that calls into question the relation between local and global, as well as the concept of purity as related to the nation and to the concealment of minority histories on the part of the national narrative. As Biswas put it in an interview,

> Inevitably, [*Second Generation*] has flashes of autobiography, but perhaps more importantly, it has stories – stories that I have seen, stories that I have heard, stories that I know and stories that I have made up knowing they could happen. All of these stories start with the journey that brought our parents to this country [...] With *Second Generation* I wanted to write something truthful – not something representative. My reason for making this distinction is that as second-generation Asians we have gone past representation.[20]

This British-Indian version of *King Lear*, where first and second generations come together in an exploration of the post 'brown Atlantic'[21] era, is a response to Biswas's desire for a kind of storytelling which also acknowledges the impossibility of the task of representation.

According to Biswas, 'second-generation Asians [...] have gone past representation', as they have already experienced the danger of essentialism resulting from the depiction of peripheral identities. By committing to an autobiographical account of a family story instead of aiming at an exemplary representation of the Indian community as a whole, Biswas pays his debt to the Black British movement of the 1990s, which demonstrated how Englishness was constructed 'only by marginalizing, dispossessing, displacing and forgetting other ethnicities'.[22]

Though media and television had a crucial role in shaping the cultural model of national identity, the reconfiguration of a more complex and heterogeneous concept of Britishness, as Kobena Mercer maintains in *Welcome to the Jungle* (1994), was equally propelled by cinema.[23] While Mercer takes into account Hanif Kureishi's work as a scriptwriter, Jigna Desai's more recent *Beyond Bollywood* (2004) looks at the work of diasporic women filmmakers and sees it as having produced 'a space for emerging identities of British and diasporic subjects to be articulated. They presented complex, nonessentialist, and nontransparent subjectivities that did not attempt to represent British Asian identity as singular and static.'[24] Biswas seems to take his cue from here when he translates for the small screen the dynamics of his Asian-British identity drama, in which hybridity is further enhanced by mixing visual and other media, most notably pop music.

In *Second Generation* music acts as an important site for the questioning of identity. The soundtrack for the serial was created by the Asian-British musician Nitin Sawhney, a flamenco guitarist, classical pianist, DJ and orchestral composer, whose hit 'Uzi's rap' featured in the TV serial and was created in collaboration with the artist UK Apache.[25] Mixing rap with the rhythms of bhangra, Sawhney's track reacts to the fetishization of Asian culture and to the related Bollywoodization of film culture, promoting instead a fusion between Eastern and Western sounds. The language of bhangra accompanies and underlines the interrelation between the fragmented pictures of Asian-British London and the scattered Shakespearean references.[26]

Music, as 'a non-representational, non-conceptual form', can help identity emerge as prismatic and multifaceted.[27] A music-related metaphor, coined by Stuart Hall, opportunely translates the process of hybridization triggered by diaspora which appears in Biswas's work: the never-ending construction of a plural identity is labelled by the Anglo-Caribbean scholar as 'cut-and-mix', a DJ editing technique based on cutting and fusing tracks together.[28] Quoting Hall, one could say that *Second Generation* portrays the Asian-British community's 'process of unsettling, recombination, hybridization and "cut-and-mix" – in short, the process of cultural diaspora-ization (to coin an ugly term) which it implies'.[29]

The sounds of bhangra communicate this hybrid nature. As Rupa Huq explains, bhangra is

> A style of music which has singing and the beat of the dhol drum [...] Bhangra has always been popular amongst Punjabi people all over the world but it has enjoyed a resurgence over the last ten years or so. Its raw traditional sound is often supplemented with contemporary musical styles.[30]

Its Punjabi roots are fused with the trends of underground British music, making it at least as quintessentially 'British' as it is 'Asian'. Huq later refers to Nitin Sawhney's music calling it 'a melting pot: an acclaimed mix of jazz and classical Indian rhythms with added spice'.[31]

In 'Uzi's rap', Sawhney uses rap and references to African-American culture to make a political statement: his music about life in an urban environment translates the young generations' battle for social affirmation.[32] Incorporating the rhythms of London, with its vernacular language and ethnic areas, and fusing them with culturally resonating music styles, Sawnhey's music constructs hybrid cultural codes. In Biswas's 'hyphenated' *King Lear*, then, the language of music, mixing English and Bengali, genres and styles, provides a key for performing identity. Plural aural contaminations tell the stories of the characters' multiple belonging and avoid any stable definition of their diasporic selves. Sawnhey's soundtrack fluctuates between genres in the same way as people's existence escapes crystallization. To quote Biswas again: 'The truth is that there are many Asian communities, all of which have thousands of stories. None of them on their own can explain or encapsulate what it is to be Asian in Britain. There is no one answer. The definition, like us, is constantly evolving.'[33]

In Biswas's work, identity and Shakespeare appear as open spaces of intervention and transformation. His remediated and renovated version of *King Lear* shows that 'Shakespeare' can emerge not only as a site where identity conflicts are performed, but also as a place where cultural change occurs, without necessarily leading to conflict resolution. The processes of intercultural dialogue and negotiation traversing the series are facilitated by the global location of 'Shakespeare' and the quintessentially hybrid status this construction has acquired through the colonial education system and a uniquely diasporic afterlife.

Notes

1. Amitava Roy, 'Here to Stay: Shakespeare, the Bengali Stage and Bengali Culture', in *Colonial and Postcolonial Shakespeares*, ed. by Amitava Roy, Debnarayan Bandopadhyay and Krishna Sen (Kolkata: Avantgarde, 2001), 2–28 (21–2).
2. Roy, 22.
3. K.R. Srinivasa Iyengar, *Shakespeare: His World and His Art* (New Delhi: Sterling, 1994), 445.
4. Joseph Warton, 'Observations on Shakespeare's *King Lear*', 'Observations on *King Lear* continued' and 'Observations on *King Lear* concluded', in *The Adventurer. Volume the Fourth* ([1753] London: H. Goldney, 1788), 58–67; 84–93; 140–8.
5. Directed by Jon Sen, *Second Generation* is the first original work written by Neil Biswas (the co-writer of *In a Land of Plenty*). It features a tremendous cast of actors, including Om Puri, Anupam Kher, Roshen Seth, Amita Dhiri, Rita Woolf, Nitin Ganatra and Parminder Nagra alongside Christopher Simpson and Danny Dyer in leading roles.
6. Homi Bhabha famously defines the hybrid place of cultural contamination as the 'third space'. The 'importance of hybridity' he states, 'is not to be able to trace two original moments from which the third emerges, rather

hybridity [to me] is the "Third Space", which enables other positions to emerge'. *Identity: Community, Culture, Difference*, ed. by Jonathan Rutherford (London: Lawrence and Wishart, 1990), 211.

7. Neil Biswas, 'Conflict between Cultures can be Positive', *Guardian*, 8 September 2003, online at http://www.guardian.co.uk/society/2003/sep/08/raceintheuk.broadcasting (accessed 11 October 2012).

8. All quotations from *Second Generation* are taken from my own transcript of the film dialogues.

9. Roy, 24.

10. All quotations are taken from William Shakespeare, *King Lear*, ed. by R.A. Foakes, The Arden Shakespeare, Third Series (London: Thomson Learning, 2005).

11. Kenneth Muir, 'Madness in *King Lear*', in *Aspects of King Lear: Articles Reprinted from Shakespeare Survey*, ed. by Kenneth Muir and Stanley W. Wells (Cambridge: Cambridge University Press, 1982), 23–33 (27).

12. Muir, 28. Interestingly, Maria Del Sapio Garbero proposes considering Tom's figure as a Derridean *pharmakon*, a remedy that at first irritates Lear's illness and finally leads to his healing; see Maria Del Sapio Garbero, *Il bene ritrovato. Le figlie di Shakespeare dal* King Lear *ai romances* (Rome: Bulzoni, 2005).

13. Margaret Whitford clarifies the figure used by the feminist writer Luce Irigaray to define mother–daughter relations: 'In *Speculum* and *This Sex Which Is Not One*, contiguity was the figure for mother and daughter: the two lips represented (among other things) the two women continually in touch with each other. But even then, Irigaray was warning that continuity in patriarchy could mean fusion and confusion of identity between women, and thus the impossibility of relations between them (since they were not separated enough for the "between" to exist, and the impossibility therefore of a maternal genealogy).' Luce Irigaray, *The Irigaray Reader*, ed. by Margaret Witford (London: Wiley-Blackwell, 1991), 160–1.

14. Coppelia Kahn, 'The Absent Mother in *King Lear*', in *Rewriting the Renaissance: The Discourses of Sexual Difference in Early Modern Europe*, ed. by Margaret W. Ferguson (Chicago: University of Chicago Press, 1986), 33–49 (36).

15. The famous contemporary book explaining the state of depression to which Lear seems to be referring is Edward Jorden's *A Briefe Discourse of a Disease Called the Suffocation of the Mother* (London: John Windet, 1603).

16. For the idea of the spectres of the past haunting the present and exposing time in its being 'out of joint', I refer to Jacques Derrida's *Specters of Marx: The State of the Debt, the Work of Mourning, and the New International* (London: Routledge, 1994).

17. Cordelia's maternal behaviour is really what differentiates her from Goneril and Regan, for whom, already at the end of Act One, Lear invokes sterility (1.4.273–9).

18. Sukhdev Sandhu, 'It's Asian life but not as we know it', *Telegraph*, 13 September 2003, online at http://www.telegraph.co.uk/culture/tvandradio/3602568/Its-Asian-life-but-not-as-we-know-it.html (accessed 11 October 2012).

19. Richard Burt, 'Shakespeare, Glo-cali-zation, Race and the Small Screens of Popular Culture', in *Shakespeare the Movie II*, ed. by Richard Burt and Lynda E. Boose (London and New York: Routledge, 2003), 14–36 (15–16).

20. Biswas, 'Conflict'.
21. The expression 'brown Atlantic' is used by Jigna Desai to refer to Asian migration in the UK. It modifies Paul Gilroy's famous title *The Black Atlantic: Modernity and Double Consciousness* (London: Verso, 1995) referring to the 'Middle Passage' of the African slaves towards America.
22. Stuart Hall, 'New Ethnicities', *Anglistica*, 1 (1997), 22.
23. Kobena Mercer, *Welcome to the Jungle: New Positions in Black Cultural Studies* (London and New York: Routledge, 1994).
24. Jigna Desai, *Beyond Bollywood: The Cultural Politics of South Asian Diasporic Film* (New York and London: Routledge, 2004), 60.
25. To listen to the hit you can log on to http://www.reverbnation.com/ tunepak/song_587758 (accessed 28 October 2011). UK Apache (real name: Abdul Wahab Lafta) is one of the most popular junglists of the British alternative music scene. In 1998, his album *Big Up* was nominated for a Grammy Award for best reggae album. During the following years, UK Apache's music became essential for the development of drum'n'bass.
26. It is interesting to note that bhangra is a central topic in Gurinder Chadha's first film, *I'm British But...* (1990), which collects interviews with second-generation immigrants of various Asian-British communities in the UK.
27. See Gilroy, 76.
28. Hall, 22. Dick Hebdige presents cut'n'mix as an Afro-Caribbean style of the 1980s. He writes: 'Cut'n'mix is the music and the style of the 1980s just as rock'n'roll and rhythm'n'blues formed the bedrock for the music and the styles that have made such an impact on our culture since the 1950s.' The story of this style is one in which 'the journey from African drums to the Roland TR 808 drum machine, or from the Nigerian "griots" to UB40 and Ranking Ann does not run in straight lines like a sentence on a page'. See Dick Hebdige, *Cut'n'mix: Culture, Identity, and Caribbean Music* (Chicago: University of Chicago Press,1987), 10.
29. Hall, 22.
30. Rupa Huq, 'Asian Kool? Bhangra and Beyond', in *Disorienting Rhythms: The Politics of the New Asian Dance Music*, ed. by J. Hutnyk et al. (London: Zed, 1996), 61–80 (66).
31. Huq, 66.
32. The political object and the purpose of demystifying the role of Asians in music are the common issues shared by several bhangra groups. These are well laid out in an interview by Rupa Huq to Annihudra, a member of the Asian Dub Foundation, quoted in Huq, 73.
33. Biswas, 'Conflict'.

Part III
Shakespeare in Times of Conflict

14
Introduction

Manfred Pfister

The chapters in this section are concerned with Shakespeare's plays and poems read, translated or staged in times of conflict rather than with conflicts staged in Shakespeare's plays and poems, though, of course, these two perspectives are closely related to each other in that frequently the conflicts staged are turned into tropes, metaphors or analogical models of the conflicts that solicit their restaging. Many of them lift Shakespeare out of his natural English habitat and take us to continental venues such as Poland, Romania or France, or to what Foucault would call heterotopes in England; they wrest Shakespeare from the hands of the English and hand him over to foreigners or persons whose Englishness, though they were born in England, did not go unchallenged by their compatriots. More importantly still, they take us outside the official sites of encounters with Shakespeare, the theatre and the classroom, confronting us with sites less sheltered than these cultural institutions and more directly exposed to the whips and scorns of times of savage conflict and war: prisons and detention or internment camps, the displacement of incarcerated dissidents, political exiles or prisoners of war. Read, translated or performed under such circumstances of extreme social duress and personal trauma, Shakespeare's texts and the conflicts they stage take on a particular poignancy and offer themselves to pointed rewritings or appropriations. Such displaced experiences of, and with, the Shakespearean text are not marginal but crucial to the total impact of Shakespeare worldwide, though Shakespeare criticism and scholarship, focused on philology, historical hermeneutics and the professional theatre, has so far largely ignored them and is only gradually beginning to take them into account, for instance in the work of Michael Dobson and Ton Hoenselaars, one of the contributors to this volume.[1]

Individually, these painful or traumatized engagements with Shakespeare may appear to be merely anecdotal, tied up within the contingencies of very special political and private circumstances; explored systematically, however, they provoke a new perception of the Shakespearean experience and its social and political functions for individuals and societies at large. A close attention to them may complement the more canonical versions of reception history and, indeed, the following studies of displacement, by confronting us with the plight of British conscientious objectors in their detention camps during the Great War or of German Jews in British internment camps and political prisoners in Fascist-occupied Romania during the Second World War, enrich and deepen both our knowledge about worlds in conflict and the uses of Shakespeare in such contexts for questioning and reshaping the social or national identity of the performers.

Unlike the kinds of amateur theatricals represented in, say, Shakespeare's own *Midsummer Night's Dream* or, closer to our concerns here, in Virginia Woolf's *Between the Acts*, written and published at the brink of the Second World War and resonant with Shakespearean echoes, the performances studied by Clara Calvo in Chapter 15 ('Work of National Importance: Shakespeare in Dartmoor') do not intend to celebrate the self-image of the society in which they are embedded, nor are the performers trusting members of it, sharing its values and aims. Her conscientious objectors engaging in Shakespearean theatricals at the Princeton Work Centre in Dartmoor, one of the detention camps set up for them in the middle of the Great War, challenge the martial ethos of the nations so fiercely displayed in that context. Disparaged by their compatriots at war as lacking in masculinity and English patriotism, they quite self-consciously incur further denigration by playacting rather than proving their mettle in the theatre of war. And, what is more, they even dress up as women in their performance of *A Midsummer Night's Dream*, thus apparently confirming the stereotype of the 'sissy' pacifist. Taking on Shakespeare, the figurehead of Englishness, is a further bold gesture in this context, a gesture that questions both the nationalist construction of the Bard and the values attributed to him: heroic masculinity and subjection of one's freedom of conscience and self-realization to harsh discipline. And *A Midsummer Night's Dream* proves an excellent option here, not only because it has always been a favourite with amateur theatre groups but, more importantly, because it deals with similar conflicts between individual freedom and stern law: Hermia's choice is one with which a conscientious objector could readily identify.

Julius Caesar, which also featured in one of the theatrical entertainments at Dartmoor, is at the centre of Ton Hoenselaars's tale of two theatres, '"A tongue in every wound of Caesar": Performing *Julius Caesar* behind Barbed Wire during the Second World War'. The diptych juxtaposes and contrasts a 1940 production of the play by German and Austrian Jews interned on the Isle of Man as potential Nazi spies with one by defeated German officers and soldiers in their POW camp in the southern French seaside town of Hyères in 1946. Both were directed by theatre professionals and in both cases the choice of a play by Shakespeare, and of this play in particular, staged in English and in German respectively, expressed a political stance beyond the warring enemy cultures and an identification with the politics of a play that questions heroism and charismatic leadership. This becomes impressively evident in the comparison of the two performances with professional theatre productions of *Julius Caesar* in England and Germany in the 1930s and early 1940s. It is against the background of performances like the 1941 Stratford production, which transported its audience from the contemporary world of the war against Fascism, and of German productions like that of Jürgen Fehling in 1941, which reflected the Nazi preoccupation with the strong-willed *Führer*, that the acute awareness of the timeliness of Shakespeare's scrutiny of dictatorship and anti-dictatorial politics in the Isle of Man production, and the shift of gravity from Caesar and Mark Antony to the sceptical Brutus in the Hyères production gain in profile and fully reveal their critical thrust. This achievement, in the face of, and even inspired by, all the limitations of amateur theatre in captivity, deserves to be recorded and celebrated, and future stage histories of *Julius Caesar* in the twentieth century which continue to disregard the unique potential of such double- or triple-displaced Shakespeares will do so at their own risk.

Of course, the quest for them is not an easy one. The materials documenting these performances are not generally to be found in the great Shakespeare research libraries of the world but often need to be sleuthed down in out-of-the-way local archives. Moreover, as prisons and POW or detention camps tend to be sealed off against the outside world and monitored by internal censorship, these materials are usually scarce and often at a second or third remove from the event. The knowledge we can gain about them is variously mediated, and the way it has been mediated can speak of new conflict zones. Monica Matei-Chesnoiu's case study, '"The play's the thing": *Hamlet* in a Romanian Wartime Political Prison' is an excellent instance of this. The performance of *Hamlet* in a political court-martial prison in Timişoara (and later in Arad) in 1942–43 turned the prison in Fascist-dominated Romania into a theatre, even a university, of self-discovery for the inmates under direct threat of execution, and it turned Hamlet's Danish prison into a metaphor for the incarceration of dissident Romanians by the German-Romanian Fascist powers. The original – extant – sketches of this production bear this out and, moreover, they suggest in their inscriptions that in this Romanian performance the English dramatist's Danish prince spoke German. In the German-speaking Romanian region of Banat this is less surprising than may at first sight appear; still, it foregrounds and problematizes national and cultural identity: what is German here – Fascism or Shakespeareomania? And what is Romanian – the collaborators with the occupying Nazi forces or the anti-Fascists inside the prison? And where is the place of doubly-displaced Shakespeare in this: with the Allied Forces, with German idealism, with the despots and their lip service to his cultural prestige, which protects the theatrical activities of the imprisoned dissidents? And there remains a last layer of entanglement in political conflict: the Timişoara *Hamlet* was first widely publicized in 1973 as part of a research project funded by the Romanian Communist Party to celebrate the 'exemplary greatness of this glorious struggle [...] of the underground Socialist and Communist circles in Romania during the war period'.[2] The imaginative theatrical appropriation of *Hamlet* by dissident prisoners awaiting execution, not all of whom can have been Communists, is here reappropriated by one of the most despotic systems of the Eastern bloc to construct and propagate its own self-legitimizing prehistory in terms of a great and heroic march towards freedom.

Of course, not all the conflicts at stake in the reception of Shakespeare worldwide are political ones; they may be private, even psychological, or they may be tied up with the rival claims of individual recipients to a fuller understanding of Shakespeare's work. The history of Shakespeare criticism provides many examples of such jealously guarded and polemically acerbic one-upmanship, in which personal antipathies between rival critics and the desire to enhance the uniqueness of one's individual insights runs higher than substantial difference of aesthetic criteria or theoretical approach. An equally – if not more – embattled minefield is translation, though studies of Shakespeare translation so far have hardly ventured to step into it. As Anna Cetera points out in Chapter 18, Translation Studies, by focusing exclusively upon the 'safe monogamy of the author-translator relation', the connection between the original and its translation, have completely faded out the competitive dynamics at work between translators and translations of the same text. Translation, particularly of canonical texts like Shakespeare's, which are translated into the same language more than once and often even in the same period, is a more complex affair than the romance of a single translator wooing one original text; it is rather a triangular, if not a polygonal relationship, in which the new translator reacts upon his or her rival or rivals by exploiting them, emulating them, trying to prove them wrong, going one better on them or, under the anxiety of influence, disregarding them. And, as Anna Cetera shows with reference mainly to Polish translators of Shakespeare, 'it is in these love triangles and their polygonal mutations that a new text is conceived and shaped'. This is a struggle about canonicity and its aim is to produce the one canonical translation in the respective language that would assume in that language the exclusive status of Shakespeare's original. This may go some way towards accounting for the proliferation of German versions of the sonnets – by now more than 70 of the entire cycle – and the heated nature of the showdowns between rival translators such as that between Stefan George and Karl Kraus: none of them has yet gained the avidly desired canonical predominance. Clearly, to regard the plethora and variety of translations existing side by side only as a sign of the plurality of meaning inherent in the Shakespearean text, as Translation Studies almost unanimously do, is to miss out on an important dimension of conflict.

Translation continues to be the topic in the last contribution to this section, though with a political vengeance, in my own observations and reflections on 'Shakespeare's Sonnets *de profundis*'. They draw attention to a fact that has been ignored in extant studies of the history of reception of the sonnets, namely, the many cases in which they have been read, or even read and translated, in prison cells, behind barbed wire, or in exile. This inserts the sonnets, though they themselves hardly ever address political matters, in scenarios of political conflict ranging from Fascism and Stalinism, the Second World War and its aftermath, to the Cold War, the Iron Curtain and the Berlin Wall. In contrast to the uses of the plays by political prisoners, internees or prisoners of war, who read and stage the Shakespearean plots as illuminating or consoling tropes of the conflict situations in which they are engulfed, there is in the sonnets no plot that could be used in this way by their politically displaced readers and translators. What is it, then, that draws those *in carcere et vinculis* to the internal struggle of the poet with love and alienation, ideal beauty and disenchantment, time-transcending constancy and subjection to the fleeting moment and the destructive work of time? This is the question that the second part of the chapter tries to answer, and the answer it suggests does not simply involve the projection of one political conflict scenario onto another, but lies instead on a more existential level.

Notes

1. See, most recently, Michael Dobson's *Shakespeare and Amateur Performance: A Cultural History* (Cambridge: Cambridge University Press, 2011) and *European Shakespeares*, ed. by Ton Hoenselaars and Clara Calvo (London: The Athlone Press, 2008).
2. Margareta Andreescu quoted in Chapter 16 below.

15
Work of National Importance: Shakespeare in Dartmoor

Clara Calvo

In the spring of 1916, Bertrand Russell argued that conscientious objectors were at the avant-garde of progress and civilization and constituted 'the greatest source of progress and moral strength to be found in the nation'.[1] Less than two months before the Shakespeare tercentenary in April and about three months before the battle of the Somme on 1 July, the introduction of conscription through the Military Service Act, enforced on 2 March 1916, divided public opinion. The Great War did not only promote chauvinistic propaganda and absurd patriotism; it also propelled pacifism, often with the aid of socialist and religious ideas, through the figures of those young men who first refused to enlist voluntarily (in spite of the white feather posted or publicly handed to them by overzealous patriots) and later defied conscription through conscientious objection. Bertrand Russell's visionary opinions took time to gain ascendancy but by the fiftieth anniversary of the 1916 Service Act, the first British men who said 'no' to conscription and war were hailed as heroes.[2] This chapter aims to reconstruct the ways in which Shakespearean drama could speak for those who in 1916 refused to fight and kill and how cross-dressing, at a time in which restrictive definitions of masculinity were dominant, turned out to be liberating. As the cultural history of Shakespeare may benefit from occasionally assuming the garb of a cultural biography of the plays in relation to other artefacts of material culture, this study examines concert programmes, written memoirs and photographs of First World War conscientious objectors. Following these traces, it is possible to partially reconstruct an amateur performance staged at Dartmoor Prison in 1919. This production shows that, in the context of European armed conflict, amateur performance could prove liberating for those engaging in it and that it can also contribute to liberating alternative meanings inscribed in Shakespeare's plays.

Conscientious objectors and Dartmoor prison

The experiences of conscientious objectors (COs) during the First World War varied considerably, but most of them had to face tribunals and endured, at one point or another, the loss of freedom.[3] Alternativist COs, men who only objected to carrying and firing weapons but were willing to wear military uniforms and to undertake work that did not involve fighting and killing, were offered the chance to join the Non-Combatant Corps (NCC). They were employed in jobs necessary for the war effort such as mining or agriculture, or worked for the Royal Army Medical Corps (RAMC) as stretcher bearers or ambulance drivers at the front. Absolutist COs, those who objected to war itself on pacifist, religious or moral grounds, were brought before tribunals and afterwards often court-martialled. In the early stages of the implementation of conscription, 35 COs were transported by force to their regiments in France and effectively sentenced to death, as any disobedience of army orders at the front was punishable by firing squad.[4] In the end, their death sentences were commuted to up to ten years of imprisonment and forced labour.[5] Other conscientious objectors were sent to prison. Conditions in jails varied, but more often than not they were appalling. Privation and illness were common. Lack of medical treatment was the rule rather than the exception. In some of their internment institutions, COs were not allowed either books or pen and paper.[6] Absolutist COs were so brutally treated in some instances that public opinion evolved from seeing them as traitors and effeminate cowards to campaigning in their favour.[7] Socialist organizations and religious groups such as the Quakers did much to help COs during the Great War. Eventually, through the work of the No-Conscription Fellowship (NCF), and sympathetic MPs, the situation of COs improved. In the summer of 1916, aware of the criticism that the treatment of COs was unleashing, the government introduced a scheme to offer absolutist COs the chance to do 'work of national importance'. COs were transferred from prisons to camps where they would work directly under the Home Office, rather than the army. The first prison camps were set up in August 1916 with tents that had been rejected as unfit for army use, but later the Home Office took over four convict prisons to provide accommodation for COs: Wakefield, Warwick, Knutsford and Dartmoor. The nature of the 'work of national importance' arranged for them was far below the qualifications of most COs; under the principle of reproducing the hardships of the front, they were forced to plough fields without horses, slave in a quarry to no apparent purpose or dig up 'roads that led from nowhere to nowhere'.[8]

On 13 March 1917, the government reopened the gloomy and insalubrious jail built by Napoleonic convicts on Dartmoor and renamed it Princetown Work Centre. Mark Hayler, absolutist CO, describes the 'work of national importance' he did there:

> The work we did was worse than futile [...] The agricultural work was absolutely penal and organised on lines as for convicts [...] There was a hand-roller to which eight men were harnessed, engaged in rolling a field. I have been one of those human horses. The work we did could have been done by one man and one horse in a third of the time [...] All spades, shovels, barrows, etc. were prodigiously heavy, weighted with lead probably. Everything was purposely out of date to make the job more irksome [...] What was the result of such a policy? This – the men revolted [...][9]

Dartmoor prison became the largest such settlement, with 1200 men in residence by November 1917, and soon acquired a reputation for its troublesome, anarchist-oriented COs.[10] Bertrand Russell, who visited Princetown Work Centre on 9 May 1917, as a representative of the National Committee of the NCF, reflected: 'The gaols have been nearly emptied of their usual population [...] they have been filled with inmates of a new sort, men who value liberty of mind more than liberty of body.'[11] Russell also equated the British government's treatment of COs to the fate of British civilians interned by Germans in POW camps. In a letter to the editor of the *Manchester Guardian*, he wrote: 'Is there really such a vast gulf between Wormwood Scrubs and Ruhleben?'[12] For Russell, the great achievement of COs was to stand up to war and law (in the form of the Military Service Act) in defence of individual liberty: 'Some may question whether their stand has done much for the moment to further the cause of peace, but none can question what they have done for individual liberty, which is perhaps an even greater cause, and one with which, in the long run, the cause of peace is indissolubly bound up.'[13] With a neat rhetorical sleight of hand, Russell portrayed COs as the only people who retained their free will and conscience intact: 'In this universal prison, the only free men remaining are the conscientious objectors.'[14]

In the light of all this, the existence of some vestiges of Shakespearean performance in the old Napoleonic prison on Dartmoor during the Great War becomes – to say the least – intriguing. An extant programme shows that a scene from *Julius Caesar* was played in Dartmoor on 26 September 1917 as part of a concert (that is, a variety show mixing

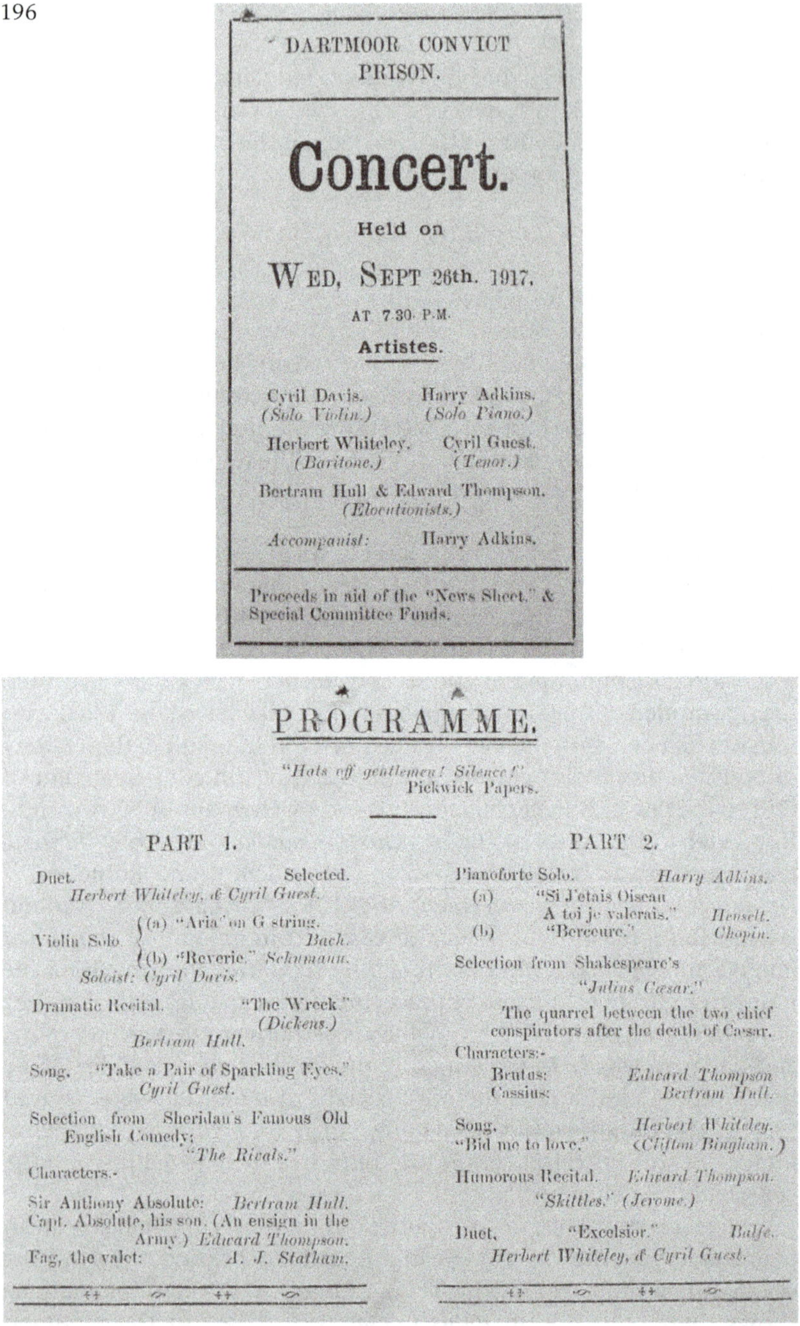

DARTMOOR CONVICT
PRISON.

Concert.

Held on

WED, SEPT 26th. 1917,

AT 7.30 P.M.

Artistes.

Cyril Davis.
(*Solo Violin.*)

Harry Adkins.
(*Solo Piano.*)

Herbert Whiteley.
(*Baritone.*)

Cyril Guest.
(*Tenor.*)

Bertram Hull & Edward Thompson.
(*Elocutionists.*)

Accompanist: Harry Adkins.

Proceeds in aid of the "News Sheet." &
Special Committee Funds.

PROGRAMME.

"*Hats off gentlemen! Silence!*"
Pickwick Papers.

PART 1.

Duet.   Selected.
Herbert Whiteley, & Cyril Guest.

Violin Solo {(a) "Aria" on G string.
                                    Bach.
             {(b) "Reverie." *Schumann.*
Soloist: Cyril Davis.

Dramatic Recital.   "The Wreck."
                                 (*Dickens.*)
Bertram Hull.

Song.   "Take a Pair of Sparkling Eyes."
Cyril Guest.

Selection from Sheridan's Famous Old
English Comedy;
              "The Rivals."

Characters.-

Sir Anthony Absolute: *Bertram Hull.*
Capt. Absolute, his son. (An ensign in the
         Army.) *Edward Thompson.*
Fag, the valet: *A. J. Statham.*

PART 2.

Pianoforte Solo.   Harry Adkins.
   (a)   "Si J'etais Oiseau
             A toi je valerais."   *Henselt.*
   (b)   "Berceure."   *Chopin.*

Selection from Shakespeare's
                "*Julius Cæsar.*"

   The quarrel between the two chief
conspirators after the death of Cæsar.
Characters:-
      Brutus: *Edward Thompson*
      Cassius: *Bertram Hull.*

Song.   Herbert Whiteley.
"Bid me to love."   (*Clifton Bingham.*)

Humorous Recital. *Edward Thompson.*
      "Skittles." (*Jerome.*)

Duet.   "Excelsior."   *Balfe.*
Herbert Whiteley, & Cyril Guest.

Figure 15.1   Concert Party Programme. Dartmoor, 26 September 1917. Courtesy of Special Collections, Leeds University Library

classical music and music-hall songs with recitations from poems or plays: see Figure 15.1).[15] The programme also included music from Bach, Schumann and Chopin, a recitation from Dickens ('The Wreck'), a scene from Sheridan's *The Rivals*, and another recitation from Jerome's *Skittles*.[16] Bertram Hull and Edward Thompson, who announced themselves as 'elocutionists', played Brutus and Cassius. Together with this Shakespearean scene, performed by professional music-hall actors, there is evidence that the inmates themselves put on an amateur production of *A Midsummer Night's Dream*, sometime between 28 December 1918 and 12 April 1919.

Shakespeare's *Dream* in Dartmoor

The performance of Shakespeare's plays for or by COs interned in a prison exemplifies the plural nature of the Shakespearean stages that sprouted during the Great War. The exploration of the role of Shakespearean performances in a disciplinary environment such as Princetown Work Centre enhances our knowledge of culture under stress, and of how culture survived in wartime. In that no man's land of British history – the months between the Armistice (11 November 1918) and the Treaty of Versailles (28 June 1919) – Shakespeare, combined with cross-dressing and cross-gender dancing, became instrumental in exposing COs to new ideas and new pleasures, offering them a chance to renegotiate their masculine identities.

The fact that Shakespearean drama was played within a disciplinary institution for COs is not in itself noteworthy. Shakespeare's plays have often been played behind bars and even behind barbed wire. In both prisons and internment camps, Shakespeare has been performed by professional actors who have taken up the challenge of acting for an unusual audience, and by the inmates themselves as part of educational programmes or for the purpose of entertainment.[17] Neither is there anything particularly extraordinary about including the performance of the quarrel scene between Brutus and Cassius from *Julius Caesar* in a variety programme: we may wonder what effect it might have had on an audience so openly opposed to warfare to see two generals sparring verbally on a stage, but this scene had long been part of the staple diet of London music-halls.[18] It had also been included in a variety concert arranged by Johnston Forbes-Robertson at the YMCA Shakespeare Hut in Bloomsbury to entertain soldiers on leave during the Christmas season in 1916.[19]

By contrast, the performance of a scene from *A Midsummer Night's Dream* was not usually part of a concert programme, even though the play had been a favourite with amateur groups for some time. As Michael

Dobson has explained, Shakespeare's *Dream* has always attracted amateur companies because, like *As You Like It* and *The Tempest*, it is a play that brings together Edwardian Hellenism, Elizabethan antiquarianism and English nationalism.[20] Dobson also attributes its popularity with amateur theatrical groups to 'its balance of strong roles, its exquisitely actor-proof structure, and its unfailingly hilarious depiction of non-professional performance', but he equally notes that this popularity is rather recent, as it rests on a 'widespread familiarity with the kinds of recreational performance established over the last century and a half'.[21] At the turn of the twentieth century, Ben Greet, Max Reinhardt and Harley Granville-Barker had turned it into a play that could easily fit into the most conventional repertoire (from the Stratford Memorial Theatre to the Old Vic) or be subjected to experimental production with avant-garde décor and lighting. It is possible that the inmates of Dartmoor had access, before or during their internment, to Ben Greet's edition of the play – published in 1912 – which contains detailed instructions for the *mise-en-scène*, clearly addressed to amateur companies.[22] They may also have heard about Granville-Barker's innovative production of the play in 1914 at the Savoy, with its apron stage, its nonfigurative curtains as backdrops, and its realistic delivery of lines. In any case, by the end of the First World War, the play had become a family favourite, as is revealed in a letter from a CO in Exeter Prison to his mother, dated September 1918. Terence Lane gives his mother a list of the books he has been reading in prison, which contains the 'Comedies of William Shakespeare', 'Including', he adds, 'our old friends, "Merchant of Venice", "Midsummer Night's Dream", etc'.[23] What is nevertheless singular about the amateur production in Dartmoor is that it was conceived and put on stage by the inmates themselves between Armistice Day and the Treaty of Versailles, when the return of COs to civilian life was imminent and those who had been deprived of liberty were already looking forward to freedom.

Traces of the Dartmoor production of *A Midsummer Night's Dream* are scarce. At some point around 1972, a First World War CO from Glasgow, William S. Cormack, was asked to write his recollections of his internment.[24] He was initially imprisoned in Wormwood Scrubs and was transferred to Princetown Work Centre on 28 December 1918, shortly after his twentieth birthday. According to Cormack, the inmates at Dartmoor had the benefit of an ample hall that was used for weekly dances and 'monthly orchestral or dramatic shows'.[25] Although he implies that there was more than one play staged in this hall, he only mentions a production of Shakespeare's *Dream*. Cormack is very reticent about details of the production. He simply writes: 'We staged Shakespeare's "Midsummer Night's Dream" in which I played the part of Hermia – sorry I have no program or photograph of this.'[26] Amongst Cormack's papers there are no photographs of his performance as Hermia, but there are a couple of snapshots showing Dartmoor's inmates dressed up for two fancy-dress balls held in March and April 1919 (Figures 15.2 and 15.3). The second ball, on 12 April, was a 'Farewell to Dartmoor', as most COs were released on 14 April 1919.[27] The photographs show Cormack and other COs in front of the stage and they give an idea of the kind of set and costumes in use at Dartmoor. For these two balls, two COs who were professional dance teachers, Stuart Campbell and Thomas Counsell, dressed up as Sir Walter Raleigh and Cardinal Wolsey, while another inmate cross-dressed as Queen Elizabeth. The producer of the drama performances staged at Dartmoor, Samuel Nathan, chose to wear the outfit of a 'Man of the Italian Renaissance'. Cormack appears very convincingly cross-dressed as a 'Maiden of Early Victorian Era' and his costume, with the bonnet removed, could very well do for Hermia.

What these pictures clearly show is a remarkable uniformity in the choice of fancy dress amongst the inmates of Dartmoor. With the exception of a CO dressed as Golliwogg[28] and another one cross-dressed as Bizet's Carmen, many of them are dressed in costumes that reinvent national identity through significant moments in British history: a man of the English Middle Ages, a girl of the early Victorian era. More significant, perhaps, is the fact that the only historical characters singled out for individualized impersonation, with the exception of Salome,[29] are all drawn from the early modern period: Queen Elizabeth, Sir Walter Raleigh and Cardinal Wolsey. The Tudorphilia that these photographs reveal seems to echo the Edwardian revival of the outdoor Tudor pageant.[30]

The photographs allow us a glimpse of the stage on which the Dartmoor *Dream* was performed – either of the sets in these pictures could have done very well for a production of the play. In the April ball (Figure 15.3), the set consists of a conventional painted backdrop, showing a tree in the foreground and the walls of a city in the background – the tree could perhaps pass for a forest and the walls in the distance for Athens. The March ball photograph (Figure 15.2) shows the stage with the curtain down, but foliage sticks out of the sides of the proscenium arch. Displaying an amateur actor's pride in emulating professionals, Cormack recollects that the hall in Dartmoor 'had a raised platform sufficiently deep to take a few pieces of scenery'.[31]

Figure 15.2 Fancy Dress Ball. Dartmoor, 4 March 1919. Courtesy of Special Collections, Leeds University Library

FARWELL to DARTMOOR - Fancy Dress Ball - Sat. 12 APRIL 1919

	CARMEN	GIRL of EARLY VICTORIAN ERA Mrs. B. Connacher	GOLLYWOG
BACK ROW Left to Right	LITTLE GIRL	MAN of ENGLISH MIDDLE AGES	MAN of ITALIAN RENAISSANCE Sam Nathan

FRONT ROW Left to Right	RED CROSS NURSE Griffiths	SIR WALTER RALEIGH Stuart Campbell	JESTER	BOLSHEVIK
	BOY in costume	SPANIARD		CARDINAL WOLSEY Tom Connacll

Regret that only a few names are now available

FANCY DRESS BALL · DARTMOOR - 12 APRIL 1919

Figure 15.3 Fancy Dress Ball. Dartmoor, 12 April 1919. Courtesy of Special Collections, Leeds University Library

Cross-dressing as Hermia

Mixed with the pleasure he took in impersonating a dramatic character on stage, Cormack's narrative betrays a certain retrospective anxiety about cross-dressing, a momentary attack of what Marjorie Garber has called 'transvestite panic', that is the fear of being 'coded, and dismissed, as effeminate':[32]

> I was also one of those who presented exhibition dances at the closing fancy dress ball. I appear in both photographs of those who really dressed up for that final function. If you want to know what like I looked [*sic*] in respectable 'go-to-meeting' clothes consult the photograph of the Education Committee, of which I was secretary and treasurer – names attached. You may then also be able to pick me out in my working habit in both photographs of the fire-brigade.[33]

Cormack's attitude is ambivalent, as he points the reader of his narrative to the photographs in which he appears in woman's weeds, only to redirect the viewer's gaze quickly to those other photographs in which he wears significant elements in a stereotypical dress code of outward masculinity: a suit and tie for the education committee and fireman's dungarees for the fire brigade. He wants to make sure that he is read sartorially in the correct manner, and that he is unambiguously, unmistakably seen as male. Writing in the 1970s, Cormack seems still aware of attitudes to COs prevalent during the Great War when they were associated with 'unmanliness'. As Bibbings has shown, First World War COs were often portrayed as cowards, shirkers, 'unmen' and dandies who had fallen prey to 'decadence' and 'sexual inversion'.[34] Having established his male identity to his satisfaction, Cormack's recollections of life in Dartmoor suggest that cross-dressing was not unpleasant to him and that he positively enjoyed cross-gender dancing. During dancing evenings in prison, he took pleasure in playing the female partner in waltzing couples and enjoyed being 'swung round':

> By the way, I may here add that at Princetown centre there were informal dances three evenings per week, to piano; also that we were allowed to bring into these dances female partners, in many instances the daughters of wardens in the village! But of course not many found that possible and so most of the waltzing pairs were males. Most often I played the female partner and I am prepared to

state that I found it quite exhilarating to be swung round instead of myself setting the time and pace. Furthermore, the hall accommodated a beverage, bun, sweets and tobacco counter and it was accepted that, although the counterfeit females dressed for the part only on special occasions, it was 'de rigueur' that the male treat his lady according to her wishes.[35]

Cross-gender roles extended beyond the actual waltzing into the rest of the evening, as we gather from the fact that, after dancing, the 'lady' was treated 'according to her wishes'. On given occasions, as Cormack indicates, cross-gender waltzing was reinforced by cross-dressing. Cross-gender dancing and cross-dressing seem to have been liberating for Cormack in several respects. His narrative pays special attention to the friendship he formed with the two professional dance teachers, Stuart Campbell and Thomas Counsell:

Both Campbell and Counsell can be detected in both fancy dress ball pictures. I mention them specially because dancing had been anathema to my Baptist parents. Campbell and Counsell found me a virgin but an apt pupil and when I came home I found that the war had altered considerably the categorisation of my parents' ideas of right and wrong. Socially I took great pleasure in dancing ever afterwards.[36]

Dancing seems to have broadened Cormack's attitude to life and enjoyment, just as much as the war opened up his parents' vision of right and wrong, previously mediated by their religion. It is perhaps one of the ironic outcomes of wartime that conflicts can expand the mind through exposure to difference.[37]

If cross-gender waltzing could alter Cormack's inherited worldview, cross-dressing to play Hermia may have provided a similarly liberating experience. To the exhilaration and fun of performing in drag, Cormack had to add the fact that Hermia is surely the character in the play with whom a First World War CO could most readily identify. The implications of choosing to perform *A Midsummer Night's Dream* for an audience of First World War COs are manifold. This is clearly a play much concerned with love and marriage, with appearances and reality, with theatre and celebration, but it is also a deeply political play that addresses the clash between a desire for freedom and the fetters imposed by the stern Athenian law. It is a play that encodes a struggle of the individual will against the state, unjust law, excessive authority and political power. It is not hard to imagine that COs in Dartmoor may have felt from the play's first scene and, particularly, in response to Hermia's predicament, that the drama ventriloquized their own situation. Like First World War COs, Hermia is confronted with a harsh choice: she must either accept patriarchal authority (and comply with her father's wish to marry her off to Demetrius) or face a death sentence. The only alternative to this senseless choice is reclusion and internment: 'to abjure / For ever the society of men' and 'to be in shady cloister mewed' (*Dream*, 1.1.65–6, 71), to withdraw, that is, to a convent.[38] A play with lines such as these might easily appeal to the inmates of Princetown Work Centre – Hermia, just as the COs had done, challenges the law when she refuses to accept orders from authority (her father and the Duke; the commanding officer in the case of a CO); her defiance is an act of self-assertion and the triumph of free will. Hermia's response to the Duke could easily be appropriated by Dartmoor COs:

> HERMIA: So I will grow, so live, so die, my lord,
> Ere I will yield my virgin patent up
> Unto his lordship whose unwishèd yoke
> My soul consents not to give sovereignty.
>
> (*Dream*, 1.1.79–82)

Read through the eyes of a First World War conscientious objector, *A Midsummer Night's Dream* becomes a play about moral choices and resistance, about how to avoid the soul's consent to 'unwishèd yokes'. Hermia's refusal to allow patriarchal authority to coerce her conscience has much in common with a CO's fight against military authority. For First World War COs, Shakespeare's play clearly articulated the value of the great lengths to which one was willing to go in order to stand up for conscience and beliefs. Like Hermia's refusal to marry Demetrius, the CO's refusal to accept conscription in 1916 was regarded as a challenge to the authority of the state.

If the questioning of patriarchal structures and of gender roles often goes together, as Marjorie Garber suggests,[39] it is easy to understand why, in order to contain the challenge that conscientious objection posed during the First World War, the CO had to be read as effeminate. On the other hand, if cross-dressing is a prerogative of the power elite, as an occasional gender inversion, as archetypal carnival,[40] and cross-dressing in the theatre is 'the norm' rather than 'the aberration',[41] Cormack's cross-dressing as Hermia and as a 'Maiden of Early Victorian Era' becomes, like the flight from Athens to the forest, an act of self-assertion, in defiance of contemporary received opinion about the gender orientation of COs. Thus, in Dartmoor, performing Shakespeare became, in an utterly unexpected fashion, 'work of national importance'. Shakespeare had a crucial role to play there, that of providing the necessary cultural currency to sanction cross-dressing as not 'unmanly' and enabling a renegotiation of masculinity. Therefore, in 1919, a play by Shakespeare, history (in the form of Victorian antiquarianism) and a sophisticated elite dance such as the waltz provided the ground for a safe transgression of gender roles.

The challenge to received gender notions that the Dartmoor performance of *A Midsummer Night's Dream* facilitated took place at a time of conflict. Between 11 November 1918 and 28 June 1919, the Great War was not yet officially over. Firing had stopped but peace had not yet been negotiated and conscientious objectors remained interned because, in spite of the Home Office Scheme, they were treated like conscripted soldiers, who were still awaiting demobilization. In this suspended moment in time, *A Midsummer Night's Dream* transcended its nature as romantic comedy and acquired specific political overtones. Like Hermia, COs had been given a choice between complying with authority and giving up the society of men. Unlike Hermia, they could not run away to a forest and did not enjoy a truly happy ending. Most COs were released from prisons and Home Office Scheme centres between April and June 1919. Disenfranchised for the following five years, return to civilian life for them was hard.[42] They found it difficult to reclaim their old jobs and nearly impossible to find new employment. Yet their refusal to fight in the war had been important for the nation as a whole. Their agricultural work was nothing but punishment and their hard toil at the quarry was useless but their resistance to the war effort is now regarded as the germ of the pacifist movement in Britain. Also, their experiences in prison, once they were released and could inform on the conditions they had endured, led to reform of the prison system. Shakespeare's *A Midsummer Night's Dream* contributed to this 'work of national importance'. If British soldiers at the front were told that God was on their side, COs in Dartmoor must have felt that Shakespeare was on theirs. For them, more than a play about love and sentimental education, *A Midsummer Night's Dream* was no doubt a political play that explored the conflict between the authority of the state and the conscience of the individual subject.

Notes

This article is a result of Research Project 12014/PHCS/09 'Great War Shakespeare II: Myths, Social Agents and Global Culture', awarded by the Fundación Séneca. I would like here to stress my gratitude to Richard Davies and the rest of the staff at the Brotherton Library (University of Leeds) for their help and guidance while consulting the Liddle Collection. I am also grateful to the staff of the Imperial War Museum and, in particular, to the librarians at the Library of the Society of Religious Friends in Britain, for supplying me with both advice and material from their archive.

1. *The Collected Papers of Bertrand Russell*, ed. by Louis Greenspan et al., 29 vols (London: Routledge, 1983–2008), XIV (*Pacifism and Revolution 1916–1918*), 67, 410–11. Bertrand Russell was actively involved in the National Committee of the No-Conscription Fellowship.
2. David Boulton, 'Rebels in Uniform', *Observer*, Weekend Review, 7 August 1966.
3. The number of COs who were tried by tribunals after conscription was implemented is estimated at 16,500. See John Rae, *Conscience and Politics: The British Government and the Conscientious Objector to Military Service 1916–1919* (London: Oxford University Press, 1970), 132.
4. Lyn Smith, *Voices against War: A Century of Protest* (Edinburgh: Mainstream, 2009), 30.
5. Howard Marten, a CO imprisoned in Rouen in 1916, described the experience of having a death sentence read to him. See Smith, 34–5.
6. See Mrs Henry Hobhouse, *I Appeal unto Caesar: The Case of the Conscientious Objector* (London: George Allen and Unwin, n.d.). It has now been established that Bertrand Russell is the ghost writer behind this booklet, which was published in July 1917, went through four editions by October 1917 and sold more than 14,000 copies – one of which was handed to King George V by Lord Milner.
7. Lois S. Bibbings has looked into how COs were portrayed and represented during the Great War in *Telling Tales about Men: Conceptions of Conscientious Objectors to Military Service during the First World War* (Manchester: Manchester University Press, 2009). Cartoons and postcards from 1916 and 1917 provide evidence for these attitudes to COs. In a satirical postcard from 1916, a German soldier pushes his bayonet against the rear of an effeminate English private with long hair and the caption reads: 'The Conscientious Objector at the Front: Oh, you naughty unkind German – really, if you don't desist, I'll forget I've got a conscience and I'll smack you on the wrist!' (Bibbings, 117). With a very different intention in mind, a series of postcards attributed to G.P. Micklewright sympathize with the plight of COs in prison and depict them as saints or martyrs who are humiliated with no regard for human rights. In one of these postcards, the CO is portrayed as a martyr sewing mail bags in prison, and his sacrifice becomes meaningful in the context of the International Brotherhood of Socialist Pacifists (see Bibbings, 10, 35, 168).
8. *Troublesome People: A Reprint of the No-Conscription Fellowship Souvenir: Describing its Work during the Years 1914–1919* (London: Central Board for Conscientious Objectors, 1940), 44.

9. Smith, 43.
10. Rae, 185.
11. *The Tribunal*, 8 March 1917. *The Tribunal* was published by the No-Conscription Fellowship between 8 March 1916 and 8 January 1920.
12. *Collected Papers*, XIV, 102.
13. *The Tribunal*, 8 March 1917.
14. *The Tribunal*, 8 March 1917.
15. Liddle Collection, CO 095 ST Tracey.
16. There is nothing very unusual about the contents of this concert programme which shows that the COs in Princetown Work Centre, still labelled Dartmoor Convict Prison on the programme, were offered the same kind of 'concert party' entertainment that was offered to soldiers in the trenches and camps of the Western and Eastern fronts.
17. See for example Amy Scott-Douglass, *Shakespeare Inside: The Bard Behind Bars* (London: Continuum, 2007) and Jean Trounstine, *Shakespeare Behind Bars: The Power of Drama in a Women's Prison* (New York: St Martin's Press, 2001). For Shakespeare in prison camps and behind 'barbed wire' see Ton Hoenselaars, 'ShakesPOW', *Linguaculture*, 2 (2011), 67–82 and Michael Dobson, *Shakespeare and Amateur Performance: A Cultural History* (Cambridge: Cambridge University Press, 2011), 134–51. See also Chapters 16 and 17 below.
18. Before the war, Basil Gill had often performed this scene as part of a music-hall programme at the London Coliseum. See Marion F. O'Connor, 'Theatre of Empire: "Shakespeare's England" at Earls Court, 1912', in *Shakespeare Reproduced: The Text in Ideology and History*, ed. by Jean Howard and Marion F. O'Connor (London: Routledge, 1987), 68–98 (87).
19. 'Christmas at Shakespeare Hut', *The Times*, 26 December 1916.
20. Michael Dobson, 'Shakespeare Exposed: Outdoor Performance and Ideology, 1880–1940', in *Shakespeare, Memory and Performance*, ed. by Peter Holland (Cambridge: Cambridge University Press, 2006), 256–78.
21. Dobson, *Shakespeare and Amateur Performance*, 200.
22. *The Ben Greet Shakespeare for Young Readers and Amateur Players, William Shakespeare's* A Midsummer Night's Dream (London: Doublesday, 1912). See also 'Ben Greet and Regent's Park', in Dobson, *Shakespeare and Amateur Performance*, 172–82.
23. Terence Lane, MS Letter, dated 18 September 1918, Library of the Society of Religious Friends in Britain, TEMP MSS 585.
24. William S. Cormack, 'Conscription and Conscientious Objection, 1914–1918', Liddle Collection, CO 022 Cormack, WS.
25. Cormack, 43.
26. Cormack, 41–2.
27. In spite of the armistice, the Army Council and the Cabinet did not think COs should be demobilized before soldiers and the government did not authorize the discharge of COs on the Home Office Scheme until 10 April 1919. See Rae, 189–90.
28. Golliwogg was a popular storybook character based on an American black minstrel doll and created by Florence Kate Upton for her book *The Adventures of Two Dutch Dolls* (1895).
29. The CO cross-dressed as Salome is clearly mimicking one of Maud Allan's dance poses. The choice of historical character, costume and pose, so

redolent of Allan's dance in her famous show *The Vision of Salome* as well as of her performance of the titular role in private productions of Oscar Wilde's *Salome* in 1918, suggests that the COs in Dartmoor were alert to news from the London theatre world. By March 1919, given the notoriety Allan had achieved as a result of the Pemberton Billing case, with its aura of decadent homosexuality and pro-German espionage, to cross-dress as Salome was a daring choice both in gender and political terms. For the Salomania that swept Europe in the first decades of the twentieth century and the connections between Maud Allan, Oscar Wilde's *Salome* and the Pemberton Billing case see Philip Hoare, *Wilde's Last Stand: Decadence, Conspiracy and the First World War* (London: Duckworth, 1997).

30. I owe my awareness of the importance of the Tudor pageant at the turn of the twentieth century to the work of Michael Dobson. See Michael Dobson, 'The Pageant of History: Nostalgia, the Tudors, and the Community Play', *SEDERI*, 20 (2010), 5–25.

31. Cormack, 41. Although Cormack never explicitly says so, the Dartmoor production of *Dream* must have had an all-male cast. This renders the amateur theatricals of the COs very much like other performances and productions up and down the Western and Eastern Fronts. Divisional concert parties generally consisted of male soldiers. Exceptions may have existed but they were rare, such as the *Twelfth Night* production at the 52nd General Hospital in Salonica, performed on 11 January 1919, with a cast consisting of officers, privates and 'sisters'.

32. Marjorie Garber, *Vested Interests: Cross-dressing and Cultural Anxiety* (New York: Routledge, 1992), 137 and ff.

33. Cormack, 42.

34. Bibbings, 89–141.

35. Cormack, 43.

36. Cormack, 42.

37. As professional dance teachers, Stuart Campbell and Thomas Counsell must have been aware of the revolution in dancing brought about by Isadora Duncan, and by Diaghilev and the Russian Ballets. The outfit of the 'Man of the Italian Renaissance' and the pose of Samuel Nathan are vaguely redolent of some costumes worn by Nijinsky. Cormack also took part in the 'exhibition dances' arranged by Campbell and Counsell for the April fancy-dress ball.

38. Quotations from *A Midsummer Night's Dream* come from Peter Holland's edition for Oxford World's Classics (Oxford: Oxford University Press, 1994).

39. Garber, 141.

40. Garber, 52 and ff.

41. Garber, 39.

42. COs were disenfranchised on 6 February 1918 under the Representation of the People Act. See Rae, 234–5 and Smith, 55.

16

'The play's the thing': *Hamlet* in a Romanian Wartime Political Prison

Monica Matei-Chesnoiu

> Life in itselfe is neither good nor evill: it is the place of
> good or evill, according as you prepare it for them.
> Michel de Montaigne, Essays[1]

Confinement, performance and self-discovery

Confinement as a form of punishment – whether served in prison or in exile – has seldom been considered as beneficial or creative. Only Lear was so overjoyed when he was reunited with Cordelia as to welcome life in prison with her as a kind of paradise, looking forward to the acquisition of wisdom through their retirement from the world. They will, he thinks, take upon themselves 'the mystery of things', comprehend the mystery of life and human destiny, which the actual participants in the game, because they are too much involved in the race, cannot understand (5.3.8–19).[2] However, this idyllic scenario, which transforms the prison, as Mariangela Tempera observes, 'in[to] a domesticated wonderland',[3] is unrealistic and is meant only to provide some form of relief in anticipation of the ensuing tragedy. Elsewhere, Claudio, in *Measure for Measure*, speaks 'so wisely' of excessive liberty which has brought about his restraining arrest (1.2.117–22), while Lucio's edgy, flippant witticism, expressive of unease, shows his preference for 'the foppery of freedom' as opposed to 'the morality of imprisonment' (1.2.125–6). Only Hamlet affirms he can be bound in a nutshell and count himself a king of infinite space, though he also admits to having bad dreams (2.2.256–8). Despite the pervading imagery suggesting that Elsinore itself is a prison where impending war and disaster are inevitable, it is not clear whether Hamlet's words to Rosencrantz and Guildenstern

(2.2.241–53) actually echo his belief that he really feels confined in Denmark's prison. Imprisoned by words and surrounded by staging, acting and seeming, Hamlet directs his own world, if only for a moment.

Real prisons, as opposed to the entrapments and confinement of discourse (albeit the Shakespearean one), are seriously different affairs. Documenting his voyage to the 'Infortunate Islands' represented by an early modern London prison, Thomas Dekker calls the place, metaphorically, 'an enchanted castle' because it produces a 'rare transformation' on people's minds, making a wise man lose his wits and a fool know himself.[4] While it is clear from the text that the misery of life in prison can break the strongest of minds, Dekker's account does not explain the second part of his statement, namely the potential to reach self-knowledge while in prison. Only in twentieth-century post-structuralist social, historical, psychological and philosophical approaches do we see attempts to deal with this issue and even here there are disagreements. Foucault is concerned with incarceration as a form of punishment, which is an expression of power,[5] but he does not offer an empirical description of penal regimes. On the other hand, early modern social historians of crime, such as Pieter Spierenburg,[6] tend to refute Foucault's account of the prison shaped as a modern form of punishment by charting the sixteenth-century origins of the institution.

The method of this chapter, however, is rather based on Bakhtin's concepts of heteroglossia, multivocality and dialogue.[7] Drama is a dialogic medium par excellence and the multiplicity of voices (source, author, players and audience) involved in the amateurish and often anonymous exchange created by productions of drama in prison may account for the possibility of ultimately reaching an elusive sense of self-knowledge for the players and the audience. In addition, the commemorative function of the performance of tragedy, as Manfred Pfister notes, involves 'the very basis of individual identity, which is constantly made, unmade, and remade on the loom of personal memories, recollections, and reminiscences'.[8] By definition, the prison space is a place of confinement and domination and life in prison in itself may be self-revelatory for some inmates, forcing them to reconsider their past experience. All the more so in the process of performing drama in prison, when the amateur actor is faced with the temporary and relative identity of the character he or she is interpreting, but also enters into a different kind of relationship with the script. The theatre discloses various social languages embedded in the play's characters but also engages the actors interpreting those characters in a personal dialogue with their own selves.

In addition to theatre performance in prison having a formative action on the individuals interpreting the role, it may also speak daggers to the play's audience. Unlike conventional productions in the public theatres, where entertainment is the main focus, theatrical productions in prison are not only meant to entertain; in addition they are expected to have a psychotherapeutic effect on both the actors and the audience.[9] In the introduction to a collection of essays seeking to explain what connects the theatre to the social world outside it, Patricia Badir and Paul Yachnin observe that theatre and the performance cultures are 'sites of individual and collective meaning-making'.[10] Is it possible that prison inmates should find meaning in rehearsing, playing or attending a play in prison? Exiled, dominated by imposed routines, numbered rather than named, inmates often evade self-knowledge and self-examination. The contrast between here and there – between prison and normal life – may explain such alienating attitudes. Yet, when faced with the make-believe world of the theatre, they are confronted with a space that is distant enough to allow them to avoid direct self-involvement, but sufficiently personal to permit some kind of self-scrutiny during the two hours' traffic of the stage.

The self-mirroring and dialogic principle is even more strongly revealed when Shakespeare – and particularly the ubiquitous *Hamlet* – is performed in prison. In analysing the rites of memory involved in how a performance is recollected by spectators, Dennis Kennedy uses the discourse of psychoanalysis and the historical method to argue that Shakespeare is part of the collective imaginary and that *Hamlet*, as Kennedy puts it facetiously, is 'the most famous play in our solar system', which 'has been part of Western thought for four hundred years'.[11] Consequently, Kennedy asks the justified question as to whether the audience's collective remembrance of *Hamlet* may play false in their encounter with the play in a particular production. Although there is no easy answer to such a multifaceted question (nor does Kennedy attempt to give one), when discussing productions of *Hamlet* in prison, the possible answers may emerge from a double perspective. On the one hand, the cultural background of the prison audience – inmates, guards, and perhaps their families – is generally not so rich as to account for a detailed knowledge of the play's many manifestations through time and space. On the other hand, members of the audience would know enough about the play's fame to be tempted to approach it with a degree of reverence due to both a literary classic and a monument of high culture.

Prison theatre in Fascist-dominated Romania

This chapter is based on material gathered from a 1973 essay by Romanian theatre critic Margareta Andreescu on the 'combative' pro-letarian theatre in Romania.[12] The article, which is subtitled 'Aspects of the anti-Fascist reaction through theatre', is meant to document the allegedly widespread anti-Nazi response of underground Socialist and Communist circles in Romania during the Second World War.[13] Andreescu's article is part of a monograph – no doubt funded by the Romanian Communist Party in the early 1970s – based on manu-scripts, memoirs and biographies recording the anti-Fascist movement in Romania during the Second World War. In addition, Andreescu mentions having consulted similar works by Iosif Pervain, which deal with working-class theatrical activity in Transylvania,[14] and an article by Simion Alterescu and Letiția Gîtză on Socialist revolutionary thea-tre in the interwar and war periods (1918–44).[15] The declared aim of Andreescu's essay is 'to evoke important moments of our working-class revolutionary movement and to make it possible for the public con-sciousness to become totally immersed in the exemplary greatness of this glorious struggle and the heroic deeds of the Romanian Communist Party, as well as in the forms they embraced along time'.[16] I have quoted the full text of Andreescu's objective to show the hackneyed phraseology and the excessively laudatory comments about the achievements of Communism, which were part of the common critical discourse of the time, in line with Socialist propaganda. In post-Communist years (and also privately among academics during Communist times), this kind of grandiose wordiness was termed 'wooden language'. Reversing Gertrude's criticism of Polonius's verbosity, Shakespeareans might describe it as too much art with less matter.

Andreescu's essay emphasizes the 'impressive' number of proletarian theatrical activities and the 'heroic' character of such productions mounted during the years when the Romanian Communist Party (PCR) was illegal and many of its members were imprisoned on political grounds. The theatre performed by working-class players for working-class audiences is described as 'a struggle and an act of bravery' which had the effect of raising spirits, especially during the years of illegality, despite government persecution, dire material conditions, poor repertoire and insufficient professional acting expertise. This was even more true, as Andreescu explains, in conditions of detention, when physical and moral survival were the main incentives, and producing plays had become a form of 'undermining from within' the suffering, despair and humiliation bred by life in prison. The result of this subversive attitude, aimed at arming oneself against the slings and arrows of outrageous fortune, was that the dark and repressive prison spaces were transformed into 'universities'.[17] This minimalist form of theatre, which mainly took the form of reciting passages from plays or, at times, collective 'chorus' recitals (in the manner of the Greek tragedy) was, as Andreescu notes, a continuation of the cultural activity the imprisoned Communist leaders had conducted in the towns from which they came (Timişoara, Ploieşti, Turnu-Severin, Reşiţa, Galaţi, Braşov). These were essentially working-class towns where the Socialist movement was considered to have been thriving, but this kind of basic theatre was also played all over the Nazi detention camps in Central Europe.

When theatre in detention took on the rarer form of organized productions, with improvised actors, costumes and stage, this action, according to Andreescu, achieved proportions of 'troubling significance'. Such a position is explained by the fact that many of these theatrical productions were mounted illegally, thereby defeating the vigilance of prison guards, and they were meant to foster a positive feeling of self-confidence and belief in a future free from the 'Fascist oppression' and 'inhuman order' represented by Nazi ideology. Andreescu gives the example of plays by Ion Luca Caragiale (the Romanian national playwright) produced in the prisons of Doftana and Dumbrăveni in the period 1938–39. Performances took place in a barn, sets and costumes were improvised from boxes and chairs covered with cloths and carpets embroidered by the women prisoners. There was no stage, the acting space was separated from the audience by means of curtains, and lighting was provided by oil lamps. Players were distinguished by tags on their costumes: a king would wear a paper crown, a queen a long cape and a crown, and the central character would wear a distinctive cap. Such improvised productions would fetch up to one thousand spectators, who applauded enthusiastically. Sometimes, they were even mounted with the approval of the prison guards, who also attended as part of the audience.[18]

A Romanian *Hamlet* behind bars

An unusual production of *Hamlet* took place in a Romanian political prison during 1942–43. There are minimal records of this production: a few sketches by a prisoner, Georg Hromadka, and the testimonies of some members of the audience. Andreescu published the sketches and some notes concerning the production. This *Hamlet* was mounted in a political prison in Timişoara, and later in Arad, and some of the prisoners were members of the Romanian Social-Democratic Party[19] from the neighbouring working-class towns of Reşiţa or Turnu-Severin. A parody of the 'To be or not to be' soliloquy paraphrased one of Hitler's speeches, in an intertextual fusion where levels of significance were suspended above the ideological void and worked around the censorship operating in a wartime political prison. Nowhere could the relevance of Denmark's prison be more topical and politically charged. There was a pun on 'to be' and the German people, and 'not to be' and the Fascist regime.[20] The scene where Polonius and Hamlet discussed the cloud as a camel allegorically satirized Hitler's acolytes. The play was used subversively against the Nazi regime and the revenge theme proved adaptable to the needs of anti-Nazi political prisoners.

The sketches by Georg Hromadka are dated 11 December 1942 and each of them represents a character in action. Hamlet appears to have uttered his 'To be or not to be' soliloquy against the setting of a prison cell (Figure 16.1), home for the inmates-actors – as Denmark would have been for Hamlet: 'To me', as the brooding prince said of both his physical and emotional location, 'it is a prison' (2.2.252–3). The iron bars in the background were also suggestive of St Michael's cross – a symbol of the pro-Fascist military group called the Legionary Movement, active in Romania at the time.[21] Hamlet sits in a crouched position – a sign of repression and submission – and holds a book in his hand (probably Hamlet's famous book or simply the play's script). Although the prison cell suggests seclusion and solitude, Hamlet is not alone; he delivers his soliloquy under the gaze of an unusually tall and very thin guard, who watches him closely and whose attitude appears to be one of domination. The implication was that, however secluded, prisoners had no privacy in their cells and that even when they wished to express their innermost thoughts, they had to do so in front of an audience of guards. Moreover, when we think of the real-life situation, the guard might represent the Romanian official government, which at that time was Fascist-dominated, or maybe even a member of the SS. It is not clear from the sketch whether this guard-figure was a real warden, who was watching the production, or just a character in this prison adaptation of *Hamlet*, but we can see from it how the world of the theatre and that of real life interpenetrate. While uttering a 'To be or not to be' monologue that spoke of 'tak[ing] arms against a sea of troubles / And, by opposing, end them', Hamlet was being watched by a representative of the very oppressors against whom arms should be raised.

Figure 16.1 Hamlet's 'To be or not to be' soliloquy in a Romanian prison cell. Timişoara, 1942. Courtesy of the Romanian Academy Library

The character of Hamlet, as the second sketch documents (Figure 16.2), was interpreted by a prisoner named Surulescu. We see him dressed in a military uniform, which appears to conflate elements of both Romanian and German uniforms, with an officer's cap but no rank insignia. The scarf around his neck is vaguely reminiscent of the green Iron Guard bandana, or perhaps of the red scarf of the Boy Scouts, which the Communists later transformed into the red 'pioneer' scarf with which they used to deck every Romanian youth as a sign of allegiance to Communist ideology; as the colour of the scarf is not distinguishable, we can only guess. Hamlet is armed with a 'bare bodkin' (3.1.78) which might serve to end his life, and he seems to be deep in conversation with an unseen interlocutor. The Hamlet in this production sports a small moustache (instead of the much-debated beard), which might be interpreted as a mockery of Hitler's absurdly small expanse of facial hair. Regardless of the interpretation we may give of this character, however, the prison context in which the play was

Figure 16.2   Hamlet, interpreted by Surulescu, in a Romanian prison production. Timişoara, 1942. Courtesy of the Romanian Academy Library

produced means that every political and ideological allusion must be weighed with both caution and care.

When we come to the figure of Queen Gertrude, played by someone called Oprea, and therefore definitely female, we have a clear indication that the language used in this production of *Hamlet* was German. A note on the right-hand corner of the sketch indicates the character as 'the Queen' (*die Königin*). This may be because Hromadka, the author of the sketches and probably the impromptu director of this production, was of German origin; it might also simply have been easier, in that region of Banat, to find a German translation of *Hamlet* than a Romanian translation.[22] Nonetheless, the political implications of a parody directed against the Nazi regime in German may be interestingly interpreted as a rejection of Fascist ideology while not denying German tradition and its cultural values. Gertrude adopts a submissive attitude – her hands folded, her eyes lowered – as was expected at that time of a woman in Romania. The setting, suggested by the bare wooden planks on which she stands, bears an uncanny resemblance to Hamlet's prison cell but might also symbolically recall the wooden boards of the stage. This – as may be inferred from the drawing – served to remind the audience that she was still in a prison, though playing a theatre queen in the impromptu theatre.

The Ghost (*der Geist*) – played by Iosif Puvak, as the sketches show – was enveloped in the white shroud commonly used to create the association with a spectre and he wore a resplendent crown, more clearly visible than Gertrude's royal diadem. The author of the sketch chose to draw a halo around his head, a common convention in the representations of saints in Romanian Orthodox icons, probably to suggest the supernatural elements in this character, which distinguished it from the others. However, this halo would have been difficult to represent in the actual production – especially with the limited means available in prison – so it invites us to draw a line between the artist/director's imagination and the actual possibilities of prison theatre productions. As in the sketch of the Queen's character, we have a clear indication that the production was in German.

This *Hamlet* behind bars was evidently dependent on the cultural capital of 'Shakespeare'. Both the script and the production would have been subject to some kind of censorship on the part of the prison authorities, but an orthodox text by Shakespeare, translated into German, could have aroused little objection. On the other hand, the improvised director and actors secretly knew that the script could be twisted into taking on a variety of subversive meanings and they went along with the game of appearance versus reality, just as Hamlet did in the 'Mousetrap'. However, this was the real world of a political court-martial wartime prison and the actors were either waiting for their death sentences to be pronounced or waiting to be executed. It is not clear whether some of the actors were actually executed but it is certain that Georg Hromadka lived to tell the tale of this production. Horatio-like, he would absent himself from the 'felicity' of death for a while (5.2.299) to tell Hamlet's tale to future audiences, to all those who would be willing to lend their ear to his account of life in Romanian political prisons. Hromadka even lived to write a book about his experience as a Social Democrat leader from the town of Reşiţa (in the region of Banat) and he died in old age, a respected German citizen.[23] From his documents of this production in prison we learn that the language of *Hamlet*, which the actors pretended to be their own, allowed them to speak truths about their lives as political prisoners. For them drama became, indeed, a thing that had to be done because, while the theatre space was makeshift, the prison (of Denmark or of Romania) was real.

In reviewing two working-class Shakespeare productions, one in New York's Harlem (1937) and the other in Birmingham (1997), Kathleen McLuskie observes that 'the appeal of the approach [to his texts] through the theatre is that it offers an immediacy of experience'.[24]

The incredible versatility of performing Shakespeare – especially *Hamlet* – makes us recognize that what we think we know is constantly eluding us. Like the direct experience of life, what we see in a theatre production is impossible to grasp; it is already past, already lost. This is all the more so if we do not see the actual production, and only have access to its material but equally elusive remains, represented in the case of the performance discussed here by little more than a handful of sketches – an interesting but distinctly speculative ride into the world of might-have-been. On the other hand, life in prison, from the perspective of the inmates, was (and is) determined not by philosophical, moral or spatial coordinates: like the rest of life, it just is. Using the metaphor of the theatre, of Shakespeare, and of *Hamlet* – each of these concepts yielding its specific layer of meaning – a quasi-anonymous group of political prisoners in Romania tried to look for a suitable (though elusive) way out of their temporal prison by adopting Hamlet's words and poses. At that specific historical time, the intent was to make a statement addressed to the authorities against a specific political situation. What we learn from their actions, however, is that it is possible to do things with words even if nobody (or very few people) listen to them.

Notes

The writing of this chapter has profited from research periods at the Shakespeare Library in Munich, funded by a grant from the Alexander von Humboldt Foundation, which I remember with gratitude. My research has greatly benefited from the collaboration with the Department für Anglistik und Amerikanistik, Institut für Englische Philologie of Ludwig-Maximilians-Universität in Munich. I gratefully acknowledge Andreas Höfele, Ingeborg Bolz and Bettina Boecker, who have followed my research with interest and have been the source of many stimulating and helpful ideas. I am also thankful to the Romanian Academy Library for the copyright approval of the two illustrations included in this chapter.

1. Michel de Montaigne, *The essayes or morall, politike and millitarie discourses*, trans. by John Florio (London: Val. Sims for Edward Blount, 1603), 37, STC 18041.
2. All the quotations from Shakespeare are taken from *The Complete Works*, ed. by Stanley Wells and Gary Taylor, 2nd edn (Oxford: Clarendon Press, 2005).
3. Mariangela Tempera, 'Le parole di Lear', in *King Lear dal testo alla scena*, ed. by Mariangela Tempera (Bologna: CLUEB, 1986), 143–58 (157); translation mine.
4. Thomas Dekker, 'English Villainies Discovered by Lantern and Candlelight' (1608), in *Shakespeare's England: Life in Elizabethan and Jacobean Times*, ed. by R.E. Pritchard, 2nd edn (Sparkford: Sutton Publishing, 2003), 236–9 (236–7). Dekker was committed to the King's Bench Prison for debt in 1612 and released in 1619.

5. Michel Foucault, *Discipline and Punish: The Birth of the Prison*, trans. by Alan Sheridan (New York: Vintage, 1975).

6. Pieter Spierenburg, *The Prison Experience: Disciplinary Institutions and their Inmates in Early Modern Europe* (New Brunswick, NJ: Rutgers University Press, 1991), 12–38 (23–6).

7. Bakhtin observes that a character's self-consciousness in Dostoevsky is 'thoroughly dialogized' (251): it is turned outward, intensely addressing itself, another, a third person. Different languages are at play in the novel, Bakhtin argues, because of its inherent heteroglossia – its tendency to multiply discourses and pit them against one another. Bakhtin does not believe this mechanism occurs in drama, which he links to poetic or single-voiced forms of discourse, but in Shakespeare there are many instances of such heteroglossia. See M.M. Bakhtin, 'Dialogue in Dostoevsky', in *Problems of Dostoevsky's Poetics*, ed. and trans. by Caryl Emerson, 8th edn (Minneapolis and London: University of Minnesota Press, 1999), 251–69.

8. Manfred Pfister, 'Shakespeare's Memory: Texts – Images – Monuments – Performances', in *Shakespearean Culture – Cultural Shakespeare*, ed. by Jurgen Kamm and Bernd Lenz (Passau: Karl Stutz, 2009), 217–39 (232–3).

9. For the current use of theatrical productions in American prisons for thera-peutic purposes see Anthony DiMatteo, 'Oedipus in Prison: The Place of Literature in the Rehabilitative Environment', *College Literature*, 19 (1992), 44–59; Michael Macmillan, '"What happened to you today that reminded you that you are a black man?": The Process of Exploring Black Masculinities in Performance', in *Theatre and Empowerment: Community Drama on the World Stage*, ed. by Richard Boon and Jane Plastow (Cambridge: Cambridge University Press, 2004), 60–93; Paul Ryder Ryan, 'Theatre as Prison Therapy', *The Drama Review: TDR*, 20 (1976), 31–42; James Thompson, 'From the Stocks to the Stage: Prison Theatre and the Theatre of Prison', in *Theatre in Prison: Theory and Practice*, ed. by Michel Balfour (Portland, OR: Intellect Books, 2004), 57–76; Jean Trounstine, *Shakespeare behind Bars: The Power of Drama in a Women's Prison* (New York: St Martin's Press, 2001); Agnes Wilcox, 'Denmark Is a Prison and You Are There', *Journal of the Midwest Modern Language Association*, 38 (2005), 116–22. Thompson discusses the relation-ship between prison theatre and prison as theatre in the US justice system and argues that the criminal justice system is a space that bears a complex relationship to performance. Prisons and punishments are performative because they construct special sites, appeal to certain audiences, involve ritu-alized acts and either entertain or appall. Discussing the 'Capital Offender Program' for young people convicted for murder in Texas prisons, which uses theatrical methodology (psychodrama) to disclose moments in the par-ticipants' past by replaying the moment of their crime in detail, Thompson observes that 'accessing emotions buried by cognitive defenses is a highly explosive therapeutic endeavor' (71).

10. Patricia Badir and Paul Yachnin, 'Introduction', in *Shakespeare and the Cultures of Performance*, ed. by Paul Yachnin and Patricia Badir (Burlington, VT: Ashgate, 2008), 1–12 (5).

11. Dennis Kennedy, 'Memory, Performance, and the Idea of the Museum', in *Shakespeare, Memory, and Performance*, ed. by Peter Holland (Cambridge: Cambridge University Press, 2006), 329–45 (341).

220 *Shakespeare and Conflict*

12. Margareta Andreescu, 'Teatrul proletar combatant în România', *Teatrul*, 11 (1973), 40–3.
13. During the Second World War, Romania tried to remain neutral but on 28 June 1940 it received a Soviet ultimatum with an implied threat of invasion in the event of noncompliance. Under pressure from Moscow and Berlin, the Romanian administration and the army were forced to retreat from Bessarabia and Northern Bukovina in order to avoid war. The authoritarian King Carol II abdicated in 1940 and was succeeded by the National Legionary State, in which power was shared by general Ion Antonescu and the Iron Guard. In 1941, Romania entered the war on the side of the Axis powers. In August 1944, Antonescu was arrested by King Michael I and Romania changed sides and joined the Allies.
14. Iosif Pervain, 'Contribuţii la cunoaşterea activităţii teatrale muncitoreşti din Transilvania', *Studii şi cercetări de istoria artei*, 1–2 (1955), 17–32.
15. Simion Alterescu and Letiţia Gîtză, 'Influenţa teatrului revoluţionar asupra mişcării noastre teatrale', *Studii şi cercetări de istoria artei*, 1–2 (1957), 10–23.
16. Andreescu, 40. All translations from Romanian are mine.
17. Andreescu, 40–1.
18. Andreescu, 41–2.
19. The Social Democratic Party of Romania (PSD), founded in 1910, was banned in 1938 under the personal dictatorship of King Carol II, but remained active in clandestine action and opposed the Fascist regime installed in Bucharest. With the ascendancy of Ion Antonescu and Romania's participation in the Second World War alongside the Axis powers, the PSD retained its favour towards the Allies and joined King Michael and other political groups in an open resistance to the regime. In 1944, the PSD and the Communist Party (PCR) united in a front whose object was to coordinate leftist actions. The united fronts succeeded in overthrowing Antonescu's government on 23 August 1944 and backed the government that declared war on the Axis. Subsequently, the PSD united with the Communists to create the Workers' Party (PMR) as the ruling party of Communist Romania.
20. If Hamlet's 'To be or not to be' soliloquy is to be interpreted as an opposition between existence and non-existence, acknowledgement and rejection, then the implication would be that while the German people are entitled to a continuous and honourable existence in the context of history, the Nazis should be refused recognition. With the benefit of hindsight, we see that this view came, in fact, to be sanctioned by history.
21. 'The Iron Guard' is the name given to a far-Right movement and political party in Romania in the period between 1927 and the early part of the Second World War. The Iron Guard was ultra-nationalistic, anti-Semitic and Fascist in character. Originally founded in 1927 as the Legion of the Archangel Michael, adherents to the movement continued to be widely referred to as 'Legionnaires' (sometimes 'Legionaries') and the organization as the 'Legion' or the 'Legionary Movement'. Its members wore green uniforms (meant as a symbol of renewal) and greeted each other using the Roman salute. The main symbol employed by the Iron Guard was a triple cross ⛨ standing for prison bars (a sign of martyrdom), which was sometimes referred to as the 'Archangel Michael Cross'. The mysticism of the Legion led to a cult of death, martyrdom, violence and self-sacrifice. These groups observed rituals

that included writing oaths in blood and drinking blood and they shared the Fascist penchant for violence.

22. Georg Hromadka was a Swabian from the Banat region. The Banat Swabians are an ethnic German population that emigrated in the eighteenth century to what was then the Austrian Banat province, which had been left sparsely populated by the wars with Turkey. A self-taught intellectual and journalist, Hromadka published the *Reschitzaer Zeitung*, a German-language journal aimed at propagating the Social Democratic ideas and at opposing the Fascist regime in Romania. Later, Hromadka, as most of the German-origin population of Banat and Transylvania during Communism, emigrated to Germany.

23. Hromadka published a monograph on the Swabians in Banat, *Kleine Chronik des Banater Berglandes* (1993), translated into Romanian as *Scurtă cronică a Banatului montan* (*Brief Chronicle of the Mountain Region of Banat*, 1996), and was posthumously awarded honorary citizenship of the Romanian city of Reşiţa.

24. Kathleen McLuskie, 'Shakespeare Goes Slumming: Harlem '37 and Birmingham '97', in *A Companion to Shakespeare and Performance*, ed. by Barbara Hodgdon and W.B. Worthen (Oxford: Blackwell Publishing, 2005), 249–66 (249).

17

'A tongue in every wound of Caesar': Performing *Julius Caesar* behind Barbed Wire during the Second World War

Ton Hoenselaars

In a moving short story entitled 'Internee Julius Caesar', the Austrian journalist Carl Weiselberger writes about the impact of internment on detainees held in a Canadian prison camp during the Second World War. To counter the monotony of camp life – which includes the choice between attending yet another lecture about the history of the homing pigeon in the recreation lounge, or the use of the compress in natural healing in the dining room – the internees decide to play a theatrical guessing game which, with a veiled allusion to Franz Kafka, they call 'Changing Identities' (*Sichverwandeln*).[1] Two internees leave the room, while the rest assign well-known *personae* to them; on their return, each of the two internees is secretly told about the other's identity, and the point of the exercise is that each has to try to uncover their own identity by interrogating the other, who also drops hints. The story recounts how the men, once they have all had their turn, draw into the game the inconspicuous and reluctant New Age internee No. 801, a man who believes in metempsychosis and is convinced that in an earlier life he was both a priest of the Astarte cult, and Julius Caesar. The men have deliberately decided to make No. 801 guess that he is indeed Julius Caesar. After several mistaken attempts – the Roman greeting of the raised arm, provided as a hint, does not mean that he is Mussolini – internee No. 801 finally guesses that he must be Julius Caesar. However, this is where the real problem begins, because No. 801 cannot be convinced that this was only a game. The conviction that he is the real Caesar immediately leads to difficulties at the next roll call, where imperious No. 801 acts insubordinately and the Canadian officer in charge interprets the raised arm as 'a political demonstration' (*IJC*, 82). Internee No. 801, now called 'Mister Caesar', is escorted to the camp prison and, having been duly intimidated, the remaining internees never play the game of 'Changing Identities' again.

This short story – written by a Jewish refugee from Hitler's Austria who, after several weeks of captivity on the Isle of Man in May 1940, was deported to the Canadian internment camp at Sherbrook, in the province of Quebec[2] – brings together a number of themes that recur in recollections of the internment camps of the Second World War. It demonstrates, by driving the issue to an absurd extreme, the desire of internees to engage in theatrical events: 'they wanted to get out of their own skins, in whichever way, even if only in the course of a game, to change their identities, to become someone else, a completely different person' (*IJC*, 75). At the same time, it demonstrates how the organization of theatrical events, despite the sharp censorial eye of camp officials who were out to quell any serious form of subversion, was often politically charged. There was a continual tug of war between the censor and the internees, as the latter sought, time and again, to express in public what should not be broached in the first place. Given the incessant political activism of Second World War internees, the focus on Julius Caesar may seem an obvious one (also in relation to Weiselberger's explicit allusion to Mussolini), but in the face of the then prevailing censorship, it also significantly marks the perhaps less obvious moral courage of the internees. Such moral courage may be discerned elsewhere too, because the fictional story of internee No. 801 was not the only appropriation of the Julius Caesar story by Second World War internees.[3]

At least two complete productions of Shakespeare's *Julius Caesar* were mounted in captivity. The first of these was the 1940 production of the play put on at the Gaiety Theatre in Douglas by Jewish refugees from National Socialism in Germany and Austria. The second was organized by German officers and soldiers who, following their country's surrender to the Allies, had become prisoners of war in the southern French seaside town of Hyères. *Julius Caesar*, of course, was a popular play during the 1930s and 1940s, but although considerable attention has been devoted to this phenomenon in recent years, these two productions mounted in captivity have so far been ignored.[4] One reason for this neglect may be that these were amateur productions. Another reason could be the persistent Anglocentrism of mainstream Shakespeareans in their approach to theatre performances, although this would (in case it were to be linguistically determined) apply only to the German-language production in southern France, and not to the Isle of Man *Julius Caesar*, since this was in broken English. The contemporary urgency and moral integrity of the two productions discussed below give them lasting relevance, but they are relevant also because they shed a special light on our discipline as it currently stands, with its geographically narrow scope, and its continued tendency – even if this was recently challenged, among others, by Michael Dobson's *Shakespeare and Amateur Performance*[5] – to favour large-scale professional productions mounted in familiar venues, important in their own right but with a political and commercial dynamic all their own, and hence geared towards the maintenance of opinion rather than the occasionally vital subversion of established modes.

Amateur refugees on the Isle of Man

In the spring of 1940, fearing an imminent Nazi invasion, the British government interned 28,000 men and women of 'enemy' nationality living in Britain. Most of them were Jewish refugees who, having fled Nazi persecution in the course of the 1930s, were appalled to find themselves imprisoned as potential Nazi spies. Fearing a German invasion of Britain assisted by a fifth column of German exile informers already in the country, Winston Churchill issued his infamous 'intern' or 'collar the lot' decree.[6] He proceeded to screen all refugees after interning them in Britain (both on the mainland and on the Isle of Man), Canada and Australia. As they waited to be cleared of suspicion, the refugees sought to continue their lives in a regular fashion, they developed a school system and produced plays.

Maxine Seller has written about the theatrical entertainments mounted by the predominantly Jewish internees on the Isle of Man, and about the type of plays that were actually put on. She notes: 'Many plays performed in the camps had strong political overtones. Not surprisingly, given the life histories of the actors and audiences, these plays dealt with issues of freedom, the fall of dictatorships, and the horrors of war.'[7] Works by liberal German authors such as Goethe and Schiller appeared on camp playbills,[8] as did Shakespeare, George Bernard Shaw and John Drinkwater. Given the traditional coupling of captivity and censorship, there would always be questions from the authorities when German playwrights like Goethe or Schiller were put on, but there seems to have been no suspicion when the native Shakespeare was chosen. Even the choice of *Julius Caesar* appears to have been unproblematic simply because of its English origin: 'Shakespeare's *Julius Caesar* was more familiar to British authorities and therefore aroused no controversy when it was presented in Sefton [Camp] in November 1940.'[9]

This November 1940 production of *Julius Caesar* was directed by the successful Swiss-born playwright and dramaturge Hans José Rehfisch (1891–1960).[10] With Erwin Piscator, Rehfisch had run the Central-Theater in Berlin (1922–23), and they had worked together as directors at the politically vocal Theater am Nollendorfplatz in Berlin (1927–28). Rehfisch's status before the Second World War is perhaps best illustrated by the fact that from 1931 until 1933 he was President of the Society of German Playwrights and Stage Composers. In 1936, he went into exile in Britain and settled in London, where he earned a living as a metal worker.

As we gather from a rare article in the internees' own *Sefton Review* – which is illustrated with evocative drawings by camp father Walter Simon[11] to complement the text (see Figure 17.1) – Rehfisch directed a modern-dress *Julius Caesar* on the Isle of Man, with the senators in business suits. With his experience of the German theatre scene and his apparent interest in the British theatrical life of the 1930s, Rehfisch was well aware that modern-dress Shakespeare, even a modern-dress *Julius Caesar*, was not original in itself: 'It is by no means an entirely new venture', he said modestly, 'to produce Shakespeare's greatest play in modern dress; it has been done before in Oxford and Cambridge, in New York and in London.'[12] Rehfisch was actually even mildly critical of using the modern setting as 'a vehicle for decreasing the remoteness of the atmosphere' and to bring the play nearer to the audience: 'the producer who will content himself with replacing the traditional [R]oman costumes with storm-troopers uniforms and with putting telephone sets on to the stage is not likely to achieve this' (*SR*, 5). Central to Rehfisch's vision were Shakespeare's characters: 'The main task in performing [*Julius Caesar*] or any other of Shakespeare's plays still is, as it always has been, the reproduction of its characters in as distinct and vivid a fashion as the author has visualized them' (*SR*, 5).

But of course Rehfisch chose to modernize because it made a vital political point. It also solved a number of practical problems. One major problem Rehfisch faced was that inexperienced actors were confronted with the demands made on them by the Shakespearean verse: how 'to prevent the amateurs from acting unnaturally or in a rigid fashion while they were speaking Shakespearean verse' (*SR*, 5). To counter the problem, Rehfisch thought of 'keeping the actors busy with commonplace occupations whenever the play would permit it' (*SR*, 5). Rehfisch looked upon such 'commonplace occupations' not as gimmicks, but as a legitimate means of bringing two-thousand-year-old history up to date. It is remarkable how the decision to aid the amateur players via a consistent modernizing practice produced potent stage images

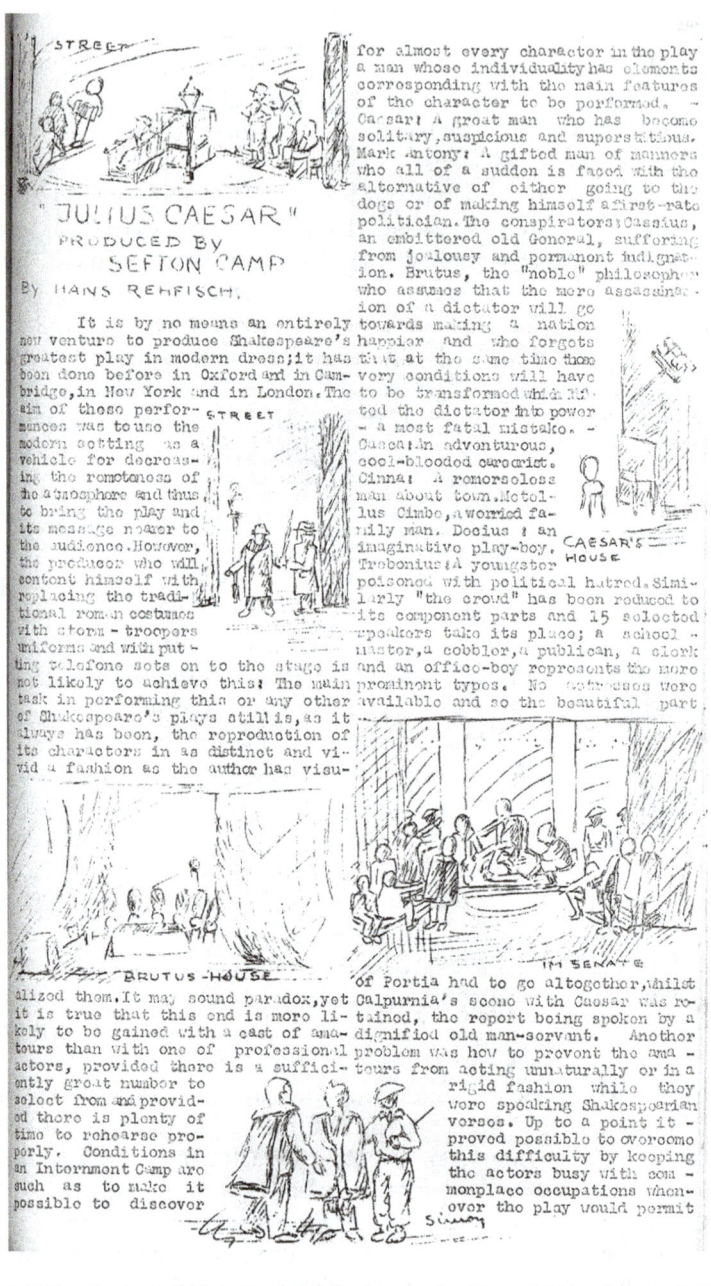

Figure 17.1 Review of Hans José Rehfisch's production of *Julius Caesar*. Sefton Camp, Isle of Man, 1940. Originally published in *The Sefton Pioneer*, 25 November 1940. Courtesy of Manx National Heritage

it: Even a dictator will have breakfast in the morning; there is no law forbidding conspirators to have a drink or a cigarette during their dangerous meetings; and when a death sentence on a political enemy has become a mere matter of daily routine the leaders may well play golf while discussing their plans.

There would be no justification for those or other details if they remained but "gags", distracting from the main theme of the play. They are justified only if they contribute to concentrate the attention of the audience on the human interest and if they help to make the audience forget the fact that they watch historic events -- which have taken place nearly 2000 years ago.

The idealism, the eagerness and the competence of all those who co-operated in the realisation of the ideas of the Sefton Camp Dramatic Society and in performing Julius Caesar on the stage, are worth recording and are a fine contribution to the history of emigration.

Press - Review

Taken as a whole the production of Julius Caesar by the dramatic group of Mr. Rehfisch was a success. For the direction was so good, the scenery such a pleasure to look at and the performing of some of the amateurs so fine that one finds it superfluous to criticise the bad English and other faults which were due to the exceedingly difficult conditions under which this production had to be made. We all, I think, look forward to more of this kind of entertainment.

GOETHES "FAUST" IN EINEM INTERNIERUNGSLAGER IN CANADA.

Ein junger Oesterreicher, der mit dem ersten Ueberseetransport von Internierten nach Canada verschifft wurde, schreibt über die Verhältnisse in einem canadischen Internierungslager u.a.:

> " Das kulturelle Leben erreichte mit der Aufführung des "Faust" einen Höhepunkt. Etwas unangenehm fiel auf, dass kein Gretchen auf der Bühne war, aber es kam trotzdem ein sehr gutes Stück zustande. Eine Reihe von Vorträgen über populär-wissenschaftliche Themen ist gerade im Rollen, ebenso Vorträge über verschiedene Länder auf den Heimabenden der Jugend... "

Figure 17.1 Continued

with contemporary political relevance. As Rehfisch said, defending his choices:

> Even a dictator will have breakfast in the morning; there is no law forbidding conspirators to have a drink or a cigarette during their dangerous meetings; and when a death sentence on a political enemy has become a matter of daily routine the leaders may well play golf while discussing their plans.
>
> *(SR, 6)*

It would appear from the archives on the Isle of Man that the Sefton production had a distinctly anti-dictatorial stance. Rehfisch's Caesar – the part he played himself – was both a 'dictator' and a 'great man who has become solitary, suspicious and superstitious' *(SR, 5)*. But Rehfisch was also critical of Brutus, interpreting his error as the inability to recognize the need, in conjunction with the regicide, for social reform. To Rehfisch, Brutus was 'the "noble" philosopher who assumes that the mere assassination of a dictator will go towards making a nation happier and who forgets that at the same time those very conditions will have to be transformed which lifted the dictator into power – a most fatal mistake' *(SR, 5)*.

The modern-dress production of *Julius Caesar* on the Isle of Man – with its obvious critique of totalitarianism – did not take place in a vacuum, and may profitably be related to a substantial body of productions in the British Isles that Rehfisch himself knew, or knew of. *Julius Caesar* had been played continuously in Britain during the 1930s,[13] and while, speaking of Britain in this period, Tony Howard has argued that 'time and again, Shakespeare seemed not to belong in any real world',[14] a number of these productions had a distinct political tinge. There was the modern-dress production at the Festival Theatre in Cambridge (May 1938), inspired by the Orson Welles venture at the Mercury Theatre a year before, and the first BBC television version of the play 'set in a fascist state', with the major characters wearing Italian-style military uniforms (July 1938).[15] Also, prepared before but premiering just after the Second World War broke out, there was Henry Cass's anti-Fascist version of the play, with Brutus symbolizing 'common humanity revolted by "the superman"', Caesar wearing 'a General Franco cap' and Mark Antony as 'the true Nazi'[16] in SS uniform.[17] Arthur Humphreys was later to argue that the production's '"relevance" failed to compensate for its lack of nobility',[18] but it did communicate to the world that – as *The Times* of 30 November 1939 also implied, and as Hans Rehfisch knew when he himself cited modern-dress productions of *Julius Caesar* in Cambridge and London – the English theatre acknowledged that 'Shakespeare knew what there is to be known about the problem of the dictator'.[19]

Recognizing the British history of *Julius Caesar* in the 1930s, and Rehfisch's contribution to it, it is remarkable that, by comparison, the two productions at the Shakespeare Memorial Theatre in Stratford-upon-Avon that are closest in time to the Isle of Man performance seem to have been so unrepresentative. The 1936 production – directed by John Wyse, starring Peter Glenville (Caesar), Donald Wolfit (Cassius), James Dale (Brutus), Donald Eccles and Trevor Howard (Octavius Caesar, Cinna) – was notable for restoring the original text of Shakespeare, but proved highly traditional in its use of costume and design, as well as in its approach to the play's exploration of tyrannicide. More remarkable, though, was the wartime production of *Julius Caesar* at the Stratford Festival of April 1941, six months after Sefton. Curiously, the production of the play at the Shakespeare Memorial Theatre did not register the political strain of the Nazi years, nor did it in any way hint at the ongoing war with Germany. In fact, the production and its atmosphere enabled most audiences to forget that a war was going on in the first place.

W.A. Darlington, who covered the festival, noted that 'nothing in England is quite as it was before the war, but nowhere can you capture the prewar illusion as easily as at the Memorial Theatre at Stratford-upon-Avon'. Whereas in London the blackout had led to the decision to start performances at 5.30 p.m., the theatre curtain at Stratford continued to be lifted at the traditional hour of 7.30, and there was undeniably 'something nostalgic and prewar about a performance which began at a normal evening hour'. There was a clock in rural Warwickshire, but it did not tell the time of the real world at war. It was not only the time of the performances in Stratford, however, that had remained unchanged. The interpretation of the plays also contributed to the prewar illusion: 'As for the performance, itself, it was exactly of the quality, tone and atmosphere which we have become used to, if never entirely resigned to, at Stratford across the years.'[20]

Reviewer John Bourne, however, wrote about the production in the full awareness that there was a war on, having, as the *Stratford-upon-Avon Herald* put it on 18 April 1941, 'returned to the town [of Stratford] after war-time misfortunes near London'. Writing of the spring season's *Julius Caesar*, Bourne commented on this anaemic production with irony bordering on sarcasm:

> It is difficult to believe in those off-stage battles. Tin helmets are too few and the clashes are too remote. Perhaps it was the civilian

population who were in the front line and who suffered most. Once upon a time – to which we should not hark back too much – men died vigorously on the Memorial Theatre stage. Now it is all very polite – even when they fall – and not a sword is bloody. Thus we go home to use our imagination on the midnight news.[21]

The Memorial production of *Julius Caesar* that premiered on 15 April 1941 – directed by Andrew Leigh, and starring the Old Bensonite Gerald Kay Souper as Julius Caesar, George Hayes as Brutus, Baliol Holloway as Cassius, and Godfrey Kenton as Antony – has been described by John Ripley as 'unremarkable'.[22] Of course, seen in context, the production was far from 'unremarkable'. That the professional Shakespeare Memorial Theatre in Stratford should have retired into a provincial and apolitical shell was in fact rather remarkable. Just as remarkable was the fact that such an unworldly production should have been possible less than six months after Rehfisch's amateur group of broken-English-speaking émigrés from the European Continent had drawn on England's national playwright to reflect on the tyrannical threat from Germany and the possibility of improving society. How remarkable that Shakespeare editions continue to list the Stratford productions, and never make any mention of Rehfisch and his exiled amateurs on the Isle of Man. How long will we be quoting authors like John Ripley, who believed that *Julius Caesar*'s 'uncongenial theme and uncommon demand for male actors kept it off the boards during the war'? Even if, as Ripley puts it, the stage history of *Julius Caesar* in the twentieth century is the 'tale of an heroic play adrift in an anti-heroic age',[23] we should no longer ignore performances such as the one mounted by Rehfisch's heroic refugees stranded on the Isle of Man. How reliable will our official stage histories be if they continue to be concerned exclusively with professional theatricals?

Hyères, France – 1946

The spring of 1946 saw a production of *Julius Caesar* almost as unusual as that which Rehfisch directed on the Isle of Man. On 7 April, the POWs at Depôt 153, in the southern French town of Hyères, staged the play under particularly difficult circumstances. As narrated by theatre aficionado and leader of the Depôt's theatre company, Ernst Dorn – who in postwar Germany was to become an actor and director, as well as the agent to his wife, the famous coloratura soprano Erika Köth – overcrowding, malnutrition and the near unbearable Mediterranean heat made dramatic productions difficult.[24] After the POWs had staged some comic theatre, as well as scenes from Tieck's *Schildbürger* (*The Simpletons*), Goethe's *Iphigenia* and *Faust*, Kleist's *Amphitryon* and *Der zerbrochne Krug* (*The Broken Jug*) and Schiller's *Wallensteins Lager* (*Wallenstein's Camp*), the French authorities allowed them to build a theatre of their own, and when the prisoners happened to lay their hands on Shakespeare's *Julius Caesar* – one continues to wonder how – it was 'with tears in their eyes' (*ShJ*, 196) that they set themselves to the difficult task of staging it.

Ernst Dorn first tackled the difficulties posed by the circumstances: the absence of women to play the female parts, the lack of acting experience among the prisoners, and the limited space available for the stage (five by four metres). Though convinced that the part of Portia was vital to set off Brutus's 'modest power and loving greatness' (*ShJ*, 197), Dorn cut it (Rehfisch had done the same on the Isle of Man) because it did not affect the plot. Matters were different with Calpurnia, because her dream vision in Act Two, Scene Two was vital to the plot. The gender problem was solved by giving the part, not as Rehfisch had done to 'a dignified old man-servant' (*SR*, 5) but to the actor playing Antony: with one or two minor alterations that did not change the plot, it proved possible to transfer the verse to Antony without any cuts.

From the various descriptions of the set and the costumes, we gather that Dorn's was not a modern-dress production but a traditional one. Forty-one white tunics were made using old naval shirts, on top of which the actors wore (presumably their own) grey woollen blankets, folded like togas. For the togas of the senators a considerable quantity of linen had been found, and in the Senate Caesar even wore a purple cape six metres long. Such apparent extravagance cannot hide the reality of the situation to us now: Dorn states very specifically that after the production the theatre togas were converted into sheets for hospital beds.

Arguably the greatest problem Dorn had to solve was that of the play's frequent scene changes. With a number of simple alterations, about which he is not very specific, Dorn managed to limit the number of scenes in the play to six without, as he says, undermining the organic development of the plot. The opening scene was cut, and the play began with Act One, Scene Two, in the marketplace. The small stage emphasized the massive throng, eagerly waiting for Caesar. In the Act Three scene showing Caesar in public, Dorn had as many as 49 people on the 20 square metres of imperial Rome available on the stage at Hyères. Yet, proper direction and discipline seem to have guaranteed great clarity from the perspective of the audience. In the next scene, five steps across the stage led up to the Capitol where Caesar and the senators sat between columns. The same forum setting was used for the oration scene. During the final battle the stage was nearly empty, the fighting suggested mainly by backstage voices and music – until the final curtain fell and Antony, standing downstage, praised Brutus and proclaimed: 'This was a man.'

The production history of *Julius Caesar* in Germany during the 1930s indicates that the play was immensely popular across the German-speaking lands, and with the assistance of the valuable census of productions in the *Shakespeare Jahrbuch*, one may also detect the play's strong relative popularity (in comparison with the rest of the Shakespeare canon) in the course of over a decade in Germany, Austria and Prague, with peaks in 1937, 1938 (in which year it was the seventh most popular play on the German-speaking stage) and 1941. The data, however, are heterogeneous in kind, making it difficult to interpret either the figures or their fluctuations; also, reviews are sparse. Thanks to the work of Wilhelm Hortmann, however, we do possess a reliable account of the most famous German *Julius Caesar* of the Nazi period, Jürgen Fehling's landmark production, which premiered in 1941 and was performed for a number of years thereafter. Fehling's *Caesar* – with Gustav Gründgens playing the lead – dominated the Nazi scene during the war years. It was not a piece of explicit propaganda but, as Hortmann notes, it was 'certainly worlds apart from agitatory theatre such as Piscator's in the twenties', and 'the reviews [were] unanimous that the director had done everything in his power to enhance the role of Caesar and mark him out as the man of the future. His fall, therefore, must appear as a historical catastrophe, and his murder a crime of mythic proportion.'[25] Given this obvious slant, one understands that Fehling had 'only limited sympathy with Brutus' careful self-examination [and] thrilled instead to the agglomerate of passions and impulses he saw contained in the part of Mark Antony'.[26]

Interestingly, the extensive production history of Fehling's pseudo-propagandist *Julius Caesar* also contains a mystifying remark (since it is not corroborated by other sources) attributed to the actor Bernhard Minetti who played a Brutus beset with emotional doubts, concerning the man behind Operation Valkyrie, Colonel Claus von Stauffenberg, who planned the coup against Hitler and famously planted the bomb in his headquarters. We have it on Minetti's authority that when von Stauffenberg was arrested, 'there was an open copy of *Julius Caesar* on his desk in which the relevant speeches by Brutus were underlined'.[27] This attractive anecdotal version of Third Reich history in Shakespearean terms – presenting Operation Valkyrie as an abortive wartime appropriation of *Julius Caesar* – presages the POW production of Shakespeare's Roman play in the French town of Hyères. With its comparable focus on Brutus, this POW *Caesar* may be said to have marked a significant new start, and one might well be grateful to Dorn for, in his own words, 'unambiguously documenting the will of German soldiers to contribute to the reconstruction of our [that is, German] cultural life' (*ShJ*, 198).

Conclusion: in exile with Shakespeare

This chapter has looked at two neglected productions of *Julius Caesar*, both of which were staged in captivity. The first was put on by continental European refugees on the Isle of Man, the second by German prisoners of war in the south of France after the cessation of hostilities in May 1945. Each of these Second World War productions in its own way uses *Julius Caesar* to formulate a version of tyranny and the individual's potential response to such misrule, in both instances yielding a stance that differs markedly from the professional stage productions of the period that we know of. Each of these productions mounted in captivity now serves as a corrective to the official history of Shakespeare's *Julius Caesar* on stage in Britain and Germany, in Stratford and Berlin respectively. While in 1941 the Shakespeare Memorial Theatre in Stratford presented *Julius Caesar* in an apolitical guise, without even hinting at the ongoing war, the émigrés in Douglas confronted the political issues of the play head-on, and even presented it in the language of the host nation. The Hyères production distanced itself from the Nazi preoccupation with the tragedy of the unappreciated tyrant, and instead pursued a reflection of the dilemmas that attend on political reform attained through more democratic principles.

By reconstructing the conditions that governed both the staging and reception of *Julius Caesar* behind barbed wire during the Second World War and afterwards, this chapter has tried to make the Roman tyrant's wounds, his 'poor dumb mouths', speak. To speak with Antony in the play, I have tried to put 'a tongue / In every wound of Caesar' (3.2.223–4), ultimately giving a voice not only to the German POWs of Hyères or the émigrés on the Isle of Man, but also to a veritable host of other amateur wartime theatricals in exile to whom few of us so far have lent their ears.

However, exile, the essential experience of the war-laden twentieth century, remains an undiscovered country. This can be illustrated by the 2009 movie *Me and Orson Welles*, directed by Richard Linklater.

Based on Robert Kaplow's smartly written novel of the same title, the movie shows how the seventeen-year-old Richard (played by Zac Efron) becomes an actor in Orson Welles's anti-Fascist Broadway production of *Julius Caesar* in 1937 – of which, as we have seen, Hans Rehfisch was aware – and obtains the part of Lucius against Welles's Brutus in the tent scene. The core of the movie is really the ambitious visual reconstruction – both meticulous and successful, and therefore most valuable – of Orson Welles's theatrical staging of the tragedy. The movie is of interest here for at least two reasons. First, it simplifies the novel, notably in its (admittedly sparse) attempts to capture the political implications of Welles's *Julius Caesar*. Absent from the movie, for example, is the cameo appearance of Clifford Odets and Albert Einstein, as they meet Orson Welles at the Mercury Theatre:

> Odets [...] gestured to a rumpled-looking man standing behind him, a man whose long greying hair stood out in massive disarray. 'Orson, I'd like you to meet Dr. Albert Einstein.'
> 'Honored,' said Welles.
> '*I'm working with him to help Jewish refugees in Europe.*'[28]

This de-politicization of the novel for Hollywood purposes also explains what is even more telling about the apolitical stance of the movie as a whole. The theatre scenes of Orson Welles's *Julius Caesar* in the Linklater movie were shot at the Gaiety Theatre, Douglas, on the Isle of Man, barely a stone's throw from Sefton Camp on the Loch Promenade where, in 1940, Hans Rehfisch's *Julius Caesar* sought to vent the internees' political frustrations with the assistance of Shakespeare. No one at the CinemaNX production company or at the local Isle of Man film agency (which co-funded the project) seems to have been aware of the coincidence, or to have felt the need to mention the irony of the geographical and political proximity of these two anti-Fascist productions of *Julius Caesar*.[29] Both the commercial instinct (seeking as much as possible to sanitize the product on offer) and a degree of academic professionalism which blinds our gaze to committed amateurs have led to a neglect of politically relevant moments and, in this instance, silenced the many refugee thespians who genuinely tried to argue an ethical point under circumstances that were extremely difficult. In the second part of *Henry VI*, Shakespeare sends the Duchess of Gloucester into exile on the Isle of Man, and the audience never hear of her again. This silence must never again be the fate of those who have gone into exile with Shakespeare.

Notes

This chapter results from Research Project EDU2008-00453 funded by the Plan Nacional de I+D+I and MICINN.

1. Carl Weiselberger, 'Internee Julius Caesar', in *Carl Weiselberger, eine Auswahl seiner Schriften*, ed. by Peter Liddell and Walter Riedel (Toronto: German-Canadian Historical Association, 1981), 74–83. Henceforth abbreviated as *IJC*.
2. For a full discussion of Carl Weiselberger in his Canadian contexts, see Nicole M.H. Brunnhuber, 'After the Prison Ships: Internment Narratives in Canada', in *'Totally Un-English'? Britain's Internment of 'Enemy Aliens' in Two World Wars*, ed. by Richard Dove (Amsterdam and New York: Rodopi, 2005), 165–78.
3. For much of the short story, Weiselberger may have drawn on his personal experience. The edited text of the short story is based on a manuscript copy dating from the time of his actual internment in Canada (see *Carl Weiselberger*, 238).
4. See *Julius Caesar: New Critical Essays*, ed. by Horst Zander (New York and London: Routledge, 2005). Of special interest is Mariangela Tempera's 'Political Caesar: *Julius Caesar* on the Italian Stage' (333–43). See also Maria Wyke, *Caesar: A Life in Western Culture* (Chicago and London: University of Chicago Press, 2008), especially 145–95 ('Liberty and Tyranny').
5. Michael Dobson, *Shakespeare and Amateur Performance: A Cultural History* (Cambridge: Cambridge University Press, 2011).
6. See Brunnhuber, *'Totally Un-English'?* and Ronald Stent, *A Bespattered Page? The Internment of His Majesty's 'most loyal enemy aliens'* (London: A. Deutsch, 1980).
7. For a more detailed account see Maxine Schwartz Seller, *We Built Up Our Lives: Education and Community among Jewish Refugees Interned by Britain in World War II* (Westport, Conn. and London: Greenwood Press, 2001), 135–7.
8. See Seller, 135–6. Sefton Camp was one of four sites on Loch Promenade in Douglas. The other main camps on the seafront were Central Camp, Palace Camp and Metropole Camp.
9. Seller, 135–6.
10. See Hamisch Ritchie, 'Rehfisch in Exile', in *Aliens-Uneingebürgerte: German and Austrian Writers in Exile*, ed. by Ian Wallace (Amsterdam and Atlanta: Rodopi, 1994), 207–22.
11. Walter Simon had fled from Germany and was working as a textile manufacturer in Greater Manchester when he was arrested by the British authorities in 1940. See also Naomi Koppel, 'Internment in the Isle of Man followed escape from Germany', *Isle of Man Examiner* (21 June 1994), 36.
12. *Sefton Review*, 2 (25 November 1940), 5–6 (6), henceforth abbreviated as *SR*. I am grateful to Alan Franklin of the Manx National Heritage Library for helping me retrieve a copy of this refugee journal.
13. One production in 1933 (The Guildhall, Winchester); three productions in 1934 (The Alhambra, London; Shakespeare Memorial Theatre, Stratford; Gate Theatre, Dublin); one production in 1935 (Old Vic, London); two productions in 1936 (Shakespeare Memorial Theatre, Stratford; Prince's Theatre,

Bristol); one production in 1937 (Open Air Theatre, Regent's Park, London); two productions in 1938 (Festival Theatre, Cambridge; BBC Television); one production in November 1939 (Embassy Theatre, London); one production in April 1941 (Shakespeare Memorial Theatre, Stratford).

14. Tony Howard, 'Blood on the Bright Young Things: Shakespeare in the 1930s', in *British Theatre between the Wars, 1918–1939*, ed. by Clive Barker and Maggie B. Gale (Cambridge: Cambridge University Press, 2000), 135–61 (151).

15. Howard, 155.

16. Howard, 156.

17. John Ripley, *'Julius Caesar' on Stage in England and America, 1599–1973* (Cambridge: Cambridge University Press, 1980), 244.

18. *Julius Caesar*, ed. by Arthur Humphreys (Oxford: Oxford University Press, 1984), 67.

19. *The Times* quoted in Howard, 156. In the same breath, Rehfisch also mentions a production in Oxford. I have not been able to identify this yet.

20. W.A. Darlington, 'The Stratford Festival', *New York Times*, 20 April 1941.

21. 'John Bourne Reviews the Festival', *Stratford-upon-Avon Herald*, 18 April 1941.

22. Ripley, 340n.

23. Ripley, 244, 214.

24. Ernst Dorn, 'Shakespeare bei deutschen Kriegsgefangenen in Frankreich', *Shakespeare Jahrbuch*, 82–3 (1948), 195–8. Henceforth abbreviated as *ShJ*.

25. Wilhelm Hortmann, *Shakespeare on the German Stage: The Twentieth Century* (Cambridge: Cambridge University Press, 1998), 146, 143–4.

26. Hortmann, 146.

27. Hortmann, 143. See also: 'After the uprising of 20 July 1944, a copy of Shakespeare's *Julius Caesar* was found on Stauffenberg's desk at Bendlerstrasse, with the part of Brutus marked'. In Bernhard Minetti, *Erinnerungen eines Schauspielers*, ed. by Günther Rühle (Reinbek: Rowohlt Taschenbuch Verlag, 1988), 108; my translation.

28. Robert Kaplow, *Me and Orson Welles* (San Francisco: MacAdam/Cage, 2003), 218 (italics added).

29. Rumour has it that while filming at the Gaiety Theatre in Douglas, the actor Zac Efron and his co-star Clare Danes saw a ghost. *The Sun* acknowledged that the Gaiety Theatre was a haunted site. Could it have been the ghost of Julius Caesar? See: http://www.digitalspy.co.uk/showbiz/news/a91467/efron-scared-by-ghost-on-orson-welles.html (accessed 24 September 2011).

18
'And, by opposing, end them': The Rhetoric of Translators' Polemics

Anna Cetera

The story of Marsyas, the great satyr-musician, who lost his musical contest with Apollo and was flayed alive for his audacity in challenging the god, bears much moral ambiguity. The first part of the contest failed to produce a winner, but then Apollo turned his lyre upside down and played again, a trick the satyr could not emulate with his double flute. If challenging the Olympian deity may indeed seem blasphemous, the unusual torment to which Marsyas was subjected suggests the equally profane thought that Apollo was a green-eyed rascal. This anxious suspicion must already have haunted ancient interpreters who tried to make sense of the story by elucidating Marsyas's guilt. A fourth-century Roman mosaic (see Figure 18.1) shows the triumphant god and the satyr, the latter seized and led to his dreadful torture. Their dramatically tense relationship is overshadowed by the presence of an odd figure, relaxed and contented, cheerfully waving good-bye to the ill-fated Marsyas. The Greek inscription, 'PLANE', denotes a unique personification of the delusion or deceitful frenzy which drove the bestial satyr to seek comparison with Apollo. And yet even the interference of the allegory hardly obscures the psychological backbone of the story: masters of art often claim their superiority by displacing rivals, and the savage cruelty of Apollo's judgement reflects in fact the gravity of the threat posed by Marsyas. After all, would Olympus still hold a place for the god defeated by a goatlike nonentity?

Traces of similar frictions can be found in the history of translation, with Shakespeare offering a particularly rich store of examples. Leaving aside the seemingly obvious acts of artistic displacement, official histories of national canons rarely do justice to the temperature and persistence of personal animosities that trouble translators' communities. *De mortuis aut bene, aut nihil*, goes the ancient saying, which, if extended beyond the

Figure 18.1   Marsyas and Apollo. The House of Aion, Paphos. Fourth century. Photo by Waldemar Jerke. Courtesy of the Polish Centre of Mediterranean Archaeology of the University of Warsaw

period of mourning, may produce little more than a wishful version of history emptied of its original nerve and pressure. In addition to this, it is also the contemporary decline of biographical research and the preference for systemic syntheses which diminish our insight into the innermost logic of the retranslation phenomenon. Once the varnish has been scratched, what comes to the surface often has the green eyes of Apollo, the daring impudence of Marsyas, or the cheerful smile of Delusion.

Claiming the territory

'Such a miserable playwright as this Korzeniowski has been proclaimed the perfect translator of Shakespeare: how worthless my translation must seem to them! [...] And thus they have given me a monstrous cap and bells to wear because no man can be made a bigger fool than by giving him the example of Korzeniowski to follow.'[1] This presumptuous, though admittedly also fanciful, complaint comes from the private correspondence of the first Polish translator of Shakespeare, Ignacy Hołowiński, apparently as a comment on the greatly unwelcome emergence of a rival in the early 1840s. The official records habitually place

Korzeniowski and Hołowiński side by side, thus confirming their share in and significance for the admission of Shakespeare into the Polish literary canon. Yet even a cursory look below the surface of authorized testimonies reveals a surprising accumulation of enmity far exceeding cleverly worded scorn. Sadly enough, the episode sets a peculiar pattern of resentment which frequently underlines the relations within the ever growing tribe of Shakespeare translators. 'I cannot approve of a translation where Romeo and Juliet speak the language of local drunkards!', snaps a postwar authority by way of welcome to the rising star of the last decade of the twentieth century,[2] only to provoke a crushing verdict from the other side: 'He hardly cares for faithfulness or for clarity, or for poetic appeal, or for theatrical effect. In his translations, all four suffer to the same degree, though not all at the same time.'[3] Are those unique outbursts of wit and animosity just literary folklore of sorts, or do they perhaps reveal a more complex psychological condition which arises whenever the safe monogamy of the author-translator relation becomes threatened by the intrusion of rival(s)?

Contrary to what one may expect from those sharing a fascination with the same author, and blessed with a similar type of creative energy, the emergent patterns of relations prove surprisingly consistent: translators are a quarrelsome tribe and are the least likely to appreciate the achievements of those engaged in a similar type of enterprise. What weapons are available to reduce undesired company? Naturally, the successive phases of reception have produced different types of challenges and, as a consequence, different types of rivalry. Whereas the pioneering translators, in supplying the first translations of Shakespeare, were anxious about those who would supersede them, the next contenders became far more preoccupied with the question of quality, and thus frequently engaged in uncompromising polemics to expose errors, discredit alternative strategies, and position themselves as worthy replacements (or in fact as the only valid ones) to be included in the literary canon. Indeed, the sound knowledge of their competitors' work alone would make translators particularly disposed to criticism. Additionally, the urge to censure, highlight errors, and secure exclusiveness for oneself found strong support in the prescriptive bias of those translation theories which prevailed in the past. When theory preached rules, practice readily supplied examples of their violation. Characteristically enough, most of the Polish critical debates on Shakespeare in the nineteenth century, in the years following the publication of first translations, focused on the (in)adequacy of these translations, and were often fuelled by examples and arguments supplied by translators themselves.[4]

Again the policies would vary from highlighting particularly inept choices to questioning the alleged strategy as if it were manifest in all individual solutions. Typically, the first battles pertained to the choice of metre and semantic equivalents, and indeed the early translations provided rich opportunities for scorn and unmerciful ridicule.

At the end of the nineteenth century and the beginning of the twentieth the disputes became more subtle as arguments focused on a loose notion of poetic effect. It was in the second half of the twentieth century that Polish translation strategies took clearly defined and sometimes very different routes; initially, this was seen in the appearance of so-called philological translations, and then of theatre-oriented rewritings based on dynamic equivalence and the subsequent omission of Elizabethan idioms and cultural references. The recent decades have preached tolerance and variety, which, rather paradoxically, has only served to fuel competitiveness, and make the claims for supposed superiority more numerous and more vocal. Setting aside those more obvious conclusions concerning human nature in general, we are left with the question of whether the inherent competitiveness of the well-established and pan-European practice of retranslating Shakespeare should be seen merely as an inevitable aspect of the reception process, or as an important driving force which in fact has a role in shaping our fleeting interpretations of Shakespeare's plays. Do the translators' quarrels impede or invigorate reception? And, last but not least: what is the impact of existing translations on new translations both in terms of the choice of strategy and of individual translation solutions?

Interpreting the difference

Quite symptomatically, most of the diachronic studies dealing with the intricacies of the reception of Shakespeare in translation are predominantly concerned with the pressure of the receiving culture in terms of its evolving aesthetics and stage practice.[5] Thus, although translation strategies are seen as resulting from the negotiations between the source text and the target culture, the latter typically consists of broadly understood conventions, expectations, interpretative habits and the like rather than being viewed as an isolated corpus of earlier translations. Also the relations of translators to their native literature are often described in terms of critical response and readership rather than of their individual attitudes, likes and dislikes, which however preponderate in private correspondence, memoirs and interviews and so on. The consistent focus on large-scale tendencies and on the clashes of conventions rather than those of huffy personalities stems to a large extent from the heritage of systemic thinking which shaped the beginnings of modern translation studies. Thus the impact of the Polysystem Theory, and the subsequent preoccupation with translation as a norm-governed activity promoted by Descriptive Translation Studies, effectively downplayed the interest in the personal or, one is tempted to say, psychological dimension of literary translation. The numerous attempts at systematizing the field and the meticulous classification of translation strategies marginalized individual motivations which, in the case of retranslation, acquire pivotal importance. A somewhat different perspective can be found in the writings of Lawrence Venuti who, in commenting on the retranslation phenomenon at large, strongly foregrounds its inherent, aggressive competitiveness.[6] However, Venuti's sober assessment of the power relations in the book market led him to interpret rivalry as a question determined more by publishing practice than by individual attitude. The basic economic rationale of the retranslation enterprise demands that the new translations establish their difference from the previous versions and strive to displace them. 'The translator's intention, then, is always already collective, determined most decisively by linguistic usage, literary canons, translation traditions, and the commissioning institution', argues Venuti, thereby evading the question of what these modern Marsyases think themselves.[7] Indeed, promotional campaigns supply numerous examples combining ardent recommendation of the new with the implicit castigation of the old such as, for example, in the intense exploitation, for promotional purposes, of academic endorsements of a Polish translator debuting in the 1990s: 'Barańczak's translations by far beat all the previous ones' (Tadeusz Nyczek) and 'A translator like this appears only once per century' (Jan Kott).[8] In both cases praise implies bitter farewell for the competing rewritings.

Similar insights can be drawn from Bourdieu's sociology of cultural production, which has already been employed to account for the contemporary struggles over the establishment of the Arabic canon of Shakespeare translations.[9] Considering the logic of cultural enterprises, insists Bourdieu, 'it is the conscious evaluation of the objective chances of profit' which prompts the challengers to overturn 'the hierarchy of the field' and displace the establishment.[10] Parallel to Venuti's line of reasoning, Bourdieu too stresses the role of the intermediaries: the true producers of cultural value, who proclaim the worth of the author and invest their prestige in their cause.[11] And yet, disillusioning as it might be, to interpret cultural activity in exclusively economic terms cannot do justice to the complexity of motives that urge translators to turn to works already available in their native tongue.[12] In fact, translators often claim the singularity of their intellectual relation to their authors, while their commitment is described in terms of artistic choice rather than commercial opportunity. By and large rewriters begin their work spurred on by a subjective conviction of its value, and often heroically cling to the task even if it lacks any prospects of immediate institutional support. Such a pattern of strong personal dedication can be observed, for example, in the poignant testimonies of the previously quoted Hołowiński:

> I sense something which as yet I have not dared to express and therefore tried to suppress by plunging into ever new translations. But none of them harmonized with the spirit of my soul until at last I heard the voice of Shakespeare. I was to love him with all my heart, I made him my world, and I gave my life to translating him. And now, while reading some of the superb passages, I recall only those blissful moments of my life when I was overwhelmed with joy at finding the right translation for them.[13]

Setting aside his Romantic diction, the essence of Hołowiński's experience consists in his strong sense of discovery, his identification with Shakespeare and the blissful joy he experiences when he finally hits on the right equivalent. His apparently idealistic attitude did not prevent him from actively searching for patronage nor from taking irritated notice of rising competition. Interestingly, it is the belief in the intensity and exclusiveness of his relationship with Shakespeare which he seems here to value most and which he presumably found was disturbed by the arrival of competitors. Of course, the practice of translation often produces the impression of an intimate acquaintance with the author, a camaraderie of sorts, as the translator feels as if he or she has been admitted to the mental life of the original writer. The sense of the deepening personal bond is frequently manifest in the translators' habit of speaking about their authors in hermeneutical terms, that is discussing their prime motives and intentions, rather than indulging in formal discourse analysis. Having befriended the author, the experience of translation opens up to its inescapable dialogic dimension. Józef Tischner, developing the philosophical thought of Emmanuel Levinas, draws attention to what he calls 'egotic solidarization', a feeling of intellectual fraternity born of the encounter with another man:

> The other c o n f i r m s [sic] my belief and my truth. Thereby, it is acknowledged that what used to have for me some personal value

is endowed also with universal dimension and partakes in a more general understanding. Such an encounter with the other not only produces a certain 'cognitive effect', but it becomes an 'existential event' which creates a special bond between individuals, a lasting acquisition as regards man's self-consciousness.[14]

Needless to say, the widely recognized status of the author may only augment the value of the postulated acquisition as well as the temptation to seek exclusiveness. As much as the joy of translation can effectively compensate for the absence of adequate recognition or financial reward, it diminishes with the appearance of fellow rewriters who disperse the illusion of intimacy and challenge the intellectual abilities of their precursors. Significantly, the decision to retranslate may itself be prompted by the double motivation of a somewhat detached fascination with the author on the one hand, and by strong, adverse reaction towards previous rewriters on the other. The latter relation in many ways resembles Bloom's doctrine of the anxiety of influence, where the aspiring artists offer a necessary misreading of their precursors. 'Every talent must unfold itself in fighting', explains Bloom, quoting Nietzsche, which only confirms the rationale of Marsyas's challenge.[15]

There is hardly a writer whose translation fortunes can serve as a better example of these tendencies and hazards than Shakespeare. Here the urge to retranslate becomes a complex combination of the ego bait stemming from the extraordinary status of the writer and the commercial opportunities linked with royalties on stage productions or generated by the potentially huge readership, which significantly includes that produced by the demands of the educational system. The resulting mixture of genuine fascination, talent and hard work with the expectation of profit makes translators of Shakespeare particularly unwilling to acknowledge the merits of their competitors, which of course does not mean that they fail to take notice of their work. And yet, the phenomenon of retranslation – viewed from the stance of Translation Studies and often described as gathering force in twenty-first-century literary translation practice at large – tends to be analysed in terms of its impact on the status of the source text rather than with regard to translators' policies and strategies. Commenting on the specificity of translated literature, Gideon Toury observes that 'there are good reasons to regard translations as constituting a special system, or "genre" of their own within a culture',[16] thus stressing both their generic autonomy and explicit ties with the target culture. However, the emphasis put on the interaction with the target culture diminishes with Toury's definition of an 'assumed translation', firmly anchored in 'the existence of another text, in another culture and language, from which it was presumably derived by transfer operations and to which it is now tied by certain relationships'.[17] Flexible as it may seem, the definition nevertheless upholds the customary binarism of one source and one copy. And what if the relationship becomes multiple and new translations are fathered by both the originals *and* some other translations? What if the new rewriters both feed on the previous translations and strive to destroy them? Or, in other words, how much time does Marsyas spend listening to Apollo before he dares to step forward and challenge him?

Facing the rival(s)

Whether willingly or not, the task of a retranslator is profoundly affected by the existence of parallel translations that indicate a path that may be followed, or – conversely – force one into taking rough side tracks to avoid plagiarism. While seemingly obvious, this aspect of translation history and practice receives somewhat marginal attention in the critical studies of the phenomenon. Even contemporary translators, in commenting on current trends or reflecting upon the future of Shakespeare in translation, prefer to expose and censure the theatrical practice of conflating existing translations (including their own) in order to produce directorial versions of Shakespeare, than to expatiate on how they themselves find their way within the existing corpus of rewritings. Are the debts too obvious to be acknowledged? Or, perhaps, they are so numerous that they need to be concealed underneath the ironic disparagement of rival policies. This is even more surprising as the question concerning familiarity with prior translations often becomes one of the first and deeply meditated preliminary choices made by the retranslator. Consequently, here the policies fall into the sphere of private ethics and range from deliberately avoiding exposure to other translations, through postponing comparisons until the text is ready and there is no fear of excessive influence, to the meticulous gathering of all available translations in the hope of capitalizing on their merits. Whatever the policy, the attitude to rival translations cannot remain completely neutral, in particular when these are close in time.

The prevailing patterns can already be observed in the initial phase of reception when the first translations into national languages were produced and published. In many European countries the myth of Shakespeare (and his theatrical reception) had long preceded the appearance of full-length literary translations. As a consequence, both translators and publishers cherished high hopes of profit on these newly compiled editions. Notwithstanding the frequent stereotype of a detached individual laboriously toiling towards overcoming the stubbornness of his or her native tongue in order to unveil the genius of Shakespeare, the consultation of unofficial sources repeatedly exposes the incredible network of intrigues and alliances that preceded the formation of national canons. The anxieties associated with (non)inclusion in these editions were further intensified by the somewhat naive assumptions concerning the possibility of producing a true, authentic, faithful translation of Shakespeare, which should serve as a permanent substitute for the original. The desire for exclusiveness, combined with the proliferation of attempts, produced further predicaments when translators were faced with alternative rewritings and discovered solutions superior, akin or identical with their own. Again, extant manuscripts reveal an astonishing spectrum of policies which range from outright stealing to bizarre substitutions introduced in textual areas where there is too much coincidental similarity, for fear of undeserved allegations of plagiarism. Whatever our assessment of these policies, all of them bear witness to the somewhat neglected truth that translators are more often than not scrupulous readers both of Shakespeare *and* of other translations of Shakespeare, and it is from these love triangles and their polygonal mutations that a new text is conceived and shaped. Revealingly, it is precisely this relationship which is later most ardently denied.

Yet another type of dependence on existing texts seems to have emerged in retranslating Shakespeare for performance. This refers in particular to situations when translators receive commissions from specific directors or are associated with theatres as dramaturges on a contract basis. Perceived as team members, they often partake in rehearsals and work towards the improvement of the translation to accommodate the vocal or physical preferences of specific actors. Occasionally, their work may resemble adaptation practices as they tamper with the textual matrix of the play to produce or strengthen interpretative coherence. Here the conflicting attitude results not so much from claims concerning enhanced faithfulness (after all, translations for performance implicitly involve a certain degree of departure from the original text to suit the needs of a particular stage), as from the fact that the originality of the new translation comes to be seen as an important asset for the ensuing production. In other words, the theatre may occasionally show preference for innovative or even controversial rewritings to boost ticket sales. As recently argued by Jan Willem Mathijssen in relation to the Dutch reception of Shakespeare, theatrical commissions often encourage a translation strategy which becomes first and foremost 'a strategy of artistic differentiation' from already assimilated rewritings.[18] What follows is that translators are asked to stand in for Shakespeare as much as to diverge from their immediate predecessors. Such a forced breach with the established tradition not only transgresses the classic dichotomy of source text and translation, but in fact gives precedence to the adverse shaping pressure of the rewritings already in existence. Of course, the very decision to retranslate may result from the disapproval or dislike of earlier rewritings, but whatever the case, a spectacular swing of the pendulum to the other side of faithfulness appears to be a necessary ingredient of success.

Paradoxically, then, the unprecedented proliferation of modern rewritings of Shakespeare may potentially threaten the very principles that underpin literary translation. In most European countries the sheer number and frequency of Shakespeare translations may appear vigorously to counter assumptions concerning the emergence of new translations as a response merely to the ageing of language. Faced with the multitude of rewritings, neither the critics, nor – least of all – the judges, seem to be in a position effectively to define and protect copyright in translation. The inevitable dangers of the situation have already been described by translators whose work has been used as a blueprint for further rewritings, or simply incorporated – in parts – into new translations.[19] What indirectly encourages the practice is the prevailing directorial style of modern theatre, and the frequent substitution of the verbal text with visual effects or even its blending with other media. With the importance of the complete text already diminished, professional rewriters or even stage directors themselves are tempted to conflate, cut, and abbreviate the full-fledged translations, and then claim authorship of the new whole. Naturally, the situation varies in particular countries, but it is important to observe that the wish to economize on royalties otherwise due to translators is just one of the motivating factors in this case. The consent or more liberal attitude towards adaptation or conflation also depends on the prevailing critical stance, and here the traditional insistence on the integrity of canonized works may lose out (or not) to the privileged position of high-profile directors whose reputation or celebrity status eclipses the status of the author and, as a consequence, of the translator.

Finally, what may also fuel conflict among translators is the development of the media which has multiplied the opportunities they have of expressing their resentment or contempt for alternative strategies.

It follows that the figure of the translator has become better defined in the public sphere which, in turn, raises further expectations concerning his or her possessing a clear-cut image and persuasive rhetoric. Opinions formerly concealed in private letters or obscure diaries burst into the public domain and are immortalized in the easily accessible Internet archive. What looms on the horizon is the gloomy prospect that translators should fall into the trap of marketing trends which capitalize on radicalizing differences and augmenting quarrels. Incidentally, according to one version of the Greek story of Marsyas, the satyr only lost when Apollo began to accompany the sound of the lyre with his voice. Thus, the forceful and uncompromising attitudes of a charismatic translator may become a shaping force in a particular culture's perception of Shakespeare.

Making amends?

And yet the profile and temperature of the debates on Shakespeare in translation do not depend on translators alone. Recent decades have witnessed a rise in the number of bilingual editions of Shakespeare where the work of a translator is accompanied by a critical commentary. Although, following tradition, the commentary focuses on interpretative matters, editors are also acutely aware of alternative translations in terms both of their diachronic development and of their concurrent plurality, and are often tempted to account for them. Thus, the intricacies of the centuries-long local reception of Shakespeare in translation represent a rough but fascinating equivalent of textual studies with their spelling variants, cruxes and successive emendations. As if under the influence of more vocal debates, editors are left pondering over their own potential role in elucidating Shakespeare. Should they – aware as they are of the tricks of the trade – respect and guard the integrity of the proposed translation, or perhaps expose the instability of meanings by recourse to some earlier or rival translations? What chances do they stand of mediating the relationships between translators without threatening the authority of the translation at hand? Worried by plagiarism in translation on the one hand, and as reluctant as lovers to share their object of veneration with another, translators have little sympathy for alternative rewritings. It is only with the passage of time (the required minimum seems to be about a century), which 'knits up the ravelled sleave of care', that translators finally become friends. Whether or not this happens faster may, in the future, crucially depend on the increasingly relevant role played by editorial management of potential conflict.

Notes

1. Ignacy Hołowiński, letter dated 17 March 1841, in *The Correspondence of J.I. Kraszewski*, Manuscript Collection of the Jagiellonian Library in Krakow, BJ 6456 IV, p. 365 v. All translations from Polish are mine.
2. Maciej Słomczyński in the Polish Television documentary by Dariusz Pawelec, *Drugi po Boy'u* (*Second Only to Boy*, 1995).
3. Stanisław Barańczak, *Ocalone w tłumaczeniu. Szkice o warsztacie tłumacza* (Krakow: Wydawnictwo a5, 2007), 204.
4. Similar tensions accompanied the establishment of the first complete Czech edition of Shakespeare (1855–72), which brought hot disputes, attempts to exclude rival translations from publication, and even authorship controversies; see Pavel Drábek, *České pokusy o Shakespeara* (Brno: Faculty of Philosophy, Masaryk University, 2010).
5. See for instance *European Shakespeare: Translating Shakespeare in the Romantic Age*, ed. by Dirk Delabastita and Lieven D'hulst (Amsterdam and Philadelphia: John Benjamins, 1993); *Four Hundred Years of Shakespeare in Europe*, ed. by Ángel-Luis Pujante and Ton Hoenselaars (Newark: University of Delaware Press, 2003); *Translating Shakespeare for the Twenty-First Century*, ed. by Rui Carvalho Homem and Ton Hoenselaars (Amsterdam and New York: Rodopi, 2004), and *Shakespeare and the Language of Translation*, ed. by Ton Hoenselaars (London: Thomson Learning, 2004).
6. See Lawrence Venuti, 'Retranslation: The Creation of Value', *Bucknell Review*, 47 (2004), 25–39.
7. Venuti, 28.
8. These quotes have featured on all volumes of the first edition of Barańczak's translations published by W. Drodze Publishing House in Poznań since 1990.
9. I refer here to the unpublished paper by Sameh F. Hanna, 'The Struggle over "Symbolic Time": Shakespeare Retranslation in Arabic', submitted for the Translation Seminar at the 2011 ESRA Conference in Weimar.
10. Pierre Bourdieu, *The Field of Cultural Production: Essays on Art and Literature* (Cambridge: Polity Press, 1993), 83.
11. Bourdieu, 77.
12. One should also take note of the evolution of the theoretical stance of Itamar Even-Zohar who advances the concept of cultural repertoires, superseding or expanding on the earlier Polysystem Theory. In his recent studies Even-Zohar draws much attention to the work of agents as initiators of cultural innovation. However, he postulates a division into various specialized functions, differentiating between, for example, the creators of new models of life and the cultural entrepreneurs engaged in the dissemination of these projects. The new model usefully integrates a sober insight into the economy and sociology of cultural evolution with an acknowledgement of the highly individualized and somewhat idealistic attitudes of artists. See Itamar Even-Zohar, 'The Making of Culture Repertoire and the Role of Transfer', *Target*, 9 (1997), 355–63; and 'Idea-Makers, Culture Entrepreneurs, Makers of Life Images, and the Prospects of Success', in *Papers in Culture Research* (Tel Aviv: Unit of Culture Research, Tel Aviv University, 2005).

13. Hołowiński, letter dated 11 November 1840, in *Correspondence of J. I. Kraszewski*, 351 r.

14. Józef Tischner, *Filozofia dramatu* (Krakow: Znak, 2006), 221.

15. Harold Bloom, *The Anxiety of Influence: A Theory of Poetry* (New York and Oxford: Oxford University Press, 1997), 52.

16. Gideon Toury, 'The Notion of "Assumed Translation" – An Invitation to a New Discussion', in *Letterlijkheid, Woordelijheid / Literality, Verbality*, ed. by Henri Bloemen, Erik Hertog and Winibert Segers (Antwerpen and Harmelen: Fantom, 1995), 135–47 (139).

17. Toury, 145.

18. See Jan Willem Mathijssen, 'The Breach and the Observance: Theatre Retranslation as a Strategy of Artistic Differentiation, with Special Reference to Retranslations of Shakespeare's *Hamlet* (1777–2001)', unpublished PhD dissertation (Utrecht: Utrecht University, 2007).

19. See Maik Hamburger, 'Translating and Copyright' in *Shakespeare and the Language of Translation*, 148–66.

19
Shakespeare's Sonnets *de profundis*

Manfred Pfister

Not the only, but perhaps the most immediate begetter of the following observations on Shakespeare's Sonnets read *in carcere et vinculis* was Radovan Karadzic. It was in 2009, the quatercentenary year of the sonnets, that I was riveted by a news item widely featured in the international press: the Serbian physician, psychiatrist, poet and ethnic cleanser Radovan Karadzic, waiting for his trial in The Hague, had asked his family to procure for him a number of books to study in his prison cell; among them, first and foremost, Shakespeare's Sonnets. The conjunction of mass murder and sonnet reading is startling and reminds one – particularly if one is German – of SS officers playing Bach's 'Goldberg Variations' or of the stark juxtaposition of Buchenwald with nearby Weimar ('A German joke is no laughing matter', as Trevor Griffiths has one of his comedians say![1]). Karadzic's trial opened in October 2009 but was immediately postponed till March 2010 and will still be grinding on painfully at least until 2013 – we do not yet know whether it has been his reading or even translating of the sonnets that has prevented him from studying the 1.2 million pages of incriminatory documents which back up his impeachment.

What came to my mind when this news first reached me was Oscar Wilde boldly and publicly invoking Shakespeare's Sonnets in self-defence at the Old Bailey and continuing to read them while imprisoned in Reading Gaol – *in carcere et vinculis*, as it is phrased in the original title of his long letter to Lord Alfred Douglas, *De Profundis*.[2] Striking as the similarity between these two cases of the sonnets read in prison may appear, one is, however, equally struck by the huge differences between the two readers' situation and motivation. 'Genocide' and 'sodomite indecency' are crucially different deviations from crucially different norms: one is a large-scale capital crime immediately linked to national and international political conflict; the other more private in nature, though connected with the sexual politics of its own times. And when it comes to the link with Shakespeare's Sonnets in both cases, there is also a crucial difference: in Wilde's case there is a direct thematic link between what he was impeached of and incarcerated for, that is the same-sex desire to which Shakespeare's Sonnets give voice, whereas in Karadzic's case there is no such immediate thematic connection. With the one notable exception of Sonnet 66, the sonnets hardly ever speak of political conflict and never of imprisonment or related forms of political displacement such as internment and exile. Though many of Shakespeare's plays do so by staging movingly and memorably the victims of political conflicts in prison or exile, and engaging the audience's sympathy and empathy with their carceral discourses and performances, nothing of that kind is present in the sonnets: nobody is imprisoned or in exile there, the word 'exile' is never sounded and the few scattered occurrences of words like 'prison' or 'jail', 'prisoner', 'imprisoned' or 'pent' in Sonnets 5, 55, 58, and 133 are mere metaphors referring to the Platonic idea of the spirit locked in the flesh or to love's or passion's slavery.

In carcere et vinculis

And yet, working at that time on a book documenting and celebrating the global and transmedial impact of Shakespeare's Sonnets in preparation for their quatercentenary that year,[3] I was alerted to the fact that what I had read about Karadzic is only a very special case of an engagement with Shakespeare's cycle *de profundis* that is part of a rich, yet so far unrecognized, tradition of the sonnets being read or translated by victims of political conflict – men as well as women – in prison, behind barbed wire, or in the equally extreme and isolating circumstances of exile.

Here are a few telling examples that have emerged from the collaborative work of more than seventy 'sonnet scouts' from all over the world reporting on the fortunes of the sonnets in their respective languages and cultures for our book. The German historian of religion Friedrich Cornelius translated Shakespeare's Sonnets between 1945 and 1946 in a French POW camp.[4] In Albania, at least three translators – Napoleon Tasi, Çezar Kurti and Mihal Hanxhari – turned to the sonnets while imprisoned, detained in labour camps or following dismissal from academic posts by the Communist regime.[5] The Hungarian Social Democrat Pál Justus, arrested by the Communist authorities in 1949 and sentenced to life imprisonment, translated them in his Budapest prison cell; he was released in 1956 and when his translation was published that year, the Hungarian expatriate Andor Klay commented in the *Shakespeare Quarterly*: 'Since Hungary, culturally an integral part of the West through nine centuries, is ruled by a handful of Communists kept in power by Soviet occupation forces, a Budapest prison cell is a proper place in which to plan literary endeavours linked to the free spirit of the West.'[6] The Latvian poet and translator Paulis Kalva worked at the sonnets secretly in his Siberian camp as a political prisoner, often calling to his mind the first line of Sonnet 66, 'Tired with all these, for restful death I cry.' When, after his return to Latvia, some of his translations were included in the first complete Latvian version of Shakespeare's cycle in 1965, as part of a semi-official collected works, the editor got into trouble for publishing work by a politically unacceptable person. Many years later, in 1990, in the period of transition to post-Soviet Latvia, Kalva gathered his translations together under the significant title *Sāpju Soneti* (*Sonnets of Pain*), 'forging a link between Shakespeare's work and his own imprisonment experience'.[7] In neighbouring Lithuania, the distinguished scholar Algis Tomas Geniušas first engaged with Shakespeare's poems in one of the 'Gulag universities' where dissident intellectuals imprisoned by the Soviet regime shared their knowledge in a *Fahrenheit 451* situation.[8] During the hegemony of the Soviet Union over the Ukraine, some of the most important translations were made by emigrant poets living in diaspora in Canada and the USA, in Argentina and West Germany; thus the first ever complete Ukrainian translation of the sonnets, that by Ihor Kostets'kyi, actually came to be written and published during his Munich exile.[9] Under quite different, yet equally menacing political circumstances, Bingen Ametzaga, a member of the Basque government during the Second Spanish Republic, sentenced to death after the outbreak of the Spanish Civil War and dying in exile in 1969, produced in 1954 one of the first two Basque translations ever of a Shakespearean Sonnet, number 66 – 'a significant choice for a political exile', as Ángel-Luis Pujante comments.[10] The same might be said of the German singer and songwriter Wolf Biermann, banished from the GDR in 1976, and of his translation and musical setting of Sonnet 66 early in 1989, only a few months before his country of exile and the country that had exiled him were reunited.[11]

And, finally, let me not forget in my roll call of sonnet readers and translators incarcerated, banished, displaced and menaced by extinction, the victims of the Holocaust, which devastated the lives of a number of sonnet translators, three of whom were women: Sophie Heiden sent her complete translation to Stratford and Washington just before she was deported to the concentration camp of Theresienstadt; Terese Robinson ended up in Auschwitz; and the cembalist Eta Harich-Schneider translated the entire cycle 'from sheer homesickness' (*aus Heimweh*) in Japan in 1943–44, while under close surveillance by the Japanese authorities for her German citizenship and her entanglement with the Communist 'master spy' Richard Sorge, who was soon to be executed there.[12]

Why the Sonnets?

What is it in Shakespeare's Sonnets that has drawn readers and translators *in extremis*, in prison cells or exile, in internment, or in POW, labour and concentration camps to them? What is it, for instance, that made the Finnish actor Jussi Lehtonen's dramatized performances of the sonnets in health care institutions, nursing homes, hospitals and prisons so successful?[13] It cannot be their manifest content, as they hardly speak of such situations nor of the frequently political conflicts and crises occasioning them. And yet they appear to offer a particular kind of consolation which helps people in the displacement of distressed isolation to cope with their plight.

On the most superficial level, the answer to this question can be the *consolatio philologiae* of engaging patiently with a long, demanding and richly rewarding poem, one of the universally acknowledged masterpieces of world poetry, puzzling over its intricacies of meaning with a concentration that detaches the mind from its immediately pressing concerns, and passing an otherwise unendurably sterile and painful time 'count[ing] the clock that tells the time' (Sonnet 12), by searching one's own language for inflections of voice, verbal ambiguities, metaphorical clusters or rhymes equivalent to those in the original.

But there is more to it than this, more than the beneficial effect of occupational therapy which would put the translation of Shakespearean Sonnets on a par with solving crossword puzzles or knitting. There is, in the first place, something about the aesthetics of the sonnet, and in particular of Shakespeare's Sonnets, which responds to, or reverberates with, the spatial constraints of the prison cell or the internment camp: the self-contained narrowness of its shape built up of three strictly-bound quartets and culminating in a yet tighter couplet. No wonder that images of small rooms or cells have frequently been employed by sonneteers reflecting on their art. In John Donne's 'The Canonization', for instance, the lover suggests to his lady that they should 'build in sonnets pretty roomes',[14] small and intimate spaces quite unlike the huge edifices or monuments with which the conquerors of the world try to impress the public, perfectly crafted and tightly filled with the riches of imagination. And when the Romantic poets rediscovered Shakespeare's Sonnets, they defended the artificiality of the form in terms of a spatial constriction which challenges the poet's shaping powers to make a virtue out of the constraints and transcend them imaginatively.[15] Wordsworth in the introductory 'meta-sonnet' to his Miscellaneous Sonnets of 1807 casts this argument emphatically in metaphors of cells and prisons:

> Nuns fret not at their convent's narrow room;
> And hermits are contented with their cells [...]
> In truth the prison, unto which we doom
> Ourselves, no prison is: and hence for me,
> In sundry moods, 'twas pastime to be bound
> Within the Sonnet's scanty plot of ground [...][16]

Though, of course, the political prisoner or exile translating Shakespeare's Sonnets has not doomed himself or herself voluntarily to incarceration, the experience of finding a new kind of freedom under constraints, which the sonnets enact in their very form, often finds expression in their work. And this work, parcelled out in translating one quartet after another, one sonnet after another, fits in perfectly with the strictly parcelled-out time and space of the prison regime.

To read or translate Shakespeare's Sonnets under such self-alienating conditions is also an act of cultural self-assertion. The translator seeking refuge in some of the greatest poems ever written turns himself or herself into a beacon in the surrounding darkness, shedding a lonely light of humane endurance and achievement against the shutters of inhumanity that have come down upon the world. In this sense, the sonnets become survival poetry; a poetry of endurance under extreme duress and suffering, humiliation and alienation. And here the translations can chime in with Shakespeare's Sonnets, which, indeed, speak frequently of survival – the survival of their own voice in the face of all oppressions seeking to silence it and make it 'tongue-tied' (Sonnets 66, 80, 140), confidently proclaiming their enduring power to assert the values they express even 'to the edge of doom' (Sonnet 116).

Such proclamations *ex carcere et vinculis* based on reading or translating the sonnets do not even need to fear the light of day, the public sphere monitored by the powers of repression. Protected by the global cultural prestige and capital of their author, engagement with them often manages to slip through the most narrow-meshed nets of censorship. Censoring the sonnets would mean censoring and tongue-tying the canonical Shakespeare himself, to whom *all* – or nearly all – authority pays lip service. This applies also, and in particular, to the one sonnet in the cycle that addresses itself directly and explicitly to the political grievances and conflicts of Shakespeare's time, namely Sonnet 66, 'Tired with all these'. Translations, adaptations and settings to music of this sonnet by artists in prison, exile, displacement or 'inner emigration' have again and again functioned as a samizdat way of ventilating the anger and despair of the disempowered and of indicting and protesting against those in power without immediately incurring legal sanctions.[17]

The sonnets bear a strong emotional charge which invites the prisoner's or exile's identification and with that offers the solace of shared aspirations and suffering. Though they hardly ever speak of politics and never of political imprisonment or exile, the speaker's situation, 'all alone beweep[ing his] outcast state' (Sonnet 29), is one which in crucial aspects coincides with that of a political prisoner or exile. There is a long sequence of sonnets in which Shakespeare's speaker laments 'the bitterness of absence', desperately trying to make sense of, and find virtue in, the separation from his beloved (as in Sonnets 27, 28, 39, 41, 43, 44, 47, 57, 97). In his loneliness, his dialogues with others are essentially reduced to imagined, internal dialogues, the kinds of soliloquies that remind one of the imprisoned protagonists of the plays, such as Richard II in Pomfret Castle. His present reduced to sterile waiting – 'I am to wait, though waiting so be hell' (Sonnet 58) – the speaker is thrown back on memories (Sonnets 29 and 39), memories of a happier past but also of past omissions or guilt, and all he anticipates is an extension of his suffering and death in the future (Sonnets 32, 60, 70 and 71).

Taken together, Shakespeare's Sonnets perform both the yearning for an ideal perfection never to be attained unless in one's dreams and imagination, and a deep dismay and disgust at the way of the world in conjunction with a crisis in self-esteem that also involves self-alienation and a threatening loss of identity. These, surely, are emotions which readers *in carcere et vinculis* can share and which make their *de profundis* translations of the sonnets a far cry from a translator's 'business as usual'. Apolitical as Shakespeare's love sonnets are, when read and translated in captivity and exile they reveal the anguish and stress suffered by the displaced victims of political conflict and crisis, and offer consolations which may help in bearing them.

Notes

1. Trevor Griffiths, *Comedians* (London: Faber, 1979), 65.
2. *The Complete Letters of Oscar Wilde*, ed. by Merlin Holland and Rupert Hart-Davis (London: Fourth Estate, 2000), 782.
3. *William Shakespeare's Sonnets, for the First Time Globally Reprinted. A Quatercentenary Anthology*, ed. by Manfred Pfister and Jürgen Gutsch (Dozwil: SIGNAThUR, 2009); in the following abbreviated as *SSG* (*Shakespeare's Sonnets Global*).
4. See 'Sonette Shakespeares: Aus einer bisher unveröffentlichten Gesamtübersetzung von Friedrich Cornelius', ed. by Dieter Mehl, *Shakespeare Jahrbuch*, 134 (1998), 164–70, and *Cupido lag im Schlummer. Drei neue Übersetzungen von Shakespeares Sonetten*, ed. by Christa Jansohn (Tübingen: Stauffenburg, 2002).
5. *SSG*, 46.
6. *SSG*, 325.
7. *SSG*, 430.
8. *SSG*, 439ff.
9. *SSG*, 690.
10. *SSG*, 183.
11. See my essay on 'Route 66: The Political Performance of Shakespeare's Sonnet 66 in Germany and Elsewhere', *Shakespeare Jahrbuch*, 137 (2001), 115–31.
12. Eta Harich-Schneider, *Charaktere und Katastrophen* (Berlin, Frankfurt and Vienna: Ullstein, 1978), 252; and *Eta Harich-Schneider: Die Sonette William Shakespeares und die Lyrik der 'Rekusanten'. Erlebnisse und Übersetzungen einer reisenden Musikerin: 1941–1982*, ed. by Christa Jansohn (Berlin: Lit-Verlag, 2011), 16ff. See also Jürgen Gutsch, '"Millions of Strange Shadows": Vom Übersetzen der Shakespeare-Sonette in jüngerer Zeit (nicht nur) ins Deutsche', *Shakespeare Jahrbuch*, 139 (2003), 161–89.
13. *SSG*, 223.
14. John Donne, *Complete Poetry and Selected Prose*, ed. by John Hayward (London: Nonesuch Press, 1930), 10. Donne's Songs and Sonnets do not, of course, contain any sonnets in the strict sense of the word but that is beside my point as what he has in mind is brief stanzaed poems that are in this respect not different from 'real' sonnets.
15. See my '"L'infini par toutes les fenêtres": Das romantische Sonett in England und die romantische Ästhetik der Entgrenzung', *Sprachkunst*, 40 (2009), 279–99.
16. William Wordsworth, *Poetical Works*, ed. by Thomas Hutchinson, rev. by Ernest de Selincourt (Oxford: Oxford University Press, 1984), 199. The same argument, without the prison metaphor, can be found in a meta-sonnet by Goethe: 'It is in working within limits that the master reveals his greatness / And the law alone can give us freedom'. See *Goethes Werke*, ed. by Erich Trunz, 7th edn, 14 vols (Hamburg: Wegner, 1962–65), I, 245; translation mine.
17. See for a historical survey my 'Route 66' and its sequel, 'Route 66 Continued: Further Fortunes of Shakespeare's Sonnet 66', in *'Not of an Age, but for All Time': Shakespeare across Lands and Ages. Essays in Honour of Holger Klein on the Occasion of His 66th Birthday*, ed. by Sabine Coelsch-Foisner and György E. Szönyi (Vienna: Braunmüller, 2004), 311–15.

Select Bibliography

Adelman, Janet, *Blood Relations: Christian and Jew in the Merchant of Venice* (Chicago: Chicago University Press, 2008).

Barker, Simon, *War and Nation in the Theatre of Shakespeare and his Contemporaries* (Edinburgh: Edinburgh University Press, 2007).

Bernardi, Claudio, Monica Dragone and Guglielmo Schininà (eds), *War Theatres and Actions for Peace / Teatri di guerra e azioni di pace* (Milan: Euresis, 2002).

Bezzola Lambert, Ladina, and Balz Engler (eds), *Shifting the Scene: Shakespeare in European Culture* (Newark: University of Delaware Press, 2004).

Blumenfeld, Odette, and Veronica Popescu (eds), *Shakespeare in Europe: Nation(s) and Boundaries* (Iaşi: Editura Universităţii 'Al. I. Cuza', 2011).

Bodwell Smith, Marion, *Dualities in Shakespeare* (Toronto: Toronto University Press, 1966).

Boorman, Stanley C., *Human Conflict in Shakespeare* (London and New York: Routledge and Kegan Paul, 1987).

Breight, Curtis C., *Surveillance, Militarism and Drama in the Elizabethan Era* (Basingstoke: Macmillan, 1996).

Bristol, Michael D., and Kathleen McLuskie (eds), *Shakespeare and Modern Theatre: the Performance of Modernity* (London: Routledge, 2001).

Calvet, Louis-Jean, *Language Wars and Linguistic Politics* (Oxford: Oxford University Press, 1998).

Cartelli, Thomas, and Catherine Rowe (eds), *New Wave Shakespeare on Screen* (Cambridge: Polity, 2007).

Carvalho Homem, Rui, and Ton Hoenselaars (eds), *Translating Shakespeare for the Twenty-First Century* (Amsterdam and New York: Rodopi, 2004).

Cinpoes, Nicoleta, *Shakespeare's Hamlet in Romania 1778–2008: A Study in Translation, Performance and Cultural Appropriation* (Lewiston, NY: Edwin Mellen Press, 2010).

Clare, Janet, and Stephen O'Neill (eds), *Shakespeare and the Irish Writer* (Dublin: University College Dublin Press, 2010).

Coolie, Rosalie L., *Paradoxia Epidemica* (Princeton: Princeton University Press, 1966).

Curti, Lidia, and Alessandra Marino (eds), *Shakespeare in India* (Rome: Editoria & Spettacolo, 2010).

Del Sapio Garbero, Maria (ed.), *La traduzione di Amleto nella cultura Europea* (Venice: Marsilio, 2002).

Delabastita, Dirk, and Lieven D'hulst (eds), *European Shakespeares: Translating Shakespeare in the Romantic Age* (Amsterdam and Philadelphia: John Benjamins, 1993).

Delabastita, Dirk, Jozef De Vos and Paul Franssen (eds), *Shakespeare and European Politics* (Newark: University of Delaware Press, 2008).

Demaria, Cristina, and Colin Wright (eds), *Post-Conflict Cultures. Rituals of Representation* (London: Zoilus Press, 2006).

Dente, Carla, and Sara Soncini (eds), *Conflict Zones: Actions Languages Mediations* (Pisa: ETS, 2004).

Dente, Carla, and Sara Soncini (eds), *Crossing Time and Space: Shakespeare Translations in Present-Day Europe* (Plus – Pisa University Press, 2008).

Desmet, Christy, and Robert Sawyer (eds), *Shakespeare and Appropriation* (London: Routledge, 1999).

Dobson, Michael, *Shakespeare and Amateur Performance: A Cultural History* (Cambridge: Cambridge University Press, 2011).

Fortunati, Vita, Daniela Fortezza and Maurizio Ascari (eds), *Conflitti: Strategie di rappresentazione della guerra nella cultura contemporanea* (Rome: Meltemi, 2008).

Franssen, Paul, and Ros King (eds), *Shakespeare and War* (Basingstoke: Palgrave Macmillan, 2008).

Gibinska, Marta, and Jerzy Limon (eds), *Hamlet East/West* (Gdansk: Theatrum Gedanense Foundation, 1998).

Gibinska, Marta, and Agnieszka Romanowska (eds), *Shakespeare in Europe: History and Memory* (Krakow: Jagiellonian University Press, 2008).

Goffman, Erwin, *Strategic Interaction* (Philadelphia: University of Pennsylvania Press, 1969).

Greenblatt, Stephen et al., *Cultural Mobility: A Manifesto* (Cambridge: Cambridge University Press, 2010).

Gregor, Keith, *Shakespeare in the Spanish Theatre 1772 to the Present* (London and New York: Continuum, 2010).

Gregor, Keith, and Ángel-Luis Pujante (eds), *More European Shakespeares*, special issue of *Quadernos de Filologia Inglesa* 7:1 (2001).

Grudin, Robert, *Mighty Opposites: Shakespeare and Renaissance Contrariety* (Berkeley and Los Angeles: University of California Press, 1979).

Habermas, Jürgen, *Theorie des kommunikativen Handelns* (Frankfurt: Suhrkamp, 1981).

Hattaway, Michael, Boika Sokolova and Derek Roper (eds), *Shakespeare in the New Europe* (Sheffield: Sheffield University Press, 1994).

Hawkes, Terence, *Meaning by Shakespeare* (London: Routledge, 1992).

Hawkes, Terence, *Shakespeare in the Present* (London: Routledge, 2002).

Hodgdon, Barbara, *The Shakespeare Trade: Performances and Appropriations* (Philadelphia: University of Pennsylvania Press, 1998).

Hoenselaars, Ton (ed.), *Shakespeare and the Language of Translation* (London: Thomson Learning, 2004).

Hoenselaars, Ton, and Clara Calvo (eds), *European Shakespeares*, special theme issue of *The Shakespearean International Yearbook* (Aldershot: Ashgate, 2008).

Holland, Peter (ed.), *Shakespeare, Memory and Performance* (Cambridge: Cambridge University Press, 2006).

Hortmann, Wilhelm, *Shakespeare on the German Stage: The Twentieth Century. With a Section on Shakespeare on Stage in the German Democratic Republic by Maik Hamburger* (Cambridge and New York: Cambridge University Press, 1998).

Howard, Jean, and Marion F. O'Connor (eds), *Shakespeare Reproduced: The Text in Ideology and History* (London: Routledge, 1987).

Jones-Davies, Marie-Thérèse (ed.), *Shakespeare et la guerre* (Paris, Les belles lettres, 1989).

Jorgensen, Paul A., *Shakespeare's Military World* (Berkeley and Los Angeles: University of California Press, 1956).

Kennedy, Dennis, *Foreign Shakespeare: Contemporary Performance* (Cambridge: Cambridge University Press, 1993).

Kingsley-Smith, Jane, *Shakespeare's Drama of Exile* (Basingstoke and New York: Palgrave Macmillan, 2003).

Littlejohns, Richard, and Sara Soncini (eds), *Myths of Europe* (Amsterdam and New York: Rodopi, 2007).

Makaryk, Irena R., and Marissa McHugh (eds), *Shakespeare and the Second World War: Memory, Culture, Identity* (Toronto: University of Toronto Press, 2012).

Makaryk, Irena R., and Joseph G. Price (eds), *Shakespeare in the Worlds of Communism and Socialism* (Toronto: University of Toronto Press, 2006).

Malley, Willy, and Margaret Tudeau-Clayton (eds), *This England, That Shakespeare: New Angles on Englishness and the Bard* (Farnham and Burlington, VT: Ashgate, 2010).

Manlove, Colin N., *The Gap in Shakespeare: The Motif of Division from* Richard II *to* The Tempest (London: Vision, 1981).

Marsden, Jean I., *The Appropriation of Shakespeare: Post-Renaissance Reconstructions of the Works and the Myth* (New York: St Martin's Press, 1992).

Martin, Randall, and Katherine Scheil (eds), *Shakespeare/Adaptation/Modern Drama: Essays in Honour of Jill L. Levenson* (Toronto: University of Toronto Press, 2011).

Massai, Sonia (ed.), *World-Wide Shakespeare: Local Appropriations in Film and Performance* (London and New York: Routledge, 2005).

Matei-Chesnoiu, Monica, *Shakespeare in the Romanian Cultural Memory* (Madison, NJ: Farleigh Dickinson University Press, 2006).

Matei-Chesnoiu, Monica, *Early Modern Drama and the Eastern European Elsewhere: Representations of Liminal Locality in Shakespeare and his Contemporaries* (Madison, NJ: Farleigh Dickinson University Press, 2009).

Matei-Chesnoiu, Monica, *Re-imagining Western European Geography in English Renaissance Drama* (Basingstoke and New York: Palgrave Macmillan, 2012).

Meron, Theodor, *Bloody Constraint: War and Chivalry in Shakespeare* (Oxford: Oxford University Press, 1998).

Miall, Hugh, Oliver Ramsbotham and Tom Woodhouse, *Contemporary Conflict Resolution: The Prevention, Management and Transformation of Deadly Conflicts* (Cambridge: Polity Press, 1999).

Mooneeram, Roshni, *From Creole to Standard: Shakespeare, Language, and Literature in a Postcolonial Context* (Amsterdam: Rodopi, 2009).

Pagnini, Marcello, *Il paradigma della specularità* (Pisa: Pacini, 1976).

Passerini, Luisa, *Il mito d'Europa: radici antiche per nuovi simboli* (Firenze: Giunti, 2002).

Pfister, Manfred, and Jürgen Gutsch (eds), *William Shakespeare's Sonnets for the First Time Globally Reprinted. A Quatercentenary Anthology 1609–2009* (Dozwil: SIGNAThUR, 2009).

Piazza, Antonella (ed.), *Shakespeare in Europa* (Naples: CUEN, 2004).

Poirier, Lucien, *Le Chantier stratégique* (Paris: Hachette, 1997).

Pugliatti, Paola, *Shakespeare and the Just War Tradition* (Aldershot: Ashgate, 2010).

Pujante, Ángel-Luis, and Ton Hoenselaars (eds), *Four Hundred Years of Shakespeare in Europe* (Newark: University of Delaware Press, 2003).

Pujante, Ángel-Luis, and Keith Gregor (eds), *Hamlet en España: las cuatro versiones neoclásicas* (Salamanca: Ediciones Universidad de Salamanca, 2010).

Roy, Amitava, Debnarayan Bandopadhyay and Krishna Sen (eds), *Colonial and Postcolonial Shakespeares* (Kolkata: Avantgarde, 2001).

Sclavi, Marianella, and Lawrence E. Susskind, *Confronto creativo. Dal diritto di parola al diritto di essere ascoltati* (Milan: Et al./ Edizioni, 2011).

Scott-Douglass, Amy, *Shakespeare Inside: The Bard Behind Bars* (London: Continuum, 2007).

Trounstine, Jean, *Shakespeare Behind Bars: The Power of Drama in a Women's Prison* (New York: St Martin's Press, 2001).

Webel, Charles, and Johan Galtung (eds), *Handbook of Peace and Conflict Studies* (London: Routledge, 2007).

Name Index

Academy of the Arts of the GDR, 147
Academy of Asturian Languages, 116
Ackermann, Zeno, 168
Adelman, Janet, 161–2, 164–5
  Blood Relations, 162, 164–5, 169
Ades, Down, 124–5
Adorno, Theodor W., 146
Adventurer (The), 171
Afghanistan, 100
Aldgate, Anthony, 144
Alexander von Humboldt Foundation, 218
Alexander von Humboldt Library, 218
Alexanderplatz, 152
Alghero, 116
Alhambra Theatre, 235
Alibert, Loïs, 117
Allan, Maud, 207–8
Almada Theatre Festival, 168
Almereyda, Michael, 143
  Hamlet 2000, 143
Alvarez, A., 91
America (Latin), 159
America (North), 5–6, 119, 129, 142, 157, 162, 183
  see also under USA
Ametzaga, Bingen, 252
Andreescu, Margareta, 192, 212, 213, 218, 220
Anglo, Sydney, 41,
Annihudra, 183
Antonescu, Ion, 220
Apollo, 237–8, 244, 247
Arad, 189, 214
Aragon, Louis, 123, 124, 125, 164
Archer, Ian W., 38
Arden of Feversham, 130
Argentina, 252
Ariosto, Ludovico, 51
Aristophanes, 88
Aristotle, 70, 97
Armistice Day, 198

Armstrong, Gareth, 168
  Shylock, 168
Arp, Jean/Hans, 123, 125
Artaud, Antonin 119, 124, 126–8, 130
  'Premier manifeste', 127
  The Theatre and its Double, 131
Arts Council of Great Britain, 138
Asian Dub Foundation, 183
Astraea, 91
Atlas of the World's Languages in Danger, 105, 116
Axis Powers, 220
Auschwitz, 253
Austria(n), 4, 148, 189, 221–3, 232, 235

Baader, Andreas, 150
Bach, Johann Sebastian, 197, 250
  'Goldberg Variations', 250
Bacon, Francis, 76
Badir, Patricia, 211, 219
Baillet, Florence, 156
Bakhtin, Mikhail, 19–22, 122, 210, 219
Balboa Echeverría, Miriam, 131
Baldick, Robert, 42, 46
Banat, 190, 216–17, 221
Bandopadhyay, Debnarayan, 181
Barańczak, Stanisław, 241, 248
Barcelona, 106, 168
Bard, Fra(u)ncis de, 28
Barker, Simon, 12
Bate, Jonathan, 101
Bautzen Festival, 147
BBC (British Broadcasting Corporation), 104, 116, 135, 143, 228, 236
Beethoven, Ludwig van, 135
Belén, Ana, 160
Benson, John, 80, 230
Berenguer, Ángel, 131
Berlin, 102, 156, 168, 220, 225, 233
Bessarabia, 220
Beswick, Jaine E., 117

Subject Index

Note: 'Shakespeare', 'conflict' and 'Europe', do not appear as self-standing entries but only in relation to specific topics.